Gender and Sexuality

in Twentieth-Century Chinese
Literature and Society

SUNY Series in Feminist Criticism and Theory
Michelle A. Massé, Editor

Gender and Sexuality

in Twentieth-Century Chinese
Literature and Society

Edited by
Tonglin Lu

STATE UNIVERSITY OF NEW YORK PRESS

Published by
State University of New York Press, Albany

© 1993 State University of New York

For information, address State University of New York
Press, State University Plaza, Albany, N.Y., 12246

Production by E. Moore
Marketing by Fran Keneston

Library of Congress Cataloging in Publication Data

Gender and sexuality in twentieth-century Chinese literature and
    society / Tonglin Lu, editor.
        p.   cm. — (SUNY Series in feminist criticism and theory)
    Includes bibliographical and references.
    ISBN 0-7914-1371-3 (alk. paper). — ISBN 0-7914-1372-1 (pbk.
    alk. paper)
        1. Chinese literature—20th century—History and criticism.
    2. Women in literature. 3. Women—China—Social conditions.
    I. Lu, Tonglin. II. Series
    PL2303.G46   1993
    891.5'09352042'0904—dc20   92-6365
                                                                CIP

10 9 8 7 6 5 4 3 2 1

For Our Mothers'
Generation

Contents

Acknowledgments

First, I would like to express my gratitude to the following organizations at the University of Iowa which, on short notice in the spring of 1991, contributed to supporting the Conference on Gender and Sexuality in Twentieth-Century Chinese Literature and Society: The Center for Asian and Pacific Studies, the Center for International and Comparative Studies, the Department of Asian Languages and Literature, the Department of Comparative Literature, the Graduate School, the Humanities Society, the International Writing Program, the Program of Women's Studies, and the University of Iowa Lecture Committee. Special thanks are reserved for Rey Chow at the University of Minnesota for her enthusiastic and generous contribution to the organization of the conference as well as to the revision of the manuscript, for Maureen Robertson for her valuable support as the chairperson of the Department of Asian Languages and Literature and as a personal friend, and for Robin Ryerson for her assistance as a tireless organizer, which was crucial to the success of the conference. I am grateful to Oney Johnson, the departmental secretary, and Tom

Rolich, the director of the Center for Asian and Pacific Studies, for their assistance in administrative matters, as well as to my students in the Seminar on Modern Chinese Literature in the Spring of 1991, Christie Block, Mark Eckholt, and Josiane Peltier, for volunteering their time and energy for this conference. I would like also to thank Arif Dirlik at Duke University, Tim Reiss at New York University, and Ellen Widmer at Wellesley College for their advice in regard to our manuscript. I would like to express my gratitude to the Mellon Program at Harvard University for its fellowship which allowed me to concentrate on editing and revising the manuscript, and to Rudolph Byrd, Karen Hansen, Janet Headley, Deborah Lyons, and Timothy Moore in the program for their useful suggestions. I am particularly grateful to Ruth Weil at the Harvard Writing Center for her aid in editing my writings. Last, but not the least, I would like to thank Elizabeth Moore and Carola Sautter, editors at the SUNY Press, whose effectiveness, understanding, and sense of humor have lightened the proces of publishing this anthology and made it more enjoyable. I hope that each of the contributors will enjoy seeing his/her fingerprints in this collection.

TONGLIN LU

Introduction

Only Women and inferior men (*xiaoren*) are
difficult to deal with.

Confucius

History has changed; men and women are now
equal.

Mao Zedong

WHY A CONFERENCE IN 1991
ON SEXUALITY AND GENDER
IN TWENTIETH-CENTURY
CHINESE LITERATURE AND SOCIETY?

From Confucius's equation of women with inferior men[1] to
Mao Zedong's definition of women as the upholders of half the
sky,[2] Chinese women have apparently completed a long march in
history. During thousands of years of civilization, Chinese women
were silenced by their highly patriarchal society. Their voices only
"emerged from the surface of history"—to borrow from a recent
book title by two mainland feminist literary critics, Meng Yue and
Dai Jinhua[3]—during the course of numerous revolutions of this
century. However, even in these revolutions Chinese women's
voices are very often marginalized as signifiers of lofty political
and ideological causes. The Chinese women's representational
power in the discourse of the Communist Party, instead of helping
them make a radical break away from traditional gender discrimination, is currently used as an excuse by some intellectuals in

China or in the field of Chinese studies overseas to formulate a misogynistic discourse in the post-Mao era. Consequently, raising the question of women's rights in these circumstances may risk having an unpleasant resonance with communist discourse.[4] As demonstrated by some essays in our collection, this supposedly subversive but misogynistic discourse underlies both traditional Confucian and modern communist ideologies in China. Both ideologies are, in the final analysis, essentially patriarchal. The intricate relationships of ideological and social forces further complicate the gender situation in contemporary China. However, this complexity makes a study of the gender situation in China timely and interesting in that it may prevent us as feminist scholars in the West from falling into the same trap as did Chinese women in their aborted emancipation movement.

We had several objectives in mind when we decided to organize a symposium on gender and sexuality in twentieth-century Chinese literature and society at the University of Iowa in March 1991. We felt it was necessary, first, to review some of the early attempts to deal with gender issues by Chinese intellectuals in the twentieth century. The papers addressing this first objective were, as expected, papers focusing on the May Fourth period. More significant was the question of the relationship between communism and gender. If women's emancipation in socialist China has made their participation in the work force not only possible but also compulsory, what are some of the social, ideological, and psychological consequences of this participation for Chinese women? A large number of the papers dealt, explicitly or implicitly, with the situation of gender and sexuality in postcommunist China. Other related issues, such as the emergence of Western individualism, intimate relations among women, and the appearance of strong women writers in China, were also discussed. Last, since we are all working in North America, it seemed appropriate to raise the question, for ourselves in particular, as to the implications of our own discourses in regard to women in China. How are we to prevent our discourses from repeating the same exploitation of women with which we charge others?

THE PERSISTENCE OF SALVATION-THINKING

In retrospect, as I was editing the symposium papers for publication, it occurred to me that the most important thematic issue that underlay all the papers, even though it was never articulated as such, was that of salvation. Women's salvation has been an obsession with Chinese intellectuals since the turn of the twentieth century. In order to illustrate the notion of women's salvation, we will take as examples two famous plays that have characterized women's positions in the two major revolutions of twentieth century China: Ibsen's *A Doll's House*[5] and Tian Han's *The White-Haired Girl.*[6] The former inspired the May Fourth generation to dream of a Chinese woman liberated from her traditional ties to kinship in the image of a Western individualistic middle class woman; the latter represented the salvation of the oppressed peasant woman by the Communist Party. Between and beyond these two plays, other attempts have been made to "save" Chinese women, including those aimed against Chinese communism. Usually, a new attempt at salvation sees itself as purer and more noble than the previous one(s).

The firm belief in the purity of their cause and in their personal purity as participants in this cause very often provides revolutionaries with an excuse to remain indifferent to other people's feelings, especially to those of others they are supposed to save. Their own "purity" justifies their injustices committed against other "impure" elements—including ironically the oppressed women they intend to save. Salvation, be it Christian, socialist, or revolutionary, implies a hierarchy, as the majority of the papers in this collection demonstrate. Women, after being saved symbolically and glamorously, finally always return to the bottom rung of a new hierarchy, which is patriarchal in yet another way. One may say that the very notion of salvation is precisely what engenders inequality in a revolution since its hierarchical structure always justifies women's oppression in a new form. To a large extent, the misogynistic discourse prevailing in contemporary Chinese literature can be traced to the salvation theory of the socialist revolution of which socialist realist literature is one of the best expressions. This discourse reinforces the underlying gender hierarchy existing in the socialist salvation theory. The Communist Party, as a collective savior in socialist realism, usually proves its ideological and political superiority by the salvation of silenced and oppressed women. In the same vein, an individual hero in contemporary fiction very often reaffirms his masculinity or individuality in opposition to women's inferiority and subordination. In other words, in order to regain his individuality repressed by the communist domination, the male individual of contemporary fiction needs to use the female body as a scapegoat for communist ideology. In both cases, women, situated at the bottom of the hierarchy, function mainly as symbols for their superiors, be they communists or individualists.[7]

Up to the beginning of the Cultural Revolution in 1966, the situation of Chinese women after the May Fourth movement in 1919 and since the socialist revolution in 1949 can be summarized by two pictures: Nora leaving her husband's house and the white-haired girl at the exit of her grotto. The former symbolizes individual freedom in the bourgeois revolution; the latter, the liberation of the labor class in the socialist revolution. The two images raise the same question: What can a woman do after abandoning, or being saved from, her previous slavery?

May Fourth Writings

In 1926, Lu Xun, a leftist May Fourth writer, painted a gloomy picture of the liberated Nora. After speculating that "Nora's sole solution after her departure is either a return to her husband's house or prostitution,"[8] the Chinese writer continues:

> Nowadays, a Nora's departure from the family is not necessarily disastrous. Because her personality and action still appear original, she may gain compassion from some people who will help her survive. However, her freedom is already limited if she needs to rely on people's compassion. Furthermore, if one hundred Noras left home, compassion would diminish. If there were thousands and thousands of them, these Noras would merely , provoke aversion. The best solution for them is to hold economic power in their own hands.[9]

Lu Xun's "best solution for women" has become a reality in socialist China, where women are indeed financially independent. Since 1949, women's massive participation in the work force has not only been encouraged by the party but also become compulsory for ideological and economic reasons. The white-haired girls, saved by the Communist Party from the grotto, apparently enjoy a better future than the run-away Chinese Noras of the 1920s. Nevertheless, Lu Xun's suggestion to women in the 1920s does not solve women's problems in the 1980s—economic independence does not necessarily lead to women's liberation. Sixty-five years after Lu Xun's prediction, a woman director of a large factory in Shanghai bitterly explained to a reporter why her fiancé had left her:

He needed a woman who could satisfy his desires at any moment, cook for him, give birth to his sons and daughters, and raise them. A woman like me who thinks about her career—heavens know what career is—is not serviceable to a man who also has his own. Finally, China is a male-centered society. Women, except for the roles of daughters, lovers, wives, mothers, and mothers-in-law that they successively play, can never enter the male-centered society. Once you rush in, you are no longer considered a complete woman.[10]

Why does the image of the "liberated" contemporary Chinese woman appear so discouraging? After thirty years of women's participation in the work force, why is contemporary Chinese society still unable to offer a solution for the dilemma faced by this woman director?

While Lu Xun was right in sensing that women's lack of economic independence played an important role in their oppression, it would be wrong to assume that economic independence—or simply the ability to earn an income—is all it takes to solve the problem of persistent misogyny. This is because the lingering power of patriarchy consists of both economics and ideology. In the field of literature, it is patriarchy as ideology that we most frequently encounter. The most thorny issue with which we as feminist literary critics must come to terms is thus not simply that of women and economic (re)production, but also that, to use Yue Mingbao's phrase, of *women and representation.*

Yue's essay, "Gendering the 'Origin' of Modern Chinese Fiction," takes us back to the question of "the silence of China" that was raised by Lu Xun. Unlike most accounts of modern Chinese literature which examine literature as *literary,* Yue asks us to examine the socio-scientific origins of modern Chinese fiction, which privileges a specific discursive model as the means to inquire into the culturally oppressed. The case study model, in which the inquirer adopts an objective point of view in order to "investigate" and "expose" the suffering of the oppressed, tends to present the suffering person in the form of an object which is visible but without a voice or subjectivity, while the voice and subjectivity of the inquirer *direct* our view of her *invisibly.* When we see that the inquirer is usually a male intellectual and the suffering person, a woman from the lower classes, the gender as well as the class implications of modern Chinese fiction become clear.

Yue's argument problematizes the masculine sexual desire in Lu Ling's fiction, which is the subject of Liu Kang's essay, "The Language of Desire, Class, and Subjectivity in Lu Ling's Fiction." Lu Ling's obsession with what Liu calls the new "symbolic order" of modernity uses a revolutionary language in which, once again, the female body becomes a visual staging of male desire. The visualization of the "preverbal" and "fragmented" female body is Lu Ling's means of asserting his own iconoclastic position and of debunking traditional literary conventions based on Confucianism. However, because such a use of the female body does not really change the patriarchal assumptions about women, Lu Ling's position as a revolutionary is subject to challenge. Among the problems created by the prevailing masculinism of May Fourth intellectuals was an indifferent if not hostile attitude toward women's new role as writers. For women writers, preoccupation with gender-related problems typically earned them the criticism of indulgence in the insignificant private sphere.[11]

The Legacies of the Socialist Revolution: Who Is the Subject of, or the Subject to, Salvation?

May Fourth writers, women and men, criticized traditional society in the hope of provoking social changes. However disillusioned they might have been, their disappointment did not completely break their faith in a better future. As the title of the leading literary journal of the May Fourth movement *New Youth* implied, what was at stake in this period was a young generation pitted against an old, as well as modernism against tradition. Women, however, were excluded from this great battlefield. Or, their presence served mainly as a means of representation. Nevertheless, despite this generally accepted convention of a silenced second sex among May Fourth intellectuals, some marginalized women writers still succeeded in resisting the attempt to objectify their own voices in the name of any lofty cause.[12]

From the May Fourth period to our time, a large number of revolutions occurred in the ancient land of China. The Communist Party took control in 1949. Traditional values, such as Confucianism, Buddhism, and Taoism, "were swept onto the rubbish heap of history"—to use a cliché of socialist China. As a consequence, communist ideology became the dominant value system. From 1966 to 1976, the decade of the Cultural Revolution not only further destroyed traditional values, but also discredited communist ideology itself. During the late 1970s and 80s, the reformers, or the technocrats in the Communist Party, headed by Deng Xiaoping, tried to encourage the adoption of Western technology on a large scale in order to fill the ideological vacuum with the slogan "Four Modernizations." Contrary to the expectations of Deng Xiaoping and his followers in the party, along with technology came Western values that increasingly offered a counterreference to the socialist regime. In May and June 1989 we witnessed on television the Chinese student demonstrations at Tian'anmen Square and the bloody repression by the communist government which followed. These demonstrations could be perceived as an outcome of Western influences serving as the counterreference to communist ideology which had already been deeply shaken by successive political struggles within the party. For many, the official recourse to mass murder marked the death of communist ideology in China, because the only thing on which the regime could rely from then on was violence.

In the course of all these revolutions and upheavals, where are Chinese women? What has become of the white-haired girl after leaving the obscure grotto? In fact, since 1949, women have not only been legally guaranteed the right to work, but have almost no other choice. Economically, the husband's salary usually cannot support the family. Ideologically, the name "housewife" invokes parasite, ignorance, as well as bourgeois and feudal decadence. Mao Zedong's well-known slogan set the standard of women's emancipation in China: "What men can do, women can also do." While women must perform men's functions in the public work place, men do not need to fulfill women's tasks in the family, since this has never been expected of them. In the new socialist climate, women must be responsible for both their new social function as workers and their old family roles as daughters, wives, and mothers. The two roles are equally demanding if a woman would like to be respected in society and in the family.

Meanwhile, men who used to monopolize every social profession except for prostitution feel threatened by the competition of the other "half of the sky" which was invisible in society for thousands of years of Chinese history. Both men and women remain largely caught within an old gender hierarchy even though the equality of the two sexes based on Mao's masculine standard has been legalized by the nation's constitution. Women's emancipation is a gift imposed by the Communist Party, which used this gesture as a marker of its progressive stance. Once their function to represent the party in public is fulfilled, women must continue to play a submissive role not necessarily in the family but in society. Both women and men need to become "obedient instruments of the party"—to use the expression of the ex-chairman of the Communist Party, Liu Shaoqi.[13]

In *Emerging from the Surface of History*, Meng Yue and Dai Jinhua write:

> Women no longer need to submit to fathers, to husbands, to sons, or even to any particular individual. But the very state of submission has not changed. The throne of the past patriarchal figure, the emperor, is nowadays occupied by a collectivity, the incarnation of the nation. Indeed, women are no longer required to be obedient to men, but women and men together equally obey this sexless collectivity or its symbol.[14]

The greater equality between men and women under the regime of the Communist Party is due less to women's empowerment than to men's loss of certain privileges vis-à-vis the party, "this sexless collectivity" sitting on "the throne of the past patriarchal figure." In this case, Mao Zedong's slogan: "what men can do, women can also do," should be rephrased as the following: "men should not do what is not permitted to women." However, because the ideological basis for the traditional patriarchy has not truly been shaken by the aborted women's emancipation in China, the Chinese people's resentment of the communist regime is very often rearticulated by men as their resentment of women's equal rights, as if Chinese men had been disempowered by women's empowerment.

In the hope of reasserting men's power, a search for masculinity has become an urgent need expressed in Chinese literature of the 1980s, especially among male authors. Masculinity in this context implies different values: such as an assertion of the male authors' individuality, a nostalgic longing for a cultural authority, and a protestation against communist ideology.[15] However, this search for masculinity is very often accompanied by a misogynistic discourse, as if the debasement of the "weaker" sex, women, were all it took to empower men.

At the beginning of 1986, a man using the pseudonym "Adam" published an essay entitled "Adam's Bewilderment" in the journal *Chinese Women (Zhongguo funü)*. The article was warmly received and highly praised by a number of male readers as the best article ever published in this journal because it was an "outlet for men's anger."[16] After dividing professions in terms of gender, "Adam" adds:

> However, generally speaking, women are not as good as men even in their specialties. For example, singing songs to induce a baby in the cradle to sleep certainly belongs to the realm of female natural instincts, but until now the best lullabies have always been composed by men. One can provide numerous similar examples. Don't try to explain them merely in terms of differences imposed by cultural and social history. To a large extent, they are proofs of men's inner superiority.[17]

Apart from the misogynistic contents of this essay, the pseudonym "Adam" itself is significant in that it reflects the fetichization of the West in post-Cultural Revolution China. Since neither Chinese ancestors nor communist leaders enjoy any more credibility, the throne of the patriarchal figure is now occupied by a white male as in the Christian tradition. Consequently, gender hierarchy is endorsed by racial and cultural domination. The man who wrote the above essay needs to become white—by turning into "Adam"—in order to regain his lost masculinity.

In the same vein, the search for masculinity prevails in literary works of the 1980s, especially in "root-searching" fiction in which masculinity very often becomes an important part of the male authors's sought roots.[18] On the one hand, these searchers for masculinity use women as objects onto which to project a "self" largely predicated on Western humanism and individualism. On the other hand, they show a nostalgia for a premodern time where Chinese women were still kept in "their places."[19] The "gender gap"[20] is made more evident by the career competition between the two sexes due, on the one hand, to women's massive participation in the public work sphere, and on the other, to the sexual segregation imposed by the Communist Party in the name of revolutionary morality.

The essays by Marie-Claire Huot, Elissa Rashkin, and Zhu Ling problematize the new search for masculinity in three contemporary male authors.

Marie-Claire Huot's essay, "Liu Heng's *Fuxi Fuxi*: What about Nüwa?," argues that *Fuxi Fuxi* is a parodic rewriting of the Chinese creation myth of the two human ancestors, Fuxi and Nüwa. The adultery between the hero, Yang Tianqing, and his uncle's wife, Wang Judou, is a reminiscence of the marriage of the two siblings, Fuxi and Nüwa. However, instead of creating an egalitarian, anarchist, and primitive atmosphere through sexual transgression, Liu Heng's tale emphasizes "the dominance of societal norms over individual ones."[21] By conspicuously omitting the woman's name Nüwa in the novel's title *Fuxi Fuxi*, Liu Heng projects a highly phallic implication into the myth.

Rashkin's essay, "Rape as Castration as Spectacle: *The Price of Frenzy*'s Politics of Confusion," also deals with problematized sexuality in a contemporary Chinese film. Zhou Xiaowen's *The Price of Frenzy* focuses on the rape of a young girl and her older sister's revenge. The "frenzy" in the film's title is less about the rape itself than about the sister's effort to track down and punish the criminal herself, thus taking the place of the incompetent legal system. The director's attempt to put the victim and the rapist on the same level in their common victimization by a "politics of confusion" existing in contemporary China intends to justify the violence against women.

Zhu Ling's essay, "A Brave New World? On the Construction of 'Masculinity' and 'Femininity' in The *Red Sorghum Family*," questions the "masculine ethos" in Mo Yan's *Red Sorghum Family*. Zhu argues that Mo Yan in his novel reconstructs male subjectivity based on a demeaning objectification of women. Mo Yan's misogynistic discourse unfortunately contributes to his ideological identification with his subverted object, the dominant ideology, because both belong to the patriarchal order, be it communist or feudal.

CONTEMPORARY CHINESE WOMEN WRITERS

If we are to establish a theoretical and ideological connection between Chinese women and women from other parts of the world, we would say that, like women elsewhere, women in twentieth-century China have been used as signifiers for one type of revolution or another, and as the link between different groups of men. While male cultural identity tends to remain stable,[22] women have always been the bearers of change, of large historical forces such as individual freedom in the May Fourth period and communist salvation after 1949. They exist either for the May Fourth intellectuals or for the Communist Party. Each of the two revolutions tried to establish a new order through the representation of the female body. The new order, however, was not much less patriarchal than the old one for which it substituted. Both the May

Fourth and the socialist revolution remain essentially masculinist in their aspirations.

After three decades of communist domination in China, Chinese writers are turning away from the collective salvation that motivated their forefathers in the May Fourth movement and are seeking alternatives in an extreme form of Western individualism. In their search for both masculinity and internationalization, they subvert communist ideology by asserting a newly constructed value: the individual self. Unfortunately, this self cannot be truly free. By submitting women to a gender hierarchy by means of a misogynistic discourse, the male individual in search for his masculinity must submit to a different form of patriarchy. In a number of literary works of the 1980s, a fictional patriarchal order of individualism (in which the individual is mostly male) replaces the "real" but dying patriarchal order of collectivism (in which the party is the symbolic father.[23]

In this violent succession of father and son, where are the women's voices?[24] During the 1980s, a number of women writers emerged. Their search for female subjecthood, caught between women's representation of the oppressed in the communist culture and their objectification as the counterpart to male subjectivity in contemporary fiction, has been seriously challenged and problematized.[25]

We no longer hear Ding Ling's daring assertion of female subjectivity, which questions the belief in free love in its sublimated form (a belief shared by Chinese intellectuals at that historical moment), through an exploration of bodily pleasure and female desire.[26] We no longer hear Xiao Hong's angry protestation against women's oppression in an unsublimated and "unsublimatable" language of the female body, which severely criticizes the predominant male-centered nationalist discourse.[27] What we hear are more problematic, dispersed, and disturbing female voices, as if women's acts of transgression have also become dispersed—if not disoriented, because the patriarchal order(s) has(ve) already been fragmented. Moreover, since the "female voice" was for so long officially appropriated by communist discourse, most women writers seem unsure about the position(s) from which they can speak.[28] At the same time, the oppression of women remains constant in daily life.[29]

In this "postideological" era, women must constantly experience the conflict between their conventional representation of the previously oppressed sex liberated by the party and the current reality of their daily oppression. Female voices are understandably ambivalent and hesitant. Nevertheless, because of this ambivalent and hesitant attitude, their voices are much less didactic thus more complex and sophisticated than those formulated by the majority of the May Fourth women writers. After the disillusionment with the myth of the revolutionary collectivity, the search for female voices can only take a highly individualized form, but as such they problematize female subjectivity more as a search than as a definite finding.

The essays by Margaret Decker, Zhong Xueping, and myself deal with contemporary Chinese women's works in this problematized search for female subjectivity in a society dominated by complicated forms of masculinist ideology.

Decker's essay, "Femininity as Imprisonment: Subjectivity, Agency, and Criminality in Ai Bei's Fiction," analyzes the descriptions of female criminals' lives in a prison controlled by the communist government in Ai Bei's novella *Red Ivy* (*Nülao*). The prison is both a female kingdom and a metaphor for Chinese women situated between tradition and modernity, between a new awareness of their selves and a traditional habit of depending on their sexual partners. Regardless of their will, these women are all deprived of sexual pleasure, of family life, and of motherhood. Nevertheless, the prison is their family in which they find a comforting sense of solidarity, in the name of their criminality and womanhood.

Zhong's essay, "Sisterhood?: Representations of Women's Relationships in Two Contemporary Chinese Texts," deals with an old but culturally silenced problem: the passionate, at times sexual, relationships among women. In intimacy, these women seriously question traditional roles imposed on their sex: daughter, wife, and mother. Zhong raises an interesting question at the end of her essay: Will women ever succeed in creating a space for themselves through the search for an individual identity? Since the notion of individual identities is predicated on male subjecthood, isn't the search necessarily doomed? Can women really approach the problem of subjectivity from the perspective of bourgeois individualism, which tends not to take gender awareness into consideration?

My essay, "Can Xue: What Is So Paranoid in Her Writings?," studies the works of an experimental woman writer of the late 1980s. Can Xue's writings radically disrupt the boundaries between signifieds and signifiers in language, between the law and criminals in society, and between the subjective and objective worlds. A number of male critics in mainland China explain the originality of Can Xue's works in terms of her alleged madness. Their accusation reveals that a woman writer's subversiveness is a threat even to the presumably avant-garde intellectuals because that subversiveness signifies a double marginality, a marginality in both language and sexuality.

WOMEN AND INFERIOR MEN: SALVATION, COMMODIFICATION, OR CRITICAL INTERVENTION?

For Confucius, women were as difficult to deal with as "inferior men." Some of us at the symposium suggested that we should perhaps call ourselves the "Inferior Men Study Group," in order that our "inferiority" may eventually disappear. Here we follow Gayatri Spivak's logic. Spivak was speaking of the name "subaltern":

> The subaltern is all that is not elite, but the trouble with those kinds of names is that if you have any kind of political interest you name it in the hope that the name will disappear.[30]

Jokingly or not, by naming ourselves "inferior men," we deny our inferiority in the very process of naming.

However, beyond the defiance of a dead male intellectual, our deliberate pose as "inferior men" is also meant as a reminder of the *artificial* nature of naming and the abuses that may follow from such naming. Such abuses are especially problematic when we speak *in the name* of a subordinate group, while hiding our own motives and intentions. Spivak's article, "Can the Subaltern Speak?," is useful, then, in a different way. Spivak convincingly shows us how the Indian ritual practice of widow burning, *sati*, was used either by certain Indian nationalists as the representation of male desire for a golden past, or more significantly, by British colonists as the justification for their colonization. While the former was eager to preserve the patriarchal order by proving the insubstantiality of a female life without a husband, through whom a woman's desire is articulated, the latter tried to justify their colonialism by abolishing this "inhuman" ritual "ethically." Caught between them, the subaltern, Spivak concludes, "cannot speak."[31] The fate of the voiceless subaltern is also the fate of tens of millions of Chinese women throughout the centuries. As intellectuals studying their fate in educational institutions in the West, we cannot simply identify with the subaltern or the Chinese woman. As Rey Chow argues in her essay, "Against the Lures of Diaspora: Minority Discourse, Chinese Women, and Intellectual Hegemony," the question remains if we can speak for/of them without reducing them to objects of representation of our own political interests only. Chinese women were already "saved" at least twice in modern history—first, by the radical May Fourth intellectuals, and then by the Communist Party. Do we want to duplicate the same mistake by "saving" them a third time through feminist theory? To paraphrase Spivak's statement "white men saving brown women from brown men," we need to ask metaphorically: Can white feminists save yellow women from yellow men?

Perhaps the absolutely negative answer Spivak gives to her own question—"the subaltern cannot speak"—should give way to a more flexible *question*: Can the subaltern be heard? And how? Spivak's own essay provides an answer when she describes the death of Bhuvaneswari Bhaduri, a young woman who committed suicide at the age of sixteen or seventeen in North Calcutta in 1924. The subaltern can indeed be heard—as Bhuvaneswari Bhaduri is through Spivak's writing. Subalterns do speak, but they do not necessarily speak as an American academician. It depends on how and to what extent intellectuals working in the First World are willing and able to understand them in their language, despite or thanks to their theoretical positions. By narrowing the definition of the term "speak" in her essay "Can the Subaltern Speak?," Spivak risks privileging the language, and thus the position, of First World intellectuals vis-à-vis Third World women despite her insightful criticism of British colonialism.[32]

Spivak herself writes earlier about French feminism:

> The point that I am trying to make is that, in order to learn enough about the Third World women and to develop a different readership, the immense heterogeneity of the field must be appreciated, and the First World feminist must learn to stop feeling privileged *as a woman*.[33]

As scholars teaching or studying at North American universities, we indeed enjoy some institutionalized privileges, such as a relatively greater freedom of speech and an easier access to certain kinds of information. But does this mean that we have nothing to learn from those who are less privileged in this respect, and who are the objects of our studies in one way or the other? In other words, are our institutionalized privileges sufficient to justify an overall privileged feeling with regard to Third World women? Why does the subaltern not have any other choice other than an objectified voice and total silence? How can we appreciate "the immense heterogeneity" of Third World women without a thorough understanding of their languages? Instead of hastening to teach them how to behave as "true women" or "true feminists" with a package of knowledge acquired in North American institutions, why can we not start to learn how to understand their positions in relation to social and historical changes? As Chow points out, we cannot avoid a certain degree of objectification when we speak for/of others. The question is how to minimize this degree.

Since China has undergone numerous upheavals and revolutions during the twentieth century, women, as the oppressed group of society, have been encouraged to participate in social changes, which are supposed to bring about their own emancipation. To a different degree, each of us, as a feminist studying Chinese literature and culture in the West, is facing the same problems as Chinese women during the revolution. Our voices, as representatives of Third World women, are easily commodified in the American academy, where Third World cultures have recently taken on a high exchange value.

The question remains as to whether we should accommodate ourselves to our commodification, or whether we should use it to resist commodification itself. The first option implies repeating whatever is fashionable in the American Academy regardless of the specificity of the gender situation in China. The second option requires a much more painstaking effort to make the voiceless subalterns, women in China, heard among Western intellectuals. This task raises the question: As feminist scholars working in the First World, are we able and willing to hear the voice(s) of women in China? The majority of our audience for the time being consists mainly of Western intellectuals, whose language is in fact different from that of the objects of our studies. In view of this situation, the first option, were we to choose it, would be far more convenient than the second, because all we need do is shape the object of our studies in the image and language of our audience according to the law of a market economy. But the price to pay would be heavy: we would contribute to our own silence by silencing the objects of our studies as in the case of the three May Fourth male authors criticized in Yue's essay. Similar to these radical intellectuals who objectively join the position of the conservative crowd in their patriarchal discourse, by suppressing the differences of Chinese women we risk reducing our voices to an echo of whatever sells in the American academy. The second option, which requires our understanding of women in China on their terms and our ability to communicate our understanding to the Western audience from a different cultural perspective, is much more difficult and hazardous, but would also be much more rewarding in the long run.

Without a genuine and painstaking effort to challenge and to go beyond the preconceived ethnocentric framework in which both we and our audience must function, multiculturalism would only be a fallacy in which representations of marginalized groups would serve as different forms of commodities in the market of First World ideology. Our complicity with the commodification of women in China as the objects of our studies, of which the commodification of our already problematized cultural and gender identities would be an unavoidable outcome, would objectively reduce us to silence by turning our voices into an echo of some Western intellectual saviors. Once again, these saviors may sit on the throne of the patriarchal figure, occupied in the past by the May Fourth radical intellectuals, the Communist Party, and presently in a devious form, by the searchers for masculinity in contemporary Chinese fiction. According to salvation logic, the culturally and sexually underprivileged group will very likely return to the bottom rung of a new hierarchy as soon as this group has accomplished its task of representation for its savior, because in the final analysis a savior is more concerned with his name than with the saved victim's life. However, the representational value of some individuals in the group may be transformed by the dominant culture into a fetichized image as in the cases of Nora in the May Fourth movement and of the white-haired girl in the socialist revolution. In both cases, the woman does not have her own voice, since she mainly functions as the speaker for her savior's ideology, which is basically masculinist in its aspirations.

Unlike Latin America, which provides a convenient "Other" for the American academy,[34] or India, which represents the thoroughly colonized Other—as well as a linguistically convenient Other, contemporary China is still a riddle to a large number of Western intellectuals in spite of their increasing interest in this culture. Because the situation of women in China in many respects differs largely from those in both First and Third World countries, it is even more difficult to speak for/of them. On the one hand, an artificial identification with women in China will unavoidably reinforce their objectification, taking into account the visible differences between their situation and ours despite our commitment to gender studies in China. On the other hand, an uncritical identification with Western feminists implies a universalization of Chinese women. This universalization treats contemporary Chinese women as duplications—most likely, inferior duplications—of middle class white women, such as their May Fourth forerunners in relation to Ibsen's Nora. In order to avoid a fallacious identification in one way or the other, we need to engage in dialogues with both our objects of studies and our audience. A dialogue, which, unlike salvation, implies exchange and equality between the two engaged parties, is the basis for mutual understanding. How can we successfully conduct dialogues with both women in China and a Western audience while respecting each other's differences? This is one of the most difficult questions and one we all hope our volume will take the lead in addressing.

At the same time, as Chow points out in her essay, it is still difficult to speak of gender in Chinese studies. If the term "gender" has been commodified outside the field of Chinese studies, inside it women have difficulties in making their voices heard either because gender as a subject is implicitly perceived as insignificant in relation to the mainstream of the field or because it echoes women's rights in communist discourse. But this difficult situation may play to our advantage if it forces us, lacking any other alternative, to become more sensitive to the problems of women in China.

Due to the current emphasis on multiculturalism in the American academy and to the greater resistance to the issues of gender studies in the field of Chinese studies, some of our problems resemble those faced by Chinese women during past revolutions. Like them, we are caught between an inflation of our representational values and a devaluation of our subjective voices. Like them, our voices are from time to time objectified as representations of various political interests, although their objectification occurred on the "battlefield of revolution,"[35] whereas ours is in the realm of the "poetics or politics of gender."[36] Consequently, women in China must pay a higher price for their representational power which serves as a weapon used on battlefields for or against communist ideology, whereas we as scholars in the West may

receive substantial "profits" for our commodified value as representatives of a minority discourse in the Western intellectual
supermarket.

In these circumstances, a thorough understanding of the
failures of women's emancipation in China may enable us to break
the spell of our own commodification. Women's emancipation in
China failed not only because a new patriarchal order attempted to
replace an old one by using women's representational power, but
also because Chinese women, for lack of gender awareness, could
not sufficiently resist their reductive roles as representations of
masculinist ideology. As feminist scholars we need to understand
that we cannot, as did Chinese women in past revolutions, indulge
ourselves in any illusion about trading our representational power
for salvation. As the failed women's emancipation in China has
demonstrated, salvation for the second sex typically amounts to a
transaction of women's representational value from one patriarchal order to another while maintaining the fundamental structure
of the traditional gender hierarchy.

However, since the acceptance of one form of domination
necessarily entails justifications for other inequalities, a fundamental change in the traditional gender hierarchy cannot come
about without the occurrence of similar changes in other existing
hierarchies, such as race and class. As part of the cultural and ideological map of a society, gender problems cannot be isolated from
other social aspects—woman does not exist as an abstract entity.
In this case, how can we contextualize the problem of women's
rights without risking falling into the same trap as did Chinese
women in their salvation? As a final note, we hope that this book
will invite our readers to join its contributors in our search for an
answer.[37]

NOTES

1. Confucius, *Analects*, Chap. 17, no. 23.

2. Mao Zedong, "The CCP Committee of the Hunan Province:
Fully Bringing Out Women's Initiative in the Revolution and Construction," *Honggi*, 1971/10, 63.

3. Meng Yue and Dai Jinhua, *Emerging from the Surface (Fuchu
lishi dibiao)* (Zhengzhou: Henan renmin chubanshe, 1989).

4. Meng Yue, for instance, told me in a phone conversation that
she could accept the misogyny manifested in the works of a great number

of male experimental writers since this is simply a sign of their attempt "to overcorrect the wrong doing (of the Communist Party)" (*jaowang guozheng*).

5. On June 15, 1918, the leading May Fourth journal *New Youth,* for example, devoted a special issue to Ibsen. This issue includes an article entitled "Ibsenism" by Hu Shih, "Ibsen's Biography." and part of translations of three of Ibsen's plays: *A Doll's House, An Enemy of the People, and Little Eyoff.*

6. *The White-Haired Girl (Baimao nü)*, a play written by a communist playwright, Tian Han, during the 1940s. A peasant girl, Xi'er, is raised by her widowed father, Yang Bailao, who works as a long-term hired hand for a rich landlord, Huang Shiren. Unable to pay the usury of his landlord, Yang is forced to commit suicide. After his death, Huang takes his daughter as payment for her father's debt. Whether or not Xi'er has been raped by her father's creditor has been an important issue in the subsequent adaptations of this play. Originally, she gives birth to a child and even has illusions about her future with the old landlord. When the play successively became a film, a ballet, and finally a film version of the revolutionary ballet during the Cultural Revolution (it was one of the only eight films to which one billion Chinese people had access during the decade of the Cultural Revolution), Xi'er is gradually turned into a brave rebel, who protects her virginity at the risk of her life. The rest of the story is less controversial than the heroine's problematic virginity. She takes refuge on a mountain top and eats wild fruits in order to survive. For want of salt, her hair turns completely white. In the end, she is saved by her run-away lover, Dachun, who has by then become a communist soldier. All ends well. The evil landlord is righteously punished, and her revolutionary lover saves her through marriage. See Meng Yue and Dai Jinhuas book, *Emerging from the Surface of History,* 265–66.

7. For a detailed analysis of the misogynistic connection between socialist realist literature and contemporary fiction, see my essay, " 'Red Sorghum:' Limits of Transgression," in Liu Kang and Tang Xiaobing, eds., *Politics, Ideology and Literary Discourse in Modern China* (Durham: Duke University Press, forthcoming).

8. Lu Xun, *Complete Works of Lu Xun (Lu Xun quanji)*, vol. 1 (Beijing: Renmin wenxue chubanshe, 1981), 159.

9. Ibid. 162.

10. Wu Jiming, "Women on the Top of the Tower" (*Tajian shang de nüxing*), Dai Qing et al., *Sexually Liberated Woman (Xing kaifang nüzi)* (Hong Kong: Yiwen tushu, 1988), 110–11.

11. This treatment of women writers was the topic of Wendy Larson's paper, "Definition and Suppression: Women's Literature in Post May

Fourth China," which was presented at the Iowa symposium. We regret that Larson's paper could not be included in this volume.

12. See Meng Yue and Dai Jinhua's chapter on Xiao Hong, "Xiao Hong: A Wise and Courageous Searcher" (*Xiao Hong: da zhiyong zhe de tansuo*), *Emerging from the Surface of History*, 174–99. Also see Lydia He Liu's paper, "The Female Body and Nationalist Discourse," presented at the Iowa symposium; she reads Xiao Hong's fiction as a protest against nationalism. We regret that Liu's paper could not be included in this volume.

13. Liu Shaoqi, *The Self-Cultivation of the Members of the Communist Party (Gongchandang yuan de xiuyang)*.

14. Meng Yue and Dai Jinhua, *Emergence from the Surface of History*, 31.

15. See my paper, " 'Red Sorghum:' Limits of Transgression," in Liu Kang and Tang Xiaobing, eds., *Politics, Ideology and literary Discourse in Modern China*.

16. Li Xiaojiang, *Eve's Search (Xiawa de tansuo)* (Zhengzhou: Henan renmin chubanshe, 1988), 222.

17. Ibid. 227.

18. On this subject, see some comments on "Root-searching Literature" by Chinese critics. For example, Guo Xiaodong, "The Totem of Motherhood: A Spiritual Variation of the Literature of Educated Young" (*Muxing tuteng: zhiqing wenxue de yizhong jingshen biange*), in *Shanghai wenxue*, 87/1, 90–96. Fan Keqiang, "Root-searchers: Primitive Tendency and Semi-primitivism" (*Xungenzhe: yuanshiqingxiang yu banyuanshizhuyi*), in *Shanghai wenxue*, 89/3, 64–69.

19. See Wang Xiaoming's analysis of the imaginary past in "Root-Searching Literature," "What One Does Not Believe and What One Does Not Want to Believe: Concerning the Literary Creation of Three 'Root-searching Writers' " (*Bu xiangxin de he bu yuanyi xiangxin de: guanyu sanwei "xungen" pai zuojia*), in *Wenxue pinglun*, 88/3.

20. Li Xiaojiang's expression in *Eve's Search*, 299.

21. See Huot's chapter in this collection.

22. See *Nüxing ren* special issue: "Can Old Men Be Modernized?," forthcoming.

23. Take for example A Cheng's three famous novellas published in the mid 1980s, "King of Chess," "King of Trees," and "King of Children" (*Qiwang, Shuwang, Haiziwang*). The protagonist of each of the three stories is a man who, by establishing a self-sufficient individual world, protects himself from the ideological and political oppression of the Commu-

nist Party during the Cultural Revolution. As the titles suggest, the heroes are superior to common people: they are "kings" in their independent masculine kingdoms. However, outside their fictional and solipsistic kingdom, the "kings" must still submit to the party line—passively and silently.

24. See Susan Suleiman's analysis of Western avant-garde writers on this subject. Susan Rubin Suleiman, "Pornography, Transgression, and the Avant-Garde: Bataille's Story of the Eye," in Nancy K. Miller, ed. *The Poetics of Gender* (New York: Columbia University Press, 1986), 132.

25. See Zhong Xueping's essay "Looking for a 'Real Man:' Female Desire in Modern Chinese Literature," forthcoming in *Signs*. This essay deals with a new form of humanism (underlying a traditional notion of sexuality) among contemporary Chinese women writers.

26. Ding Ling, "The Diary of Miss Sophia." For critical discussions of Ding Ling as a woman writer, see Tani Barlow's introduction to a collection of Ding Ling's short stories in English translation, *I Myself Am a Woman*, Tani Barlow and Gary Bjorge, eds. (Boston: Beacon Press, 1989), 1–45; and Yi-tsi Feuerwerker's *Ding Ling's Fiction: Ideology and Narrative in Modern Chinese Literature* (Cambridge: Harvard University Press, 1982). Rey Chow offers an insightful reading of the "Diary" story in *Woman and Chinese Modernity* (Minneapolis: University of Minnesota Press, 1991), 162–70.

27. See Meng Yue and Dai Jinhua's chapter on Xiao Hong in *Emerging from the Surface of History* (174–99) and Lydia He Liu's paper, "The Female Body and Nationalist Discourse."

28. See note 4.

29. See, for example, Dai Qing's report on women who committed the "double-marriage crime." Dai Qing, *"Double-Marriage Criminals"* (*Chonghun zui*), *Nüxing ren*, 1989/2.

30. Gayatri Spivak, "The New Historicism: Political Commitment and the Postmodern Critic," *The Post-Colonial Critic: Interviews, Strategies, Dialogues*, Sarah Harasym, ed. (New York and London: Rutledge, 1990), 158.

31. Gayatri Spivak, "Can the Subaltern Speak?," Gary Nelson and Lawrence Grossberg, eds. *Marxism and Interpretation of Culture* (Urbana: University of Illinois Press, 1988), 271–308.

32. As Henry Louis Gates points out: "My claim is that what Jacques Derrida calls writing, Spivak, in a brilliant reversal, has renamed colonial discourse. So it is no accident that the two terms share precisely the same functionality. The Derridian *mot*, that is nothing outside the text, is reprised as the argument that there is nothing outside (the dis-

course of) colonialism . . . Indeed, I think Spivak's argument, put in its strongest form, entails the corollary that all discourse is colonial discourse" (Henry Louis Gates, Jr., "Critical Fanonism," *Critical Inquiry,* Spring 1991, 466).

33. Gayatri Spivak, *In Other Worlds: Essays in Cultural Politics* (London: Routledge, 1988), 136, italicized by the author herself.

34. On March 7, 1991, at the University of Iowa, Jean Franco spoke of the internationalization of Latin American literature. According to Franco, for many South American women writers of the 1970s, the demand for their works in the publishing market of the United States existed before they even started writing. Latin American literature is easy to "access" because of the geographical proximity of the countries to the U.S.A. and the relatively wide use of Spanish in certain American states.

35. Meng Yue and Dai Jinhua, *Emerging from the Surface of History,* 59.

36. Susan Rubin Suleiman, "Pornography, Transgression, and the Avant-Garde: Bataille's Story of the Eye," in Nancy K. Miller, ed. *The Poetics of Gender,* 132.

37. I am grateful to Rey Chow for her painstaking effort to help me edit and restructure the first version of this essay, to Ruth Weil for her final editing, to Yue Ming-bao, and to Zhong Xueping for their constructive suggestions, as well as to Liu Kang for his reading which helped me view certain problems from a different perspective.

1

Against the Lures of Diaspora:
Minority Discourse, Chinese
Women, and Intellectual
Hegemony

MODERN CHINESE LITERATURE AS "MINORITY DISCOURSE"

The questions I should like to address in this chapter can be stated very simply: Why is it so difficult to bring up the topic of women in the field of Chinese studies? What can the critical spotlight on "Chinese women" tell us about the discursive politics in play?

These questions are not only questions about women and Chinese studies. They have to do with the problematic of post-colonial discursive space in which many Third World intellectuals who choose to function in the First World. Within that space, these intellectuals are not only natives but spokespersons for natives in the Third World. Currently, the prosperity of that space is closely tied up with the vast changes taking place in Western academic institutions, notably in North America, where many intellectuals "of color" are serving as providers of knowledge about their nations and cultures. The way these intellectuals function is therefore inseparable from their status as cultural workers/brokers in diaspora, which may be a result of graduate studies, research, visiting or permanent appointments, immigration, and, in some cases, exile or political asylum.

In this chapter, I want to use the increasing interest in women in the field of Chinese studies as a way to focus the problems of the Third World intellectual in diaspora. The implications of these problems go far beyond narrow institutional designators such as "women's studies" and "area studies" in which the study of Third World women is most commonly lodged.

Superficial developments in the humanities across the U.S.A. indicate the opposite of the first of my opening questions. Following the legitimation of feminist interests in the West, receptivity to women's issues in other parts of the world seems now without precedents. In the Asian field, it is not difficult to find research projects, dissertations, books, and conferences devoted to women. Perhaps for the first time in Asian history, we can identify a visible group of scholars, largely female, whose work centers on women. And yet the spotlight on women in our field seems also to make the shape and sound of the enemy more pronounced than ever.

I use "enemy" to refer not to an individual but to the attitude that "women" is still not a legitimate scholarly concern. Depending on the occasion, this enemy uses a number of different but related tactics. The first tactic may be described as habitual myopia: "You don't exist because I don't see you," The second is conscience-clearing genitalism:[1] "Women? Well, of course! . . . But I am not a woman myself, so I will keep my mouth shut." The third is scholarly dismissal: "Yes, women's issues are interesting, but they are separate and the feminist approach is too narrow to merit serious study." The fourth is strategic ghettoization: since "women" are all talking about the same thing over and over again, give them a place in every conference all in one corner, let them have their say, and let's get on with our business. These tactics of the enemy—and it is important for us to think of the enemy in terms of a dominant symbolism rather than in terms of individuals; that is, a corpus of attitudes, expressions, discourses, and the *value* espoused in them—are not limited to the China field. They are descriptive of the problems characteristic of the study of non-hegemonic subjects in general.

Leaving aside the issue of women for the time being, I should like to argue that the notion of modern Chinese literature as we know it today depends, implicitly, on the notion of a minority discourse in the postcolonial era. As two critics define it, "minority discourse is, in the first instance, the product of damage, of damage more or less systematically inflicted on cultures produced as minorities by the dominant culture."[2] Modern Chinese literature is, in this respect, not different from other postcolonial national literatures. Its problems are symptomatic of the histories of non-Western cultures' struggles for cultural as well as national autonomy in the aftermath of Western imperialism. Because postcolonial literatures are linked to the hegemonic discourse of the West as such, they are, in spite of the typical nativist argument for their continuity with the indigenous traditions,[3] always effectively viewed as a kind of minority discourse whose existence has been victimized and whose articulation has been suppressed.

While the worldwide significance of modern Chinese literature derives from its status as a minority discourse, it is precisely this minority status that makes it so difficult for modern Chinese literature to be legitimized as world literature. Other *national* literatures—notably English, French, and Russian—have had much wider claims to an international modernity in spite of their historical and geographical specificity. In spite—and because—of the current clamor for minority discourses, there are not a few voices supporting the opposite viewpoint. The debates in the U.S.A. on the issue of canonicity, for instance, are driven by the urge to perpetuate what has been established as the universals of cultural literacy. In fact, the more frequently that minor voices are heard, the greater is the need expressed by the likes of Allan Bloom and E. D. Hirsch, Jr., for maintaining a canon, so that a Western notion of humanity can remain as the norm.[4] We understand from the Gulf war that it is by resorting to the rhetoric of preserving universals—love, knowledge, justice, tradition, civilization, and so forth, argued both in George Bush's "new world order" and Saddam Hussein's pan-Arabism—that political power sustains its ideological hold on the populace. The rhetoric of universals, in other words, as what assures the ghettoized existence of the other, be it in the form of a different culture, religion, race, or sex. As is well known, the battle against the ideology embedded in the rhetoric of universals is also one faced by those working on the theme of women in the China field.

The proposal I want to make, however, is that, for the investigators of Chinese women, this battle *cannot* simply be fought by recourse to minority discourse, or to Chinese women as the suppressed and victimized other. I will explain by discussing the precarious relation between minority discourse and women in the China field, with a special emphasis on the difficult and challenging role of Chinese women intellectuals today.

Consider one of the primary tasks faced by Chinese intellectuals in the twentieth century—that of establishing, in the throes of imperialism, a national literature. If the desire to establish a national literature is a desire for a kind of universal justice—a justice in the eyes of which Chinese literature and culture would become legitimate internationally rather than simply Chinese—how is this desire pursued? While there are many efforts to demonstrate the continuity of modern Chinese literature with past literary achievements, what distinguishes modern Chinese writings is an investment in suffering, an investment that aims at exposing social injustice. This investment in—or cathexis to—suffering runs through Chinese cultural production from the beginning of the twentieth century to the present—from the upsurge of interest in romantic love in popular Mandarin Duck and Butterfly stories of the 1910s, to the proscience and prodemocracy attempts at national self-strengthening in May Fourth writings, to the focuses on class struggle in the literature of the 1930s and 40s, to the official communist practice of "speaking bitterness" (*suku*), by which peasants were encouraged by cadres of the liberation forces to voice their sufferings at mass meetings in the 1950s and 60s, and to the outcries of pain and betrayal in the "wounded literature" (*shanghen wenxue*) of the post-Cultural Revolution period. In other words, the attempt to establish a *national* literature in the postcolonial era requires a critical edge other than belief in a magnificent past. For twentieth-century Chinese intellectuals, this critical edge has been *class consciousness*. In orthodox Marxist terms, class is the contradiction between the surplus of capital on the one hand, and labor on the other. The surplus of capital leads to a situation in which those who do the least work enjoy the most privileges, while those who work continue to have the products of their labor taken or alienated from them. The category of class thus supplies a means of analyzing social injustice in economic terms, as the unequal distribution of wealth between the rich and the poor.⁵ In the Chinese context, in which intellectual work was formerly part of the hegemony of the state, class consciousness is inseparable from *cultural* revolution, a revolution that seems not only to overthrow the economic but specifically the ideological dominance of the ruling classes. Thus even in the crudest usage by Chinese communists, alienated labor carries ideological as well as economic implications.

The historian Arif Dirlik refers to the use of class for nation-building as the practice of the proletarian nation. Commenting on a passage from *The Crisis of the Arab Intellectual* by Abdallah Laroui (who derived much of his historicism from Joseph Levenson's work on China), Dirlik writes:

[The new China is] the "proletarian" nation of revolutionary intellectuals (Li Dazhao, Sun Yat-sen, Mao Zedong come to mind immediately). If it does not bring the proletariat (or the oppressed classes) into the forefront of history, it at least makes them into a central component of the national struggle—as a referent against which the fate of ideas and values must be judged.⁶

We cannot understand modern Chinese literature without understanding the ways in which nationhood and class are intertwined in literary discourse. The use of class consciousness as a way to build a national culture is one of the most important signs of Chinese literary modernity, a modernity that is, as May Fourth and subsequent writings show, self-consciously revolutionary. If modern Chinese literature emerges as an other, a minor literature in the global scene, it also emerges by putting the spotlight on its oppressed classes, among which women occupy one, but not the only, place.

In its investment in suffering, in social oppression, and in the victimization and silencing of the unprivileged, modern Chinese literature partakes of the many issues of minority discourse that now surface with urgency in the field of cultural studies/cultural criticism in North America today. Central to such issues is the question: "Can the subaltern speak?," as we find it in Gayatri Spivak's essay of the same title.⁷ In this regard, the history of modern Chinese literature can be seen as a paradigm for contemporary cultural studies, simply because the most written figure in this history is none other than the subaltern, whose speech has been coming to us through fiction, poetry, political debates, historical writings, journalistic representations, as well as radio plays, films, operas, and regional cultural practices. In a fashion paralleling the theorizations of minority discourse that emphasize the production of postcolonial subjects whose speeches or writings disrupt the hegemonic discourse of the imperialist, modern Chinese literature specializes, one might argue, in producing figures of minority whose overall effect has been an ongoing protest against the cultural violence they experience as physical, familial, institutional, and national levels. At the same time, the conscious representation of the minor as such also leads to a situation in which it is locked in opposition to the hegemonic in a permanent bind. The minor cannot rid itself of its minority status, because it is that status that gives it its only legitimacy.[8] Support for the minor, however sincere, always becomes support for the center. In communist China, one could even say that class consciousness, as it becomes an ideological weapon of the state, offers a critical edge only insofar as it permanently regenerates the reality of social injustice rather than its dissolution.

How is this so? Let me explain by relating class consciousness to the conceptualization of social change *through language.* Among Marxist critics working in the West, the advocacy of class consciousness is often closely related to a specific theory of language. For instance, speaking of the subaltern, Gayatri Spivak says:

> The subaltern is all that is not elite, but the trouble with those kinds of names is that, if you have any kind of political interest you name it in the hope that the name will disappear. That's what class consciousness is in the interest of: the class disappearing. What politically we want to see is that the name would not be possible.[9]

The theory of language offered here is that the act of articulating something moves and changes it, and therefore may cause it to disappear. In China, however, the relation between language and reality has been very differently conceived, because of the lingering force of Confucius's concept of *zhengming*—the rectification of names. The Confucian attitude toward language is expressed in a well-known passage in *Lunyü* (The analects):

> If names be not correct, language is not in accordance with the truth of things. If language be not in accordance with the truth of things, affairs cannot be carried on to success. . . .

Therefore a superior man considers it necessary that the names he uses may be spoken *appropriately*, and also that what he speaks may be carried out *appropriately*. What the superior man requires is just that in his words there may be nothing incorrect.[10]

For Confucius as for the majority of Chinese people, naming is the opposite of what Spivak suggests. Instead of causing the reality to disappear, naming is the way to make a certain reality proper— that is, to make it real. That is why it is so important to have the right name and the right language.

To use the words of Slavoj Zizek, we may say that Confucius understood "the radical contingency of naming, the fact that naming itself retroactively constitutes its reference." It is "the name itself, the signifier, which supports the identity of the object."[11] "In other words," Zizek writes, "the only possible definition of an object in its identity is that this is the object which is always designated by the same signifier—tied to the same signifier. It is the signifier which constitute the kernel of the object's 'identity.' "[12] Strictly speaking, there is nothing false or misleading about Confucius's theory of language. As a process, *zhengming* demonstrates the practical politics involved in any claim to visibility and existence—namely, that such a claim must be at the same time a claim to and in language. Hence, even though—in fact, precisely because—it is *no more than a claim*, language is the absolutely essential means of access to power. In their struggles to be seen and heard, minority groups all prove the truth of Confucius's theory: before dismantling and decentering power in the way taught by deconstructionists, they argue, they must first have power and be named—that is, recognized.

The act of naming, then, is not intrinsically essentialist or hierarchical. It is the social relationships in which names are inserted that may lead to essentialist, hierarchical, and thus detrimental consequences.[13] Historically, the problem with Confucius's teaching was that it was used to address civil servants in their service to the state. A very astute understanding of language was thus instrumentalized in organizing political hierarchy and consolidating centralized state power, with all the reactionary implications that followed. *Zhengming* became a weapon that assured the immovability of an already established political hegemony and in that sense a paradigmatic case, in Derrida's terms, of *logocentric* governance.

By extension, we understand why, in their mobilization of class consciousness, the Chinese communists have actually been following the Confucian model of language as it is inherited in Chinese politics in spite of their overt ideological contempt for the Master. The raising of class consciousness as official reeducational policy during the two decades following 1949 did not so much lead to the disappearance of class as it did to a reification/rectification of the name class as the absolute reality to which all citizens had to submit in order to clear their conscience. Hence, in pursuit of the ideal of the proletarian nation, strengthening national culture became equal to hunting down the class enemy, even though class enemy was *simply a name*. In a discussion of the contemporary Chinese political situation by way of Jacques Lacan's notion of *jouissance*, Kwai-cheung Lo writes:

> The "class enemy" in the Chinese Cultural Revolution is, in a sense, a fetish structuring the jouissance. The whole country is summoned to ferret out the class enemy, to uncover the hidden counter-revolutionaries. The class enemy is everywhere, in every nook and corner of our social life, but it is also nowhere, invisible and arcane. It is clear that the class enemy is jouissance, which is an impossibility but can produce traumatic effects. It is also the *objet petit à*, a pure void which keeps symbolic order working and sets the Cultural Revolution in motion. The paradoxical character of the class enemy is that it always returns to the same place, exerts effects on the reality of the subject, and it is itself a nothing, a negativity. Thus, in the end, when we have looked in every corner to ferret out the class enemy, we then have to uncover the enemy in our heart. The Cultural Revolution turns out to be a Stalinist trial. Everyone must examine their whole life, their entire past, down to the smallest detail, to search for the hidden fault and, finally, confess themselves as sinners. . . . When the people are asked to confess, to "open their hearts to" (*jiaoxin*) the Party, and they look deep into their hearts, what they find is not a subject who is unable to express the signified, but a void, a lack which has to be filled out by the object, the sin, the incarnation of impossible enjoyment, jouissance.[14]

In their obsession with the name class enemy, the rectification of which led to the madness of the Cultural Revolution, the Chinese communists thus proved themselves to be loyal disciples of Confucius's teaching about state control.

Perhaps the greatest and most useful lesson modern Chinese culture has to offer the world is the pitfall of building a nation—the People's Republic of China—on a theory of social change—class consciousness—in the illusion that the hope offered by that theory—the disappearance of class itself—can actually materialize in human society. Chinese communism was the dream of materializing that theory of officializing a concept of language and literature in which the minorities, the oppressed, and the exploited are to be vindicated. But when the force of class consciousness is elevated to official ideology rather than kept strictly as an analytic instrument (as it was in the texts of Marx), it also becomes mechanical and indistinguishable from other ideological strongholds of governmental power. To date, the mainland government is still trying to keep this rhetoric of class consciousness alive after its latest abuse of the peaceful seekers of democratic reform. When a government that was originally founded on the ideal of social justice dwindles to the level of open injustice and continual deception of its people, as the Chinese government does today, we must seek strategies that are alternative to a continual investment in minority, in suffering, and in victimization.

MASCULINIST POSITIONS IN THE CHINA FIELD: WOMEN TO THE WEST, FATHERS TO CHINESE WOMEN

The clarified relation between nation and class in twentieth-century China allows one to ask: How do women intervene? How can we articulate women's *difference* without having that difference turned into a cultural ghettoization of women while the enemy remains intact? How can women "speak"?

Current trends in contemporary cultural studies, while being always supportive of categories of difference, also tend to reinscribe those categories in the form of fixed identities. As in *zhengming*, categories such as race, class, and gender were originally named in order to point out what has been omitted in mainstream categorizations and thus what still remains to be named, seen, and heard. Names of difference as such are meant as ways for the marginalized to have some access to the center. And yet one feels that these categories of difference are often used in such a way as to stabilize, rather than challenge, a preestablished method of examining cultural diversity, whereby difference becomes a sheer

matter of adding new names in an ever-expanding pluralistic hori-
zon. If categories such as race, class, and gender are to remain useful means of critical intervention, they must not be lined up with
one another in a predictable refrain and attached to all investigations alike as packaging. Instead, as terms of intervention, they
must be used to analyze, decode, and criticize one another. Thus,
for instance, gender is not only gender but what has been muted in
orthodox discussions of class, while class is often what notions
such as woman or even sexual difference tend to downplay in
order to forge a gendered politics. How do we conceive of gender
within class and distinguish class within gender? How is it that
scholars, including Asianists, seem more ready to accept gender
when it is spoken of *generally* across the disciplines, while to
bring it up in the interpretation so specific texts within a particular field, such as Chinese studies, one still runs the risk of being
considered unscholarly and nonobjective?

A valid point made by Dirlik is that in order to destroy cul-
turalist hegemony, it is not enough to concentrate on unequal relations between nations (such as those between the First and Third
worlds). What is of similar importance is an investigation of the
unequal relations *within* societies. In the context of China, the
narrative of class as a way to address the unequal relations within
society has proved itself inadequate, because of its official abuse,
an abuse which takes the form of an armed appropriation—a turning into property and propriety—of a particular language, the language of the oppressed or what we have been calling minority discourse. That is to say, if the past forty years of Chinese political
history has been a failed revolution, it is in part because the revolution has been a secret cohabitation between Confucius and the
communists, between *zhengming* and a theory of language in
which naming is, ideally, the first step to changing social reality.
In this cohabitation, Confucius, saturated with practices of
bureaucratic hierarchy, remains on top.

After June 4, 1989, it is unlikely that the Chinese intellectuals who have begun careers in the West will return to China. In
their diaspora, Chinese intellectuals will emerge as a group whose
distinction from the objects they use for their research will be
more and more pronounced. Geographic, linguistic, and political
differences are going to turn internationalized Chinese women
intellectuals, for instance, into a privileged class vis-à-vis the
women in China. As we continue to use Chinese women's writings and lives as the raw materials for our research in the West,

the relationship between us as intellectuals overseas and them at home will increasingly take on the coloration of a kind of master discourse/native informant relationship. The inequality of this relationship should now be emphasized as that inequality *within* a social group that Dirlik mentions. While intellectuals are rewarded for their work in the West, voices of the oppressed continue to be unheard and intellectual work continues to be persecuted in China. There is very little we can do overseas to change the political situation back there. The attention bestowed upon Chinese events by the world media is arbitrary. In early 1991, for instance, as global attention was directed toward the Gulf war, the Chinese government's trial and sentencing of the June 4 protesters went largely unnoticed. Whether we like it or not, our position with regard to China is waiting and hoping.

As minority discourse becomes a hot topic in cultural studies in the West, some overseas Chinese intellectuals are now choosing to speak and write from a minor position. While enjoying the privilege of living in the West, they cling, in their discourse, to the status of the neglected other. While this espousal of minority status may not be stated as such, it is most often detected in discourses which moralistically criticize the West in the name of real Chinese difference or otherness. Depending on the political interest of the person, Chinese difference (by which is usually meant Chinese identity) may take the form of a reactionary confirmation of traditional, humanistic attitudes toward culture and knowledge, or it may assume a liberalist guise by reading Chinese culture in terms of the Bakhtinian dialogic and carnivalesque. In some cases, while being fashionably skeptical of Western theory, these intellectuals nonetheless revere Fredric Jameson's ethnocentric notion that all Third World texts are necessarily to be read as "national allegories"[15] and proceed to read Chinese culture accordingly. However, to nationalize Third World cultural productions allegorically is also to "other" them uniformly with a logic of production that originates in the West. What is being forgotten here is how First World production comprises not only the production of tangible goods but also intangible value. The latter, as I will argue in the following pages, is exported as ideological exploitation, which plays a far more crucial role in structuring lives of peoples in the non-West. Without a discussion of value as such, the notion that all Third World texts are "national allegories" is quite preposterous.[16] In Jameson's model, Third World intellectuals are, regardless of their class and gender, made to speak uniformly as minors and women to the West. Following Jameson, many contemporary Chinese intellectuals' desire to play the role of the other confirms what Nancy Armstrong, writing about the historicization of sexuality in the British novel, says: "the modern individual was first and foremost a woman."[17]

Vis-à-vis insiders of the China field, on the other hand, these intellectuals' strategy is decidedly different. There, faced with new types of research and new interests such as women's issues, their attitude becomes, once again, patriarchal and mainstream; women's issues do not interest them in the way *their own minority* in relation to the West does. Faced with women, their attitude resembles that of right-wingers in the American academy. They defend tradition, sinocentrism, and heritage, and denounce feminist scholarship as unscholarly. It is as if, dealing with insiders, they no longer remember the political significance of the minority discourse which they speak only when it is opportune for them to do so. They are minors and women when faced with foreigners; they are fathers when faced with insiders, especially women.

To return, then, to the question of why it is so difficult to bring up the topic of women in the field of Chinese studies. It is difficult not because women's issues are insignificant—there has been interest in woman and the new woman in Chinese writings since before the 1910s. Quite to the contrary, it is because woman, like the minor, offers such an indispensable position *in discourse*, traditional and modern, that feminists have difficulty claiming her. One question that traditionalists in the field often ask feminists is: But there is no lack of femininity in classical Chinese literature! Why are you saying that the feminine has been suppressed? A look at the Chinese literary language would suggest that these traditionalists are, literally, right: *Chinese literary history has been a history of men who want to become women.* In the past, male authors adopted women's voices and wrote in feminine styles; in the modern period, male authors are fascinated by women as a new kind of literary as well as social content. We may therefore argue that it is in the sense of men preempting women's place as the minor (vis-à-vis both tradition and the West) and claiming that place for themselves that "the Chinese woman," to use Mao Zedong's words to André Malraux, "doesn't yet exist."[18] Chinese women are, in terms of the structure of discourse, a kind of minor of the minor, the other to the woman that is Chinese man.

Throughout the twentieth century, it is the continual creation of alternative *official minor positions* that continually puts off a direct attack on the subjugation of women. To defend Chinese culture, pairs of oppositions are always set up: tradition and modernity, China and the West, China and Japan, the communists and the nationalists, and feudal landlords and the people, the rich and the poor, and so forth. The place of a minor discourse—as that which must struggle to speak—is therefore always already filled as long as there is always a new political target to fight against. The common view that women's issues always seem to be subsumed under the larger historical issues of the nation, the people, and so forth, is therefore true but also a reversal of what happens in the process of discourse construction. For in order for us to construct a large historical issue, a position of the victim/minor must always already be present. In terms of language, this means for a (new) signifier to emerge as a positive presence, there must always be a lack/negative supporting it. The producer of the new signifier, however, always occupies (or identifies with) the space of the lack/negative (since it is empty) in order to articulate. This goes to show why, for instance, among all the Chinese people, it is the peasants, the ones who are most illiterate, most removed from the intellectuals, and therefore most lacking in terms of the dominant symbolic, who most compel progressive Chinese intellectuals' fantasy.[19] Chinese women, on the other hand, are always said to be as powerful as Chinese men: we keep hearing that they "hold up half the sky." If minority discourse is, like all discourse, not simply a fight for the content of the oppression that it is ostensibly about, but also a fight for the ownership—the propriety, the property—of speaking (that is, for *zhengming*), then Chinese women are precluded from that ownership, because it has always been assumed by others in the name of the people, the oppressed classes, and the nation.

Precisely because the truly minor is the voiceless, it can be seized upon and spoken for. As Spivak says, "If the subaltern can speak . . . the subaltern is not a subaltern any more."[20] The Chinese communist government serves a good example of an agency speaking for minorities in order to mobilize an entire nation. As such, its governance is in accordance with a notion of marginality "which implicitly valorizes the center."[21] For intellectuals working on women in the China field, therefore, the first critical task is to break alliance with this kind of official sponsorship of minority discourse. Instead, they need to use their work on Chinese women to deconstruct the paternalistic social consequences resulting from a hegemonic practice of *zhengming* itself.

THE DISSOLUTE WOMAN AND THE FEMALE SAINT

In a recent interview with the press in Hong Kong, the Taiwanese feminist Xü Xiaodan, well known for her nudity in political campaigns, described her ambition in the following way: "I will enter Congress in the image of a dissolute woman; I will love the people with the soul of a female saint."[22] What is remarkable about Xü Xiaodan's statements is the introduction of a feminist practice that refuses conformity with the Chinese elite. The meaning of the term elite varies from society to society,[23] and I use it here to designate those among the Chinese who have had the privilege of being highly educated and whose views of female sexuality remain in accordance with the Confucian and neo-Confucian notions of female chastity. The point, however, is not for Chinese intellectuals to exclude/excuse themselves from the elite, but rather to break up the traditional alliance between education and Confucian standards of female sexuality.

While being well educated herself, Xü Xiaodan challenges the traditional morality that demands Chinese women to be chaste, self-sacrificing, and thus virtuous. Her politics is different from the sentimental sponsorship of the oppressed that we often encounter in minority discourse. For if traditional morality organizes female sexuality by upholding the female saint and condemning the dissolute woman, Xü Xiaodan does not simply criticize that morality by speaking up as the minor—the dissolute woman—only. Instead she shows that it is by straddling the positive and the negative, the clear distinction between which is absolutely essential for traditional morality's functioning, that she speaks and acts as a feminist. Instead of speaking from the position of minority, then, she offers a model that by its very impure nature defies the epistemic violence underlying the perpetual dependence of the minor on the center. Women's sexuality, hitherto strictly organized according to the difference between the female saint and the dissolute woman, returns to a freedom that is not an arbitrary freedom to act as one wishes, but rather a freedom *from* the mutual reinforcement between education and morality, which are welded together by stratifying female sexuality.

Where the notion of class allows us the negative capacity to criticize privilege but never identify with it, the notion of gender can operate both from and against privilege, allowing us the possibility of both identification and opposition. This means that we can, as we must, attack social injustice without losing sight of the fact that even as women speaking for other women, for instance, we speak from a privileged position. While an orthodox class consciousness would have us repress the self-reflexive knowledge of the speaking intellectual's social position as such (since to reflect on one's own privileged voice would be to destroy the illusion that one is speaking purely for universal justice), gender, insofar as it shows the organization of female sexuality in ways that are related but not restricted to class, makes it easier (though not necessary) to reflect on the difference between the speaking subject and the spoken object. This is because that difference (between the privileged and unprivileged) has not been prescribed as the definitive object of attack as it is in class consciousness. Paradoxically, therefore, it is because class consciousness has chosen social injustice as its target and its content that it cannot reflect on the form of its own possibly privileged, unjust utterances. Self-reflection of this kind leads only to paralysis, as we see in many examples of May Fourth literature.

Lu Xun's literary texts, I think, best illustrate this point. The question that his stories often imply is: How can intellectuals pretend to be speaking for the oppressed classes since, precisely, we have a voice while they do not? Do not speaking and writing already mark our social privilege and permanently separate us from them? If it is true that our speech takes its raw materials from the suffering of the oppressed, it is also true that it takes its capital from the scholarly tradition, from the machineries of literacy and education, which are affordable only to a privileged few.

On the other hand, because its target and content is the inequality between the sexes, an issue which is not limited to a narrow definition of class difference (in which having privileges equals bad and not having privilege equals good), gender has room for enabling reflection on the inequality inherent in the construction of discourse—that is, the difference that separates those who speak and those who are spoken of/for. Precisely because its content is not necessarily economic (in the narrow sense described above), the discourse of gender *can* know its own economic privilege. Knowing its own form as such does not, unlike in the case of a practice of class consciousness that must remain blind to itself, annul its project.

In the field of China studies, gender and women's issues are likely to emerge as the predominant critical paradigm in the years to come. This will be so not *only* because of Chinese women's traditionally minor status. Rather, it will be because, even while they may choose, from time to time, to forsake the claims of their femininity, *intellectual* Chinese women who speak of Chinese women will, I hope, not forget their own social position. While they do not lose sight of the oppression of women, these intellectuals should admit rather than repress the inequality inherent in discourse and the difference between them and their objects. They should articulate women's issues both as dissolute women and as female saints, but never as either one only. If the relative freedom in intellectual work that the Chinese living in the liberal West enjoy is a privilege, Chinese intellectuals must use this privilege as truthfully and as strategically as they can—not merely to speak as exotic minors, but to fight the crippling effects of Western imperialism and Chinese paternalism at once.

POSTSCRIPT: THE LURES OF DIASPORA

At the two conferences where this chapter was presented,[24] there were questions as to whether what I am doing is not a kind of essentialist identity politics in which, once again, the authenticity of a particular group is privileged. These questions demand a detailed response.

If we describe the postcolonial space in Hegelian terms, we can say that it is a space in which the object (women, minorities, other peoples) encounters its Notion (criterion for testing object), or in which the being-in-itself encounters the being-for-an-other. In this encounter, consciousness undergoes a transformation, so that it is no longer only consciousness of the object but also consciousness of itself, of its own knowledge. What consciousness previously took to be the object *in-itself,* Hegel writes, is not an *in-itself* but an in-itself (an object) *for consciousness.* Hence consciousness has, in truth, *two* objects—object and knowledge of object—which do not mutually correspond but are related in a movement Hegel calls experience:

> Since consciousness thus finds that its knowledge does not correspond to its object, the object itself does not stand the test; in other words, the criterion for testing is altered when that for which it was to have been the criterion fails to pass

the test; and the testing is not only a testing of what we know, but also a testing of the criterion of what knowing is. . . . *Inasmuch as the new true object issues from it*, this *dialectical* movement which consciousness exercises on itself and which affects both its knowledge and its object, is precisely what is called *experience (Erfahrung)*.[25]

Supplementing Hegel, we may say that this *dialectics of experience* finds one of its most compelling personifications in the Third world intellectual in diaspora. While their cultures once existed for Western historians and anthropologists as objects of inquiry within well-defined geographic domains, the growing presence of these intellectuals in First World intellectual circles fundamentally disrupts the production of knowledge—what Edward Said calls Orientalism—that has hitherto proceeded by hiding the agenda of inquirers and naturalizing the objects as givens. To paraphrase Hegel, First World inquirers must now cope with the fact that their objects no longer correspond to their consciousness. Third World intellectuals, for their part, acquire and affirm their own consciousness only to find, continually, that it is a consciousness laden with the history of their objecthood. This history confronts them all the more acutely once they live in the First World, where they discover that, regardless of personal circumstances, they are beheld as the other.

The explosive nature of this dialectics of experience deals the death blow to older forms of protest that were bound to native territorial and cultural propriety. *For Third World intellectuals especially*, this means that the recourse to alterity—the other culture, nation, sex, or body in another historical time and geographic space—no longer suffices as a means of intervention simply because alterity as such is still the older pure object (the being-in-itself) that has not been dialectically grasped. Such recourse to alterity is repeatedly trapped within the lures of a self-image—a nativism—that is, precisely, imperialism's other.

In naming Chinese women intellectuals, thus, my intention is not to establish them as a more authentic group of investigators whose claim to women in the Chinese field would exclude that of other investigators. Naming here is, first and foremost, a way to avoid repeating the well-worn discursive paradigm of Orientalism, in which the peoples of the non-West are taken factographically as objects without consciousness, while the historical privileges of

speaking subjects—in particular the privileges of having consciousness—remain unarticulated.

Second, naming is also a way of *not giving in* to the charms
of an alterity in which so many of the West's others are now called
upon to speak. Naming is not so much an act of consolidating
power as it is an act of making explicit the historical predicament
of investigating China and Chinese women, especially as it pertains to those who are ethnically Chinese and/or sexually women.

Third, it follows that naming the investigators amid the current multicultural interest in women in non-Western fields is also
a means of accentuating the otherwise *muted* fact of intellectual
women's privilege as intellectuals and thus (particularly in the
Chinese context) as members of the elite. While this privilege is,
at this point, hardly acknowledged in the masculinist explorations
of modernity, nationhood, and literature—because masculinist
explorations are themselves preoccupied with their own minority
and womanhood vis-à-vis the West—it is peremptory that women
investigators, especially Chinese women investigators investigating the history of Chinese women's subordination, handle the
mode of their speech—which historically straddles the elite and
the subaltern—with deliberate care. In naming them as such,
therefore, my point is to place on them the burden of a kind of
critical awareness that has yet to be articulated in their field. The
weight of each of the terms under which they work—Chinese,
women, intellectual—means that their alliances with other discursive groups, as well as their self-reflection on their own positions,
must always be astute. Both practices, allying with others and
reflecting on oneself, are by necessity more demanding than a
blanket dismissal of names and identities as essentialist.[26] Such a
dismissal is often the result of an ahistorical espousal of difference
and femininity as is found in some influential theories which, by
equating the feminine with the negative and the unrepresentable,
dismiss all processes of identification as positivistic. (A good case
in point is the work of Julia Kristeva, which is popular with many
feminist critics despite Kristeva's unwillingness to name woman[27]
and to name herself feminist.) The question on which to insist,
however, is not to name or not to name but: What is to be gained
or lost in naming what and whom, and by whom?

What I am arguing can also be stated in a different way: What
are we doing talking about modern Chinese literature and Chinese
women in the North American academy in the 1990s? As such
activities of speaking and writing are tied less to the oppressed

women in Chinese communities in China than to our own intellectual careers in the West, we need to unmask ourselves through a scrupulous declaration of self-interest. Such declaration does not clean our hands, but it prevents the continuance of a tendency, rather strong among Third World intellectuals in diaspora as well as researchers of non-Western cultures in First World nations, to sentimentalize precisely those day-to-day realities from which they are distanced.

The diasporic postcolonial space is, as I already indicate, neither the space of the native intellectual protesting against the intrusive presence of foreign imperialists in the indigenous territory, nor is it the space of the postcolonial critic working against the lasting effects of cultural domination in the home country (now an independent "nation") after the phase of territorial imperialism. In the case of China, it is necessary to remember that Chinese territory, with the exception of Taiwan from 1895 to 1945 and Hong Kong from 1842 to 1997, was never completely colonized over a long period by any one foreign power, even though the cultural effects of imperialism are as strong as in other formerly colonized countries in Asia, Africa, and Latin America. One could perhaps say that such cultural effects of foreign dominance are, in fact, *stronger*: they are most explicit, paradoxically, when one sees how the mainland Chinese can hold onto the illusion—born of modern Western imperialism but itself no less imperialistic—of a native land, a *zuguo*, that was never entirely captured and that therefore remains glorious to this day.

The space of the Third World intellectuals in diaspora is a space that is removed from the ground of earlier struggles that were still tied to the native land. Physical alienation, however, can mean precisely the intensification and estheticization of the values of minority positions that had developed in the earlier struggles and that have now, in Third World intellectuals' actual circumstances in the West, become defunct. The unself-reflexive sponsorship of Third World culture, including Third World women's culture, becomes a mask that conceals the hegemony of these intellectuals over those who are stuck at home.

For Third World intellectuals, the lures of diaspora consist in this masked hegemony. As in the case of what I call masculinist positions in the China field, their resort to minority discourse, including the discourse of class and gender struggles, veils their own fatherhood over the ethnics at home even while it continues to legitimize them as ethnics and minorities in the West. In their hands, minority discourse and class struggle, especially when they take the name of another nation, another culture, another sex, or another body, turn into signifiers whose major function is that of discursive exchange for the intellectuals' self-profit. Like the people, real people, the populace, the peasants, the poor, the homeless, and all such names, these signifiers *work* insofar as they gesture toward another place (the lack in discourse-construction) that is authentic but that cannot be admitted into the circuit of exchange.

What happens eventually is that this Third World that is produced, circulated, and purchased by Third World intellectuals in the cosmopolitan diasporic space will be exported "back home" in the form of values—intangible goods—in such a way as to obstruct the development of the native industry. To be sure, one can perhaps no longer even speak of a native industry as such in the multinational corporate postmodernity, but it remains for these intellectuals to face up to their truthful relation to those objects of study behind which they can easily hide—as voyeurs, as fellow victims, and as self-appointed custodians.

Hence the necessity to read and write against the lures of diaspora. Any attempt to deal with women or the oppressed classes in the Third World that does not at the same time come to terms with the historical conditions of its own articulation is bound to repeat the exploitativeness that used to and still characterizes most exchanges between West and East. Such attempts will also be expediently assimilated within the plenitude of the hegemonic establishment, with all the reward that that entails. No one can do without some rewards. What one can do without is the illusion that, through privileged speech, one is helping to save the wretched of the earth.[28]

NOTES

1. "Genitalism," per Gayatri Spivak, is the attitude that "depending on what kind of genitals you have, you can or cannot speak in certain situations" ("Questions of Multi-culturalism," *The Post-Colonial Critic: Interview, Strategies, Dialogues*, Sarah Harasym, ed. [New York and London: Routledge, 1990], 62).

2. Abdul R. JanMohamed and David Lloyd, "Introduction: Minority Discourse—What is to be Done?," *Cultural Critique*, no. 7 (Fall 1987), 7.

3. Nativism is not necessarily an attitude held by natives. Scholars who study a particular culture can espouse nativism as a way to fence off

disciplinary territories, and this often happens in non-Western fields such as Asian studies. For an extended argument on this point, see my "The Politics and Pedagogy of Asian Literatures in American Universities," *differences*, vol. 2, no.*3*, 29–51.

4. I have in mind Allan Bloom, *The Closing of the American Mind* (New York: Simon & Schuster, 1987) and E. D. Hirsch, Jr., *Cultural Literacy* (Boston: Houghton Mifflin, 1987).

5. In his study of the history of Chinese communism, Arif Dirlik shows that, beginning in the earliest period of their acquaintance with the ideas of Marx, the Chinese communists have tended to be most fascinated with what is arguably Marx's most problematic area—his economism. See Dirlik, *The Origins of Chinese Communism* (New York and Oxford: Oxford University Press, 1989), especially chapters 2–6.

6. Arif Dirlik, "Culturalism as Hegemonic Ideology and Liberating Practice," *Cultural Critique*, no. 6 (Spring 1987), 37.

7. Gayatri Spivak, "Can the Subaltern Speak?," in Cary Nelson and Lawrence Grossberg, eds., *Marxism and the Interpretation of Culture* (Urbana: University of Illinois Press, 1988), 271–313.

8. For an argument of this predicament characterizing minority discourse, see Abdul R. JanMoham*ed*, *Manichean Aesthetics: The Politics of Literature in Colonial Africa*.

9. Gayatri Spivak, "The New Historicism: Political Commitment and the Postmodern Critic," *The Post-Colonial Critic*, 158.

10. *Confucian Analects*, chapter III, 5, 7; *The Four Books: The Great Learning, The Doctrine of the Mean, Confucian Analects, and The Works of Mencius*, with English translation and notes by James Legge (Taipei: Culture Book Co., 1973), 298.

11. Slavoj Zizek, *The Sublime Object of Ideology* (London and New York: Verso, 1989), 95.

12. Zizek, *Sublime Object*, 98.

13. As I am writing this in April 1991, a controversy over the ethics of naming rape victims has just broken out across the U.S. media. The immediate cause is the naming by several news institutions (*The Globe*, NBC, and *The New York Times*) of the female victim in the alleged case of rape by a member of the Kennedy family. The pros and cons of whether the victim should be named touch on individual rights to privacy, media consumer needs, the dissemination of news for financial profit, abuses suffered by rape victims at legal proceedings, and more, all of which have to do with social relationships rather than with the pure act of naming itself.

14. Kwai-cheung Lo, "The Real in Lacan: Some Reflections on 'Chinese Symptoms,' " *Polygraph*, no. 4, 86–87.

15. Fredric Jameson, "Third World Literature in the Era of Multinational Capital," *Social Text*, no. 15 (Fall 1986), 69.

16. See Spivak's discussion of this point in "The New Historicism," 161–62.

17. Nancy Armstrong, *Desire and Domestic Fiction: A Political History of the Novel* (New York and Oxford: Oxford University Press, 1987), 8.

18. Quoted in Juliet Mitchell, *Psychoanalysis and Feminism* (New York: Vintage Books, 1975), 416.

19. Kwai-cheung Lo, "The Real in Lacan," 89.

20. Spivak, "The New Historicism," 158.

21. Ibid., 156.

22. *Overseas Chinese Economic Journal* (*xinbao*) (the U.S. edition of *The Hong Kong Economic Journal*), January 1991.

23. Writing about colonial India, Ranajit Guha uses the term *elite* to describe the dominant social groups, made up of "mainly British officials of the colonial state and foreign industrialists, merchants, financiers, planters, landlords and missionaries" on the one hand, and of powerful indigenous elements at the all-India and the regional and local levels, on the other. See "On Some Aspects of the Historiography of Colonial India," *Subaltern Studies I: Writings on South Asian History and Society*, Ranajit Guha, ed. (Delhi: Oxford University Press, 1986), 8. Spivak, while defining the subaltern as "all that is not elite" ("The New Historicism," 158), points also to the gendered subaltern as being paradigmatic of the subaltern subject ("Politics of the Open End," *The Post-Colonial Critic*, 103). Because education traditionally plays such an important role in determining class difference in Chinese society, I think the relation between the elite and the subaltern in China needs to be formulated *primarily* in terms of the way education and gender work together.

24. The conference on "Sexuality and Gender in Twentieth-Century Chinese Literature and Society" at the University of Iowa, March 1991, and the panel on "Gender, Class, and Twentieth-Century Chinese Fiction" at the annual meeting of the Association for Asian Studies, New Orleans, April 1991.

25. *Hegel's 'Phenomenology of Spirit,'* with Analysis of the Text and Foreword by J. N. Findlay (New York: Oxford University Press, 1977), 54–55.

26. The extensiveness of the philosophical, political, and feminist argument about essentialism is such that I can merely point to it here. Two recent publications that readers can consult are Diana Fuss, *Essentially Speaking* (New York: Routledge, 1989) and *differences*, vol. 1, no. 2 (Summer 1989), a special issue on essentialism.

27. "In 'woman' I see something that cannot be represented, something that is not said, something above and beyond nomenclatures and ideologies" (Kristeva, "Woman Can Never Be Defined," in Elaine Marks and Isabelle de Courtivron, eds., *New French Feminisms* [New York: Schocken Books, 1981], 137).

28. I want to acknowledge those who have contributed to the final version of this chapter. I have benefitted from comments made by Wendy Larson and Lydia Liu at the conferences at Iowa and in New Orleans. Continual discussions with Lo Kwai-cheung , Lu Tonglin, and Yue Ming-bao about this paper and other related issues give me the support of a strong critical community. Most of all, I am indebted to Yu-shih Chen for a forceful and enabling critique, which made me restate my concerns with a clarity that had been previously missing.

2

Gendering the Origins of Modern Chinese Fiction

"SILENCE" AS A PROBLEM OF REPRESENTATION

In 1927, Lu Xun, China's most renowned modern writer, was invited to the YMCA in Hong Kong to give a talk on the current situation in mainland China. In his talk entitled "Silent China" (*wusheng de zhongguo*), Lu Xun emphatically called for support "to restore speech to China because there is fighting now in Zhejiang and Shanxi, but we don't know whether folks are laughing or crying."[1] According to Lu Xun, the inability of China to "break her silence" had to do with the traditional written script, the *wenyan*, which he saw as a linguistic tool for the oppressive neo-Confucian ideology of the Sung and Ming dynasties.

Like so many of Lu Xun's critical essays, "Silent China" demands our critical attention not so much because it contains a cogent analysis of social problems but because of the rare insight it offers into China's cultural-political dynamics in the 1920s. According to Lu Xun, classic Chinese writing had muted the voices of China. It followed that the building of a new Chinese culture and nation depended upon the abolition of this older language.

But today we should ask whether linguistic reform was all that was needed "to restore speech to China." In this essay, I will argue that it was not. I will show that many female voices which had historically been silenced by the tools of representation continued to be muffled by the new linguistic tools advocated by the revolutionary intellectuals of the May Fourth period.

Lu Xun was not insensitive to the oppression of women. He wrote extensively about this oppression as an impediment to modernization. But like many Chinese intellectuals, he viewed this as a sociological issue that was separate from the larger historical problems of language and culture. So, although he linked the fate of the nation both to language and to women's suffering, he failed to take the further step of linking women's issues to language itself.

That such a link exists and plays a crucial role in representations of femininity has long been argued by feminist scholars. Teresa de Lauretis, for example, has shown that language is instrumental in the ideological formation of gender-specific subjectivities.[2] Like Kaja Silverman, she also maintains that gender is an *effect* of semiotics and, by extension, of language defined as a system of signification.[3] Following this argument, I will show that the failure on the part of Lu Xun and other May Fourth intellectuals to recognize the connection between women and language led to the perpetuation of the silencing of female voices. I will examine the representation of women in three short narratives written in the period between 1919 and 1934, and argue that the rhetoric of revolution in fact rejoins many conventionalized figures of femininity in such a way as to *displace*, rather than to overcome, the silence. While these narratives are ostensibly about the need to reform the unfair social conditions in the China of that period, they are in fact also about conceptual changes in notions of femininity. In this regard, this essay resituates "silence" within a project of gendering the "origins" of modern Chinese fiction. My purpose in doing so is to open up an ideological closure in China's cultural politics of the 1920s that has haunted critical discussion to this day.

The Origins of Modern Chinese Fiction

Lu Xun's interpretation of China's cultural-political predicament in the 1920s represents the popular beliefs of many May Fourth intellectuals. Triggered in 1919 by a Beijing student demonstration against the national government's compromising policies to twenty-one Japanese demands concluded at the Versailles peace conference, the term May Fourth has come to signify the emergence of "modern Chinese" consciousness. The subsequent May Fourth movement, which evolved into a nationwide euphoria for "New Culture," today stands as a historic landmark for the beginning of a modern Chinese literature.[4] Eager to build a modern culture and nation through a new concept of language and literature, May Fourth intellectuals consciously adopted a Western-oriented rhetoric based on the values of science and democracy. As early as 1917, Chen Duxiu and Hu Shi, the most prominent spokesmen of the May Fourth "new culture" euphoria, vigorously advocated in the monthly *New Youth* (*xin qingnian*) the ideas of "Mr. Science" and "Mr. Democracy." According to Chen and Hu, these two Mr.'s were ideological prerequisites for the process of cultural change which China needed to undergo before entering the world as an equal nation.[5] In the field of literary production, this concern translated into a rejection of traditional conventions in writing.

Hu Shi's programmatic formula for a modern China called on a reform in language and literature which immediately triggered a heated debate on the abolition of the traditional *wenyan* script.[6] Published in 1917 and known as the "Eight Don't-isms" (*babu zhuyi*), this boldly written manifesto centered around the issue of truthful or realistic representation. In his epoch-making essay, "A Proposal for Reform in Literature" (*wenxue gailiang chuyi*), Hu Shi argued for the adaptation of *baihua*, because it was a living language which could truthfully reflect China's oppressive social reality.[7] At the root of this language and literature reform lay the impassioned belief that this would save China from the hands of aggressive foreign encroachment and a corrupted domestic government.

In modern Chinese literary history, this complete rejection of traditional achievements stands as the major characteristic of May Fourth intellectuals and their attempts to create an entirely new basis for writing. Instead of looking to the past, May Fourth intellectuals sought the origins of the new language and literature in the confusions of their contemporary society, all of which had to do with the future—that is, the reproduction—of China. Their attempts to rethink literature, therefore, were *sociological* rather than purely literary in origin. A case in point is the advocacy of *baihua*. Although May Fourth intellectuals consciously adopted a progressive, Western-oriented rhetoric in arguing for the use of *baihua,* its legitimacy largely came from late Qing sociolinguistic trends and elitist politics on mass culture.[8] As pointed out by a number of scholars, the use of *baihua* as a written medium was already widespread during the late Qing, long before May Fourth intellectuals devoted their attention to this issue.[9]

On the whole, May Fourth intellectuals can be regarded as the modern perpetrators of a reformist tradition of thinking. Especially with regard to perceiving themselves as the voices of China, May Fourth intellectuals were faithfully echoing the Hundred Days reformers in 1898, who had urgently called for the "cultural regeneration" of their country.[10] Foremost in this self-consciously progressive program was a process of spiritual purification targeted toward the traditional novel genre, which flourished at that time in the form of popular fiction tailored for a rapidly growing urban readership. Frequently dealing with the topic of love and written in a semiliterary style, these popular narratives still continued traditional literary convention on a formal level.[11] Against this putatively corrupted form of writing, Liang Qichao—the representative voice of the aborted Hundred Days reform movement—who believed in social reform through the means of fiction writing, championed the use of realist fiction as more suitable for conveying the espoused ideas of Western science and democracy.[12]

Without these sociological developments, the May Fourth project in language and literature would not have been conceivable. Yet, precisely because of the *impurity* of the societal situation in which many issues remained murky, the most formidable task Chinese writers faced during the May Fourth period was *how* to come up with a clear new concept of fiction. Invoking the example of Europe, Chen Duxiu and Hu Shi thus began to propagate a "realist fiction" because, in their opinion, the traditional art of writing fiction was "not truthful to China's modern society."[13] Debunking the *wenyan* as a "dead language," May Fourth intellectuals advocated the use of *baihua* as the only suitable medium for conveying the "living reality" of China.

This line of reasoning was most forcefully adopted by Mao Dun, whose theoretical preoccupation with analytical method and objective description exerted a strong influence on the concept of fiction in the decades to come.[14] However, convinced that Chinese society's most pressing problems could be solved by means of a new writing that was purified of the old *literature,* May Fourth intellectuals adopted methods which were from the very outset more scientific than literary. Interestingly, the most popular of such methods was their use of the case study genre in conjunction with the portrayal of women's oppression.

In her study of Mao Zedong's early writings on female suicide cases, Roxane Witke makes the important observation that the preoccupation with female oppression became very popular during the May Fourth period. However, she believes that the popularity had less to do with an interest in women's issues per se than with the fact that the case study approach was developing as a polemic genre.[15] In the heated atmosphere of reform and enlightenment, many intellectuals engaged in writing about women's oppression because it functioned as an irrefutable signifier for marking one's own revolutionary stance.[16] Thus, the emergence of the "woman question" (*funü wenti*) in reform literature and fictional writings during this period was less a conscious effort to change the oppressive structure of a *patriarchal* society than an attempt to utilize women's issues as a political stratagem for advancing China's nation-building program.

Beginning in late Qing China, the "woman question" was brought to the fore by an increasing number of Christian missionaries. For them, female illiteracy and the practice of foot-binding provided a conducive sociocultural climate for promoting a Judeo-Christian ideology that presented itself as more sympathetic to women. However, according to Chen Dungyuan's *A History of Chinese Women's Lives*, it was not until Liang Qichao published his essay "Lun nüxue" (On women's education) in 1897 that the "woman question" gained real momentum.[17]

An ardent believer in social Darwinism, Liang appealed to the notion of equality in arguing for women's education as an important prerequisite for national wealth and power. For Liang, women's education was essential to a reconception of China from family (*jia*) to nation (*guo*). China's future was seen in terms of its survival as a nation among nations. By emphasizing women's reproductive capacities, Liang advocated education for this other half of the population because, we can say, one of the most fundamental functions for ensuring evolution (that is, the continual production of patriotic citizens) lay in women's use of their bodies.[18] While a repudiation of women's oppression became increasingly untenable, this awareness of women was determined by and large by the parameters of patriarchal concerns: women deserved attention not in their own right but rather because their illiteracy had prevented China from entering the world as an equal nation.

It is important to note here that "female literacy" *merely* meant educating women for their feminine role, and that therefore uneducated women became the major target of this educational program. Beneath many intellectual reformers' functionalist eagerness lay a set of traditionalistic assumptions about women's education and femininity. And while these undoubtedly sincere attempts to reform society should be acknowledged in their own right, the gender-specific assumptions require a more critical kind of attention.

The Case Study as a "Modern" Approach to Fiction

Roxane Witke seriously questions the May Fourth valorization of the case study genre as representing a revolutionary and modern perspective on women. In recording female suicide cases, Witke maintains, Mao Zedong and most writers rarely investigated the social and historical determinations that were, through language, shaping women's lives. Instead, they were preoccupied with the construction of a cause-effect narrative pattern that would present women as victims vis-à-vis society as the victimizer. Notably, it is always a male intellectual narrator who recounts the tragic fate of a lower-class, uneducated woman, and often nameless woman, whose sad existence reinscribes her historical status as an object.

More than anything else, the narrativization of oppressed women emerged as a modern topic of *writing* in the hands of May Fourth intellectuals who were concerned with defining a new concept of fiction. For their purpose, the case study approach was ideal: as a critical tool, it equipped the young intellectuals with the desired amount of sociological awareness by allowing them to focus on lower class, uneducated women; as a form or style, the case study approach provided them with a new way of writing that was clearly relevant to, rather than divorced from, society.

Its modern appearance notwithstanding, the May Fourth tendency to use the case study approach to investigate the oppression of women replicates in an interesting way the traditional genre of *Lienü zhuan* (Biographies of virtuous women). For many centuries, this canonical work was instrumental in instructing Chinese women for their feminine role.[19] When this genre appeared—for instance, in local gazetteers—it was used to record brief episodes in which nameless and virtuous women readily sacrificed their lives for their husbands, brothers, and families. Significantly, the notion of femininity that underlies the *Lienü* genre of writing is a violent form of silence, of femininity-reduced-to-silence, which is esthetically recuperated as feminine self-representation. In the name of morality, Chinese women thereby received a lesson on patriarchal indoctrination by voluntarily assisting in their own self-destruction.

Unlike the *Lienü* genre, the case study approach did not operate on the premise of upholding chastity. Nevertheless, it still left unquestioned the construction of female virtue as self-immolation. Roxane Witke makes an interesting observation regarding this point. She argues that the case study approach gave the *Lienü* genre an ironic modern twist because Mao Zedong saw female suicide as an expression of hate these women felt for their husbands. Because Witke subscribes to the standard interpretation of female suicide in the *Lienü* genre as women showing respect to their husbands, Mao's reading necessarily comes across as a "modern"— that is, revolutionary—variation. However, in neither case is the institutionalization of suicide as a distinctive feminine mode of expression called into question. The need to question the reinforcement of femininity in suicide, whether suicide is for or against patriarchy, is the point I am making.

In most case studies, female suicide was always blamed on society's reinforcement of a feudal marriage system. Placed within the context of the May Fourth campaign against the traditional family structure, suicide immediately came to denote revolution. However, the interpretation of this violent act of destruction as a revolutionary stance for women is problematic precisely because historically suicide had always already been seen as a specific form of female self-expression.[20] While the *Lienü* genre commonly interpreted female suicide as a sign of women's belief in chastity, the modern case studies now argued that women committed suicide because they revolted against their husbands or their in-laws. But what remains problematic in this kind of interpretation of female suicide, modern or past, is the fact that female suicide could be appropriated for the ideology in vogue. In this way, the conceptualization of female *virtue* in the modern age ironically resumed the form of self-immolation, this time, however, for the smooth functioning of a discourse on revolution which putatively operated in the name of emancipation.

Strictly speaking, the case study cannot be considered literary. Even today, the case study is a method most often used by social scientists rather than literary critics in the investigation and presentation of social problems. Central to this method is the division of the world into an investigating subject and an investigated object. The object may then be studied from a variety of perspectives in order to bring out its problems. These problems purportedly inform us about the functioning and problems of the society to which the object belongs. At no point does the case study provide a critique of the investigator himself/herself. Rather, the investigator remains an authority whose scientific presentation of the object dictates our perception of it. While the object's world is rendered transparent, the investigator's own history remains invisible.

This unequal distribution of narrative power in the case study approach brings out a particular problem in May Fourth fiction. Even though the writers are sincere in their intentions to defend women, their writing betrays the discursive habits of a patriarchal tradition which excludes women's experiences from its articulation. In the following readings, I will address three forms of such exclusion. The three stories I have chosen for this purpose have hitherto been ignored by literary critics, although the authors are recognized as established May Fourth writers. However, as stories portraying the oppression of women, they demand our attention, not least because they typify as well as problematize the May Fourth concern with a realist mode of writing. All three narratives employ silence as a way of reinscribing femininity. Together they indicate, in the modern period, a repetition of the *Lienü* genre, a fascination not simply with the female body, but with *woman-as-body*, and finally an ambivalence with regard to the possibility of a female *mind*.

The Fictional "Construction" of Women in May Fourth Stories

Thematically, much of May Fourth fiction written in the name of revolution deals with the oppression of predominantly uneducated females.[21] On the formal level, the use of a third-person narrative stance and matter-of-fact language appropriately fits the case study approach. More often than not, the narrative pattern is that of an intellectual male who lends his voice to silent, lower-class, and uneducated women. Unlike intellectual, self-reflective female characters in May Fourth fiction, these illiterate women are usually described in terms of their feminine physique. The life accounts of these women that accompany the detailed and, at times, lurid descriptions of their bodies convey an impression of female existence that is, above all, iconographic. As a result, this mode of writing merely produces a narrative of women in which female oppression is seen as ontological fate.

The best example of this is Ye Shengtao's *One Life* (*Yisheng*) (1919), which was originally published under the title *Is This a Human Being Too?* (*Zhe yeshi yigeren?*)[22] The story exemplifies the classic May Fourth habit of recounting the victimization of an uneducated woman from the countryside. Writing short, straightforward sentences with hardly any dialogue, the narrator begins the story with a summary of the first two decades of an oppressed female existence that remarkably matches the very economy of the short story genre:

> She was born into a peasant family; never having enjoyed the privilege of being waited upon by maids or using rouge and powder, nor having received any formal education, she was no more than a simple animal. After she left her mother's womb and grew until she could walk, she helped her parents in the fields. At fifteen, her parents married her off. Since she was going to be someone else's sooner or later, keeping her a year longer only meant spending a year's more expenses on food and board. So what could be better than marrying her off early, thus sparing the energy and money it would take to raise this capital for other people? As for her husband's family, they were in need of help in the fields and had planned to hire someone. With her now marrying into the family, they no longer could afford the help, but at least she saved them the money needed for raising half a cow! [Ye, 204]

As a formal strategy, this third-person narrative stance inscribes the objective attitude required of a realistic depiction. By implication, the narrator's progressive outlook becomes an issue of innocence—that is, establishing his *absence* from the "scene of the crime" where the oppression of women takes place. To give credit to this impression, female subjugation is presented as factual and without critical elaboration.

For example, in a series of events which include the death of the woman's infant child, a physical assault by her husband, and finally the escalation of her in-laws' verbal harassments, the only explanation we are given is the fact that she's a woman. Not only is her reaction presented as silence but also as typically feminine. When she finds out that her husband pawned her winter clothes to pay off his gambling debts, her complaint, albeit soft, immediately earns her a physical assault. When this happens, her mother-in-law not only passively stands aside but also angrily bursts out: "Crying again? You've cried the whole family to its end!" (Ye, 205). When subsequently, driven by fear, this woman runs away, her new and happy experience as a maid in an urban household is only temporary. Before long, she is discovered by her in-laws. After several failed attempts to force her back home, they send her father to exert moral pressure on her. Under the protection of her new employers, she initially manages to evade the demands for her return. But when her husband suddenly dies, they send her home. Arriving there, she discovers that she has been sold to another family as quickly as she was acquired by her in-laws the first time. Her value has never been more than that of a commodity, which is eloquently summed up at the end of the story:

> Her father, her in-laws . . . all thought that this was the most appropriate solution. They drew on this analogy: if the cow ceased to work in the fields, it ought to be sold. Like a cow, she did not have an opinion of her own. Now that there was no longer any need for her, she was simply to be sold off. Thus, to cover her husband's funeral expenses with the money exchanged for her body—this was her final duty! [Ye, 207]

As a result of this third-person narrative stance, the oppressive conditions in the story are construed as *society's* maltreatment of women. But does the narrator's fictional absence really prove his avowed innocence and objective attitude? And if not, how does the narrative mode give him away?

We notice that in the factual description of the woman's misery, she merely becomes a means to a narrative end. That the narrative itself serves as an example of how female experience continues to be appropriated for patriarchal purposes can be seen in the way femininity is conceptualized *exclusively* in terms of motherhood. In the story, after the woman gives birth to the child, the narrative deliberately draws attention to the poverty of material conditions: "Her child did not have a warm crib to sleep in, nor any soft clothes to wear, no fresh air to breathe, nor bright sunlight to enjoy. And even the luxury of being close to his mother was only granted at night, during the day he was just dumped in a dark corner of the room" (Ye, 204). This reference to the woman's class background is largely intended as proof of the narrator's objective attitude—that is, his unbiased presentation of class differences or exploitation. But when the woman's child dies because of a lack of emotional care and severe malnutrition which the narrator alluded to earlier on, the woman's reaction is described as follows: "She cried incessantly, and never felt so heartbroken before in her whole life" (Ye, 204).

As a member of the oppressed class, the woman is seen as the product of her socioeconomic predicament. Yet, when she assumes her social role as a mother, she is simply seen as woman. The implication here is a kind of natural or instinctive affection a mother feels toward her child, and which is above socioeconomic determinations. However, as Nancy Chodorow argues in her study, the emotional bond so commonly assumed to be natural between mother and child is more the result of a culturally and socially conditioned process of care-taking or what she calls "mothering."[23] It goes without saying the Chodorow's point here is neither to dismiss the physiological effects nor to belittle the psychological experience of motherhood. Rather, she is concerned with drawing attention to a notion of motherhood that could be seen as complicit with patriarchal conceptions of femininity.

By emphasizing the sociocultural conditioning of women as caretakers, Chodorow calls into question an understanding of femininity which simplistically theorizes women's perceptual realm in terms of biological determinism. That such a naturalized notion of femininity is at work in our story is evident in the narrator's description of motherhood anchored as women's intrinsic quality. By exempting the notion of motherhood from any socioeconomic considerations, the narrator unwittingly employs a notion of femininity that silently reproduces patriarchal assumptions about women.

Xiao Qian's *The Raining Dusk (Yuxi)* recounts the narrator's haunting childhood memory of a lower-class uneducated woman whose oppressive conditions are "beyond his comprehension."[24] After being abandoned by her husband in favor of a more westernized type from the city, this woman—who had been sold to her husband's family as a child-bride—roams around in the fields until she is raped one night and subsequently turns mad. The story ends on the narrator's second encounter with the woman several days later, when he "incidentally" passes by a hidden courtyard and overhears her singing a self-lamenting tune that is interspersed with "unhealthy laughter" (Xiao, 223).

This story is interesting because it exemplifies how the objective attitude can become untenable as a revolutionary mode of writing when the narrative focuses on the female body. Also noteworthy is the way the story illustrates how a traditional notion of femininity undergoes its modern permutation in spite of, or perhaps because of, claims to the contrary. Let us look carefully at the opening paragraph and examine how the narrator goes about marking his own progressive attitude:

> Talking about seeking shelter from rain, the intelligent reader will, of course, have no problems recalling many stories of how a talented scholar, on his way to take the civil service examination, is forced by a torrential rainstorm to seek shelter at a deserted temple or secluded bamboo garden of a private residence where he then meets either an intriguing female spirit or a delicate beauty of a well-to-do background. Although the old days are gone and wiped out, these absurd images still exist in the minds of many young men and women as they leisurely walk to such quiet places. [Xiao, 217–18]

By invoking the process of narration and the presence of the reader, the narrator pursues a twofold goal: to distance himself both from traditional representations of women and from the fictionality of his own narrative. This ideological double-stroke safely anchors the revolutionary stance of the narrative. Consequently, the subjective mode of the first-person narrative stance is neutralized as truthful so that his depictions of the outside world can be considered objective.

However, within this same narrative mode, there is a noticeably *erotic* preoccupation with feminine physical features: "a slender hand that grabbed a corner of the brick wall at the entrance to the grinding shed," or "her white little blouse had been drenched to the extent that one could almost see the flesh under it trembling" (Xiao, 219). Compared to traditional Chinese literature in which descriptions of female breasts are taboo, this candid indulgence in visual presentations of the female body is a formalistic indication of the narrator's revolutionary outlook. On an ideological level, however, these descriptions merely constitute contemporary variations of femininity because lower-class, uneducated women are now subsumed under the category of feminine. And like the traditional notion of femininity, this modern permutation also fails to capture the complexity of women's sociohistorical experiences. Hardly surprising, then, a sense of incomprehensibility permeates the narrator's mind and generates his perturbed reaction to the woman's physical presence—"I hastily dropped the shoe which had occupied my mind and raised my head to look at this strange woman"—or his subsequent perplexed confession: "my interest in hearing more about her story grew stronger but my friend urged me to leave, and because he was so persistent, my drenched shoe suddenly came back to my memory" (Xiao, 221–22). In spite of his intention to explicate the oppressive conditions of a lower-class woman, this focus on the body merely reduces her oppression to ontological fate. Consequently, this "revolutionary" discourse on woman *en-genders* a paralyzing sense of silence that finds no other outlet than in a cryptic remark on which the narrative expands: "Well, she has the look of someone *fated* to suffer, doesn't she!" (Xiao, 222, italics added).

Ye Zi's *On the Yangzi ferry* (*Changjiang lun shang*) explores how female literacy is important for revolution through the figures of two women: the narrator's educated mother and a poverty-driven, pregnant woman from the countryside.[25] The unbridgeable class difference between these two women is sustained in the narrative focus through a highlighting of the former's mental activity as opposed to the latter's passivity. This classical conception of class distinction qualifies the story as an objective depiction of social reality. However, as the narrative develops, we recognize the workings of an underlying gender-structure that suggests a masculinist bias in this presentation. The dichotomization of mental power and physical labor is not simply a matter of class but also one of gender.

The story recounts a brief episode on the ferry in which the narrator's mother is trying to save the pregnant woman's life. Notably, the mother's active involvement never remains only on the level of physical engagement. Upon the discovery and rescue of the pregnant woman, who tried to hang herself in an act of desperation, the mother's physical activity is presented as the reenactment of her mind (Ye, 224). For example, when she helps the pregnant woman and not only delivers the baby but also solicits money for the woman's travel, it is in the name of humanism that her physical activity is justified (Ye, 225). As the story evolves, we are given the figure of an educated woman whose body is of secondary importance in comparison with her mind.

By contrast, the pregnant woman's medium of expression is her body; and her maternity, as signified by her breasts, becomes of crucial significance. As in Xiao Qian's story, the description of this other woman is confined to references to her physical features and the most simplistic life-accounts. Hence her "simple and sad story" (Ye, 223) is presented in this manner: driven by poverty, she and her family left the village in order to seek refuge with her relatives on the other side of the Yangzi River. But having no money for the fare, her husband and children were thrown off the ferry before it left, while she managed to hide herself in a dark corner. We notice that the narrative completely eliminates the mental dimension of the woman. Furthermore, in presenting her oppressive conditions, the narrative becomes caught up with a visual presentation of her body. For example, in the dramatic moment of her rescue, which actually makes the first encounter between the narrator and the woman, all the narrative registers is that "her armpits and her breasts were swollen from hanging onto the rope" (Ye, 225). Later on, after bypassing an analysis of the sociopsychological factors that might have motivated her suicide attempt, the woman's suffering from childbirth provides the occasion for curious imagistic indulgence: "her temples were covered with bean-size drops of sweat, and her entire body was struggling in pain. As soon as she saw me, she turned her head away *in embarrassment*" (Ye, 226, italics added).

As in Xiao Qian's story, such explicit references to the female body do not in themselves invalidate progressive thinking. Rather, it is the uncompromising pairing of lower-class, uneducated females as mindless and intellectual females as bodiless which undermines the progressive stance of the narrative. For ultimately this neat division of representing intellectual woman as possessing no body, while uneducated women lack a mind, recuperates a traditional notion of femininity that denies women any authentic claim to social mobility. As the narrative mode explicitly renders lower-class, uneducated women as *female* bodies while the intellectual mother's mind is *defeminized*, it implies that women can climb up the public social ladder only by leaving their sex at home.

Schematically speaking, these two figures of woman embody a 1920s enlightenment vision of China which is seen, on the one hand, as bound to a traditional body, and on the other, committed to a progressive mind. But what are the gender-coded assumptions underlying such a discourse on revolution in which a notion of truth is probed through the figure of an educated woman? The story ends with the mother's bitter recognition of human indifference: not only does her uneducated counterpart throw the newly born baby girl into the river but worse, nobody else shares her humanistic ideal of saving two marginal lives. Hence, the inability of progressive thinking to assert itself when confronted with a traditional body ideologically transpires into a notion of passivity—of feminine reluctance to act in public despite an enlightened mind. The mother's hesitation to take the initiative for acting in front of a large, male-dominated crowd silently gestures toward a conservative mark of femininity that weighs on her progressive thinking even while she openly disavows it.

THE INDISPENSABILITY OF GENDER

As the voices of China continue to reproduce patriarchal models of female experiences, the silence thus generated betrays the enlightened vision of a modern nation that is built upon linguistic and literary reform. This surfacing of silence in the rhetoric of revolution calls into question a notion of representation that keeps ignoring the importance of gender as an analytical category.[26] To demonstrate that such a conceptual perspective is not only useful but absolutely necessary has been the major concern of this essay. For, in the final analysis, the question that keeps nagging at feminist scholarship is not the representation of woman but also the relationship between woman *and* representation.

The literary representations of women in May Fourth fiction stand in stark distinction to the many sociohistorical studies that document the activities of women's suffrage movements and other forms of public engagement at the turn of the twentieth century.[27] As female literacy increased, new economic options became available. Many educated women assumed teaching positions in girls' schools which were operated by Christian missionaries. The expansion of the industrial sector created the opportunity for many uneducated women from the countryside to escape their double exploitation which was built into the economic structure with the agrarian family as the productive unit. To a large extent, then, these socioeconomic developments provided women with an opportunity to explore new types of subjectivities. By invoking these studies, my point is not to claim that the "sociological" representations of women are more truthful. Rather, it is that such sociological findings can alert us to the problems of literary representations, while literary representations in turn inform us of the methodological limitations of social-scientific studies.

As they wrote their literary case studies, May Fourth writers repeated the traditional consignment of women to silence regardless of their antitraditional intentions. In their hands, the case study became a practical tool for nation-building. Believing in language as a transparent medium of expression that simply conveys problems, they failed to realize that language is always already social and historical, and therefore *itself* the problem. Their dream of a transparent, scientific language and literature became most untenable when they studied the most violent problem in Chinese society—the oppression of lower-class women.[28] Although they meant to liberate women from traditional bondage, their language remained mortgaged to the residues of traditional representation. As we see in the three stories, this dilemma is most vivid in the asymmetry between the writers themselves as investigators and the women as objects of study.

I hope my discussion of the May Fourth literary situation has shown that the problem of silent China is very much a problem of gendered representation, even though it is seldom stated as such. Naomi Schor, who analyzes the intricate ramifications of femininity in representation, also arrives at this proposition. Schor's philosophical reflection is worth keeping in mind, for she suggests that modernism "might very well be that ambivalent moment of history which can neither reconcile the *otherness* of woman nor exist entirely without it."[29] I should like to add that this uneasy relationship between woman and representation can no longer be explicated on a purely linguistic or literary level but needs to be rethought from an ideological perspective as well.

NOTES

I would like to thank Karen Ravn for her meticulous editing. Rey Chow's suggestions have been instrumental in helping me to bring out my major argument. To Lu Tonglin, I am grateful for a careful reading of an earlier version of this paper.

1. Lu Xun, "*Wusheng de zhongguo*" (Silent China), *Lu Xun quanji* (Complete works of Lu Xun) (Beijing: Renmin wenxue chuban she, 1981), IV, 11–18.

2. See Teresa de Lauretis, *Technologies of Gender: Essays on Theory, Film and Fiction* (Bloomington and Indianapolis: Indiana University Press, 1987). In her first chapter, "Technology and Gender," de Lauretis develops this theoretical understanding on page 6. Her second chapter, "The Violence of Representation: Considerations on Representation and Gender," is an illustration of the gendered subject-position in ideologies.

3. Kaja Silverman, *The Subject of Semiotics* (New York and Oxford: Oxford University Press, 1983), 139.

4. See Chow Tse-tsung, *The May Fourth Cultural Movement* (Cambridge: Harvard University Press, 1964), 293–99.

5. Chen Duxiu, *"Benkazuan zhi dabian shu"* (A letter in response and defense of accusation toward this magazine) in *Zhongguo xin wenxue daxi* (A comprehensive anthology of the new literature of China), Zhao Jiabi, ed. (Shanghai: Liangyou tushu yinshua gongsi, 1935), II, 81–82. For a partial translation, see Chow Tse-tsung, *The May Fourth Cultural Movement*, 269–88.

6. Hu Shi, *"Ji Chen Duxiu"* (A letter to Chen Duxiu) in *Zhongguo xin wenxue daxi*, I, 31–33.

7. Hu Shi, *"Wenxue gailiang chuyi"* (A proposal for reform in literature), in *Zhongguo xin wenxue daxi*, I, 34–43.

8. Shu-Ying Tsau, "The Rise of 'New Fiction' " in *The Novel at the Turn of the 19th Century*, Milena Dolezelová-Velingerová, ed. (Toronto: University of Toronto Press, 1980), 18–37. See also Milena Dolezelová-Velingerová, "The Origins of Modern Chinese Literature" in *Modern Chinese Literature in the May Fourth Era*, Merle Goldman, ed. (Cambridge: Harvard University Press, 1977), 17–36.

9. Tan Biyan, *Wan qing de baihua wen yundong* (The Baihua language movement in late Qing) (Wuhan: Hubei renmin chuban she, 1956).

10. See C. T. Hsia, "Yen Fu and Liang Ch'i-ch'ao as Advocates of New Fiction" in *Chinese Approaches to Literature*, Adele Rickett, ed. (Princeton: Princeton University Press, 1978), 221–57.

11. For discussion of popular urban-fiction in the 1910s, see Rey Chow's "Mandarin Ducks and Butterflies: Towards a Rewriting of Modern Chinese Literary History," Ph.D. dissertation, Stanford University, 1986.

12. For a comprehensive understanding of the intellectual debates on the new literature reform, see *Zhongguo xin wenxue daxi*, I, 31–60.

13. For Hu Shi's *"Wenxue gailiang chuyi"* (Proposal for a reform of literature) and Chen Duxiu's *"Wenxue geming lun"* (On literary revolution) see *Zhongguo xin wenxue daxi*, I, 34–44; 44–48. For English translations of both articles, see *Sources of Chinese Tradition*, William T. de Barry et al. (New York: Columbia University Press, 1960), II, 818–29; and Chow Tse-tsung, *The May Fourth Movement*, 271–79.

14. Mao Dun, *"Ziran zhuyi yü zhongguo xiandai xiaoshuo"* (Naturalism and modern Chinese short stories) in *Zhongguo xin wenxue daxi*, II, 379–80.

15. Roxane Witke, "Mao Tse-tung, Women and Suicide," in *Women in China: Studies in Social Change and Feminism*, Marilyn B. Young, ed. (Ann Arbor: Center for Chinese Studies, University of Michigan, 1973), 7–31.

16. Charlotte L. Beahan, "The Women's Movement and Nationalism in Late Ching China," Ph.D. dissertation (Columbia University, 1976), 156. See also Helen Foster Snow's chapter on "Women and Christianity" in her *Women in Modern China* (The Hague and Paris: Mouton, 1967), 70–90.

17. Liang Qichao, *"Lun Nüxue"* (On women's education) in *Yinbing shi heji wenji* (Shanghai: Zhonghua shuju, 1932), 1.1: 37–43.

18. Chen Dongyuan, *Zhongguo funü shenghuo shi* (A history of Chinese women's lives) (Shanghai: Shangwu yinshu guan, 1928), 328–29.

19. For a discussion on the *Lienü zhuan*, see Marina H. Sung, "The Chinese Lieh-Nü Tradition," in *Women in China, Current Directions in Historical Scholarship*, Richard Guisso and Stanley Johannesen, eds. (Youngstown: Philo Press, 1981), 63–74.

20. See Margery Wolf, "Women and Suicide in China," in *Women in Chinese Society* (Stanford: Stanford University Press, 1975), 111–42.

21. See for instance *Zhongguo xiandai duanpian xiaoshuo xuan* (A selection of modern Chinese short stories) (Hong Kong: Shanghai shuju, 1963), 2 volumes, which present a variegated selection of stories displaying this narrative pattern.

22. Ye Shengtao, "Zhe yeshi yigeren?" (Is this a human being too?), *Duanpian xiaoshuo xuan* (Selected short stories), *Zhongguo xiandai wenxue cankao ziliao*, (Materials on modern Chinese literature) (Shanghai: jiaoyu chuban she, 1979), I, 204–7. All translations mine.

23. Nancy Chodorow, *Reproductions of Mothering: Psychoanalysis and the Sociology of Gender* (Berkeley, Los Angeles, and London: University of California Press, 1978). See especially her first chapter, "Why Woman Mother," 3–40. Although it is by now a fairly well-established fact, what Chodorow affirms bears repeating, namely, that "human behavior is not instinctually determined but culturally mediated" because the instinctual or biological basis for parenting is based on indirect research on human beings (p. 13). Chodorow's major argument is summarized in the following passage:

"Women's mothering as an organization of parenting is embedded in and fundamental to the social organization of gender. In any historical period, women's mothering and the sexual division of labor are also structurally linked to other institutions and other aspects of social organization. In industrial capitalist societies, women's mothering is central to the links between the organization of gender—in particular, the family system—and economic organization." (34)

24. Xiao Qian, *"Yüxi"* (Rain at dusk), in *Zhongguo xiandai duanpian xiaoshuo xuan*, II, 217–23. All translations are mine.

25. Ye Zi, *"Changjiang lun shang"* (On the Yangzi Ferry), in *Zhongguo xiandai duanpian xiaoshuo xuan*, II, 223–29. All translations are mine.

26. See Teresa de Lauretis, *Technologies of Gender*, footnote 2.

27. A number of sociohistorical studies are useful here: Mary Backus Rankin, "The Emergence of Women at the End of the Ch'ing: The Case of Ch'iu Chin," in *Women in Chinese Society*, 39–66. Roxane Witke, "Women as Politicians in China of the 1920's," 33–45. Susan Leith, "Chinese Women in the Early Communist Movement," 47–72. Delia Davin, "Women in the Liberated Areas," 73–91. Charlotte L. Beahan, "In the Public Eye: Women in Early Twentieth-Century China," all in *Women in China*.

28. For a similar argument, see Rey Chow, "'It's You, and Not Me': Domination and 'Othering' in the Theorizing of the 'Third World'," in *Coming to Terms, Feminism, Theory and Politics*, Elizabeth Weed, ed. (New York and London: Routledge, 1989), 152–61.

29. Naomi Schor, *Breaking the Chain: Women, Theory, French Realist Fiction* (New York: Columbia University Press, 1985), see especially her Introduction.

3

The Language of Desire, Class, and Subjectivity in Lu Ling's Fiction

Writing between two wars—the Sino-Japanese war of national defense and resistance (1937–1945) and the civil war of communist revolution (1946–1949), Lu Ling's work epitomizes the antagonistic and contradictory nature of modern Chinese literature. If the two catchwords, modernity and revolution, can somehow characterize twentieth-century China's obsession or predicament, then any attempt to bypass or to square the psychic state of desire—the primordial drives of the unconscious, configured in primarily sexual terms—by way of valorizing the above two grand narratives, will miss a key point in the whole debate of modern Chinese culture and history. Such is the fate of Lu Ling. His work has been marginalized because of its naturalistic depiction of sexual drives, which is said to grossly distort the heroic images of his working-class and revolutionary characters.

Born in 1923, Lu Ling's writing career started at the age of fifteen, when his first short story was published by the literary journal *July* in Chongqing. Thus began his highly productive, eventful, and tormented affiliations with Hu Feng's literary group associated with *July*. Lu Ling is arguably the most talented novelist of the *July* group, with about a dozen volumes of more than sixty short stories, six novella, three novels, and four plays to his credit at the age of 26. This was the year 1949, when the Chinese revolution broke new ground. The revolution also broke Lu Ling's ambition and excitement in its wake. From 1955 on, Lu Ling spent twenty years behind bars, imprisoned by the very regime which he had fought for so passionately in his youth. Like his mentor Hu Feng, he suffered from schizophrenia. Hu Feng died in 1987; Lu Ling is still alive. There has been a revived interest in his forgotten work in recent years, so he may still dimly hope that Hu Feng's prophecy that Lu Ling's work will be recognized as a major event in modern Chinese literature will come true some day.[1]

Lu Ling's uncouth and cumbersome language straddles two antithetical poles of the literary conventions of modern China. On the one hand, his language is charged with libidinal passion, focusing exclusively on the inner tortures of men and women, expressed in spontaneous utterances. On the other hand, Lu Ling is deeply preoccupied with the grand themes of enlightenment and national salvation. These latter two terms, coined by China's foremost philosopher and cultural critic Li Zehou to describe modern China's struggle for modernity, neatly summarize the two antithetical poles at political and ideological levels: Western individualism as the thrust of the enlightenment theme, and revolutionary collectivity as the absolute mandate of national salvation.[2] Lu Ling's focus on the private, lived experience of the individual, repressed sexual desires in particular, can be said to align well with the theme of the enlightenment. Yet as a dedicated leftist writer, Lu Ling's zeal for revolution and national salvation is attested to by the bulk of his writings dealing with battles, wars, and conflicts at every sector of social life.

We will miss the point once again if we read Lu Ling's work according to the paradigms of the grand narratives in Li Zehou's terms. The heterogeneity and contradictoriness of Lu Ling's language and form need to be read from a different perspective—a perspective less concerned with formal and textual consistency and continuity, but one more attentive to the phenomena of displacement and rupture. The May Fourth tradition of modern Chinese literature can be conceptualized as a process of grasping China's new reality through decoding the traditional discursive conventions and paradigms, and reinscribing a new symbolic order. At heart lies the issue of subjectivity, characterized by Li Zehou as the opposition between the individual and the collective in terms of his grand narratives. But the formation of subjectivity in modern China entails radical discontinuity and confusion of both social and psychological orders irreducible to a simple polarity of individuality and collectivity.

We need, therefore, to examine these social and psychological aspects more closely. A dialectical way to look at social disorientation and its ensuing psychic disorder and fragmentation will benefit from Lacan's conception of three orders (the imaginary, the symbolic, and the real). I want to argue that historical and social criticism of modern Chinese culture and literature has to confront the difficult problem of conceptualizing the process of subject formation, or subjectivity, by way of psychological explanations. My reading of Lu Ling's work will venture into this problematic domain, in order to describe certain phenomena in Lu Ling's texts from psychosocial perspectives. For Lacan, the imaginary means the preverbal, visual stage of subject formation, best dramatized in the mirror stage. The symbolic order is primarily the function of language, the semiotic world in which the human being's subjectivity is shaped and differentiated from the other. The real is that which cannot be grasped without the mediation of the symbolic, but resists symbolization and constitutes the absolute ground for the two correlative functions, the imaginary and the symbolic. Real as such is properly understood as history.[3] If we look at May Fourth literature, however, we need not insist on Lacan's mirror stage of the imaginary as the initial step of the individual's subject formation. It seems that understood this way, the imaginary still remains locked within the categories of the individual ego-psychology. We need to transform, creatively, Lacan's concepts into a dynamic interpretive strategy capable of grasping complex processes of becoming, and moments of change. The imaginary is thus understood, as Jameson puts it, as "moments in which their mature relationship to each has broken down, moments that present a serious imbalance in favor of one or the other registers. Most frequently, this imbalance would seem to take the form of a degradation of the Symbolic to an Imaginary level."[4] May Fourth seems to constitute such a moment, except that it is not necessarily a degradation, but rather a bold movement of disruption and reorganization.

The imaginary, as predominantly presocial and archaic or unconscious experience of desire, with all its specularity, visuality, and fluidity, is celebrated and deployed by the iconoclastic May Fourth writers to debunk the Confucian ethical and moral constraints. If this is called the mirror stage, then it is a stage whereby a subject tries to break free from the previous fixed symbolic order in order to arrive at a new sense of self. This celebration of the visual (imago) has an esthetic resonance. In Freud's and Lacan's context of Western culture, the esthetic organization of the world of bodies in the imaginary is deprived of phenomenological center and fixed point of view of preindividualistic and premimetic, whereas in China, it may be just the opposite. The Confucian symbolic has long dominated China. And with the overwhelming emphasis of Confucian ideology on kinship as the fundamental ethical and social principle of organization, the mirror stage of the primary narcissism and aggressivity seems to have been bypassed or at least willfully ignored by Confucian ethical rationality.

The twentieth century, however, witnesses the resurgence of fundamental human aggressivity, as well as the disintegration of the self from the other, and the self from its own body in violent fashions. The twentieth century is for China a century of revolution—*geming*—a violent annihilation of lives and the attendant explosion of, and intoxication in, the pent up desires to possess what has been lacking in the self, to deprive what has been plenty in the other, and to turn everything in this world upside down. This continued carnival, as it were, has its favorite mode of expression: the spectacle of the dismembered and fragmented images of the body, the body without a soul, or the feminine body as the other. In a nutshell, what dominates the early May Fourth writings is a figuration of bodies or embodiment of objects, rather than a representation which intends to institute an orderly, relatively fixed symbolic order. A short list will suffice: Lu Xun's obsession with the mob spectacle; Yu Dafu's masochistic obsession with sexual drives and self-abuse of the body; Mao Dun's meticulous description of erotic details; Shen Congwen's idyllic figurations and refigurations of concrete sensuous experience; Ding Ling's bold depiction of young women's self-consciousness of their bodily sensation and yearnings.

The root-seeking novels of the 1980s of Mo Yan and Han Shaogong,[5] the avant-garde experimental novels of Yu Hua, seem invariably to have zeroed in on the visual, or the imaginary, from divergent angles and with different intentions. The tendency toward visual and specular mode by which body stands in sharp relief is thus a mode of figuration rather than representation. As Barthes puts it, "figuration is the way in which the erotic body appears in the profile of the text," whereas in representation, "desire never leaves the frame, the picture; it circulates among the characters; if it has a recipient, that recipient remains interior to the fiction."[6] In other words, figuration invites participation, as well as commitment to process and practice; figuration entails *jouissance* as bodily pleasure and joyful corporality of carnival. Representation, on the other hand, aims to objectify the body and establish a distinction, an order of subject and object, pointing to a new symbolic order.

In the course of over eighty years, modern Chinese writers have embraced specular figuration of the imaginary so as to break down the traditional symbolic; but inevitably, they embarked on representational mode for the purpose of creating subjectivity. They have created various subjectivities, each of which may correspond to an ideal subjectivity for each individual writer. They all take these subjectivities as *the* subjectivity for modern China. An optical illusion, I may venture to say, to pose itself as a perpetual other, which duplicates itself infinitely and therefore is always out of reach.

The symbolic is an inescapable and inevitable way to grasp the real. For a reconstitution of the symbolic, modern Chinese writers resort to various strategies of sublimation. The Marxist sublime, the ideology of class struggle and social revolution, orders the most attractive path for a new symbolic order that can grasp the real as such. Thus the eruption of sexual desires, entwined with the unleashing of class antagonism, is displaced by a discourse of revolutionary sublime—the conventions of revolutionary realism and revolutionary romanticism. Desire, which opens up the gap between the self and the other, and intends, phenomenologically, to reach the ultimate other, is dissolved in representations of the revolutionary sublime. Sexuality and femininity in the once glorified realm of the imaginary are reduced to an object of representation, a metonymic device for a greater, deeper, symbolic meaning—the inevitable victory of the revolution and liberation.

Many modern Chinese writers, men and women, seem to have succumbed ultimately to such a temptation for the symbolic order, for it guarantees not only the safe path to history but also the subjectivity they so anxiously strive to create. Ding Ling is a much talked about figure in this respect. She is taken as a fine example of the abandonment of bourgeois individualistic feminism for the sake of social revolution and class struggle. Zhang Ailing may represent another extreme, a recalcitrant, metropolitan feminist who defied the leftist ideological interventions in the formation of feminine subjectivity.[7]

How about the wartime writers, then, especially the so-called northeastern writers of Xiao Hong, Duanmu Hongliang? And the *July* writers such as Lu Ling? It seems to me that these authors instill into their works of revolution and war a plethora of feminine and bodily desires and fantasies of the oppressed peasants and students, against a backdrop of intense class conflicts and national interests. For them, the individual, psychic world of desires and fantasies constitutes elemental forces of resistance and revolution. So what happens in their narrative discourses is a constant transgression and transference of the primordial rivalry, the indistinction of primary narcissism and aggressivity that characterize the imaginary, with the transindividual, historical relationships sedimented in the symbolic.

The symbolic, however, often assuming a masculine position of the sublime, tends to domesticate the optical multiplicity of the imaginary, or to monologize the heteroglot terrain of the unconscious. But to make use of Lacan's best-known sentence, "the Unconscious is the discourse of the Other," and his two schemas, especially the schema R, we may see that the path of the subject to its other is a tortuous detour.[8] Although the ego, according to Lacan, finally "identifies itself from its specular *Urbild* to the paternal identification of the ego-ideal,"[9] the economy of the unconscious is such that a perpetual "slippage of signified," shifting ground from the imaginary to the symbolic and vice versa, would seem to make the ultimate domination of the phallic symbolization impossible. If we view modern Chinese literature from such a social-psychological perspective, we may see the battles at formal and discursive levels as manifestations of modern China's cultural and social unconscious. We may perhaps understand better the dialogic nature of Xiao Hong's, and in our present text Lu Ling's discourse of desire, class, and sexuality.[10]

In one of the early short stores, "He Shaode is arrested" (1941), Lu Ling captures the conflictual moment of desires, both masculine and feminine, in a cinematic overlay of disjunct snapshots. He Shaode is a runaway soldier from the Guomingdang army, who hides in a remote mining area and earns his living by toiling in a mine pit. He is in love with a girl named Lianjin. The girl's father turns out to be the wicked landlord who has finally informed the police against him. He Shaode is arrested; thus his affair with the girl ends. This affair has remained strictly at the level of thoughts, involving merely talking and fantasizing, without any physical contact or touch.

Lu Ling's heroes and heroines are not ignorant and stupid peasants, although many of them have humble backgrounds and low social status. He Shaode has wandered around the country for a long time, and is a quite intelligent autodidact. "The spleen in He Shaode's soul was unmatched by any one of his age and class; he was always lonesome, sorrowful. The world unfolded before his eyes. He walked in this world in the full glory of his youth. But he was always depressed, his desires never satisfied, and he was afflicted with pains for the unobtainable objects he longed for."[11] Such a person might seem an unlikely candidate for romantic love; but Lu Ling's He Shaode possesses an idealistic vision of love that nevertheless coexists with a sense of life's complexity:

> His mind now was suffused with a true and serious existence. He walked toward her [Lianjin's] shop, without a bit of the lust of someone looking for a woman. He figured he was going to solve the most serious problem in his life. . . . Yet an inner voice warned him that this problem could never be solved. He sank into utter despair. Forget her—that's the best solution. Since he could not figure out what "hope" is, and what his hope might be, thus despair itself become absurd and meaningless to him. [59]

He Shaode's self-consciousness as registered in a discourse of existential sublime only reveals, as we will quickly learn, a repressed lust, a physical desire, the very lexicon of which betrays the tension of the moral and ethical symbolic order into which He Shaode and the narrator remain locked. The scene of romantic confession of love displays poignantly the transaction between the desire-ridden male gaze and the inscrutable world of the other in both the man's and the woman's inner self:

> Her eyes sparked with curiosity, which made her face amiable. She gently tossed her very slender shoulders. Her full bosom: she just looked like a blossoming maiden.—But He

Shaode mistook this for "love." He was wrong. He was excited; and in the meantime he felt a dull pang piercing his heart. It was inexplicable. He thought this was love and joy, too. "I am a vagrant," he mumbled. He didn't dare to look at her, fearful that his passion would collapse at once.

"I've wandered many places. . . . So I know what life is. Life—life is a very serious thing. For instance, I meet you. . . . I have never been so close to a woman like you, although I've met lots of women in my life. . . . But you are different. . . ." He realized he was wrong; actually he wanted to say "You make me feel different." But he didn't want to correct it. He looked at her courageously. Her cheek turned pale, barely recognizable. He was gripped with an unnameable fear.

"I don't understand what you are talking about," Lianjin murmured, lowering her head. She had never seen a man as trembling and solemn as He Shaode was on such an occasion. She was perplexed, because this never occurred to her before. It scared her. Never would a man be so stupid; he would just grab her into his arms and do it—that's it. He and she just need that right now. Nothing was more meaningful in life than this. Ah, just this instant attraction—only a fleeting second—and he and she became so far apart now.

Lianjin always looked for novelty and mystery. He Shaode used to look like a mysterious guy, but now he seemed stupid and repulsive. He inflicted a sharp pain on her, as if someone were forcing others to acknowledge some horrifying thing. He Shaode broke open a door in front of her to the other side of life. There were a lot of strange things inside, but she dare not, and could not come close to it. So she almost all of sudden sensed the void and meaninglessness of her life. . . .

He Shaode cast a formidable shadow on her mind. She could not erase it. And it became more and more compelling. It clutched her heart tightly, so much so that all she could sense now was something unintelligible, ineffable and terrifying. There was an incomprehensible solemnity and seriousness in her relationship with He Shaode. This feeling caused her so much pain, and in the meantime it allured her irresistibly. [69–77]

In the gaze of He Shaode, there is a blatant sexual intent. The desire to possess her, to embrace her, and to penetrate her is acted out at both imaginary and symbolic levels: while fixing his desire-ridden eyes on her body, He Shaode lectures Lianjin on the meaning of life. And by the end of the story we come to realize that this existential meaning is indissolubly tied to He Shaode's class consciousness, when he finds out that she and her father, the landlord, have betrayed him the proletarian miner. But the gaze and the visual spectacle are reciprocal. For Lianjin, the gaze is introverted, and it therefore seems more disturbing. He Shaode's self-revelation is mystified and reified into a "door full of strange things inside." The door may be conceptually ethical/moral, and physical/sensual at once. It stands manifestly for the moral solemnity as well as the unasserted masculinity and sexual potency. Lianjin's vague sense of ego verges on sensual and sexual drives, and a mysterious solemnity, as confused and contradictory as He Shaode's state of mind.

On the other hand, the self-reflexiveness of He Shaode amounts to something of a true revelation of the trajectory of the repressed desire and its discourse. It is a kind of psychic disorder which nevertheless possesses an affective power to influence and to hypnotize both interlocutors. The narrator seems to be hypnotized to some degree, too. For the ambiguous and contradictory connotations of meaning of life (from his perspective? her perspective?) are indicative of a second-degree of metanarrative disorder— namely, the unevenness and indeterminancy of the narrating discourse vis-à-vis the meaning of the narrated speeches. This constitutes Lu Ling's stylistic peculiarity, characterized by an imbalanced profusion of quasilyrical prose and metaphors, and graphic depiction of grotesque details of the body. This linguistic and stylistic discordance or disorder may coincide with the psychic torture and the rivalry at the level of the unconscious in Lu Ling's characters.

In Lu Ling's best-known novel, *Hungry Guo Su'e* (1942), the subjectivity of the proletarian leader Zhang Zhenshan and of the sex-hungry peasant girl Guo Su'e is interwoven by class consciousness and sexual drives, registered in a carnival mode of figuration. The carnival body in its violent movement of participation, transgression, and transformation is the central figure of the novel, which constantly undermines the attempt to represent desire, body, and class consciousness from the perspective of the sublime. The representation and objectification of feminine desires and bodies is consistently thwarted through Lu Ling's carnival mode. The traditional value system that holds woman as the incarnation of sin and temptation of the flesh, and the revolutionary ethics that places the male as the liberator of the feminine victim, are equally jeopardized in the carnival celebration of the body. Woman in the carnival mode, as Bakhtin puts it, "is essentially related to the material bodily lower stratum. . . . She is ambivalent. She debases, brings down to earth, lends a bodily substance to things, and destroys; but, first of all, she is the principle that gives birth."[12] This can also be said of Guo Su'e. She comes to a self-awareness through her bodily experience, her sexuality, in defiance of social norms. Her desire and femininity come forward not as a primary object of representation for some higher goals, but as the very site in which self-other relationship and the process of subject formation are unfolded. Her awakened sense of feminine sexuality is a life-giving force, a "primitive vitality," as Lu Ling puts it.

Guo Su'e is a peasant's daughter from northwestern China. Her mother is dead, and her father abandons her. She leaves her home village, drifting southward. She becomes the wife of the middle-aged opium addict Liu Shouchun, because he saves her from starvation. At the beginning of the novel, Guo Su'e is attracted to Zhang Zhenshan, an intelligent and strong young worker. Zhang Zhenshan is a social outlaw since his childhood. Their affair is discovered by Liu Shouchun. He summons the local clansmen to have a clan's inquisition. Guo Su'e is brutally mutilated and raped by the mob clansmen, and dies. In the meantime, Zhang Zhenshan is fired by his boss for his instigation of a strike in the factory. It is too late for him to learn that Guo Su'e has been abducted and murdered. He burns down Liu Shouchun's cabin and returns to the world of wandering outlaws. Wei Haiqin, another admirer of Guo Su'e, tries to avenge her by fighting with her murderer, but is killed by his rival at the lantern festival. The carnival of the festival does not end with the death of Wei, but with the unbroken festivity of the dragon dances performed by Wei's children. The dragon dance is an ambivalent expression of the primitive vitality, brutality, and wantonness of life.

The self-other relationship unfolds in a series of violent sexual encounters between Guo Su'e and Zhang Zhenshan. The narrative discourse is characterized by frequent shifts of points of view and disjunct stylistic tropes. Visualization is a main figure. Graphic, sexual images abound. The narrative point of view is traversed by Lu Ling's frequent use of *style indirect libre* and psychological descriptions shifting inside and outside the character's mind freely. But desire, sexuality, and the grotesque body have by no means been privatized. A transindividual and collective class consciousness, and a metanarrative impulse of sublimation at the level of the symbolic order are always entangled with private fantasies and primordial drives. The first scene of their rendezvous in the novel:

"Here I am." He walked to the table. He shrugged, and smiled a firm smile. Guo Su'e opened her sluggish eyes widely and stared at him, as if he was a stranger. But as she brushed her hair and raised her hand unintentionally toward her face, her eyes sparkled with a blazing flame of mixed agony and rapture. Zhang Zhenshan grinned broadly, with his huge white teeth sticking out, and fixed his smoke-obscured, desirous eyes squarely on the two brownish, big, and full breasts of the woman, bulging out of her underwear. [6]

Guo Su'e stuck her nose feverishly into the muscular and sweating chest of the young man, sniffing wildly the sulphurous and stuffy odors emitted from his armpit. Her naked legs intertwined with his hairy ones, twitching in convulsions. Her heart now sank into a dreamy tranquility, now quivered in a gale of paroxysm. Her whole body was shivering. It was only at this moment that she was in possession of her life. As though all her days in the past had all been unstirred slumber in darkness; afterward, it would be the inevitable destruction and crash. . . . Zhang Zhenshan clumsily turned around his body and shovelled Guo's breasts with his enormous palms, snorting heavily like a horse. [9–10][13]

There is an eruption of desire from both man and woman. The sexual act is presented in animalistic images. It is a carnivalization of the body as the negation of the social symbolic order, as a way to negotiate between the self and the other. For Guo Su'e, the sexual act is a moment of subversion and transgression of social and ethical norms, as well as a moment to assert her own subjectivity: "it was only at this moment that she was in possession of her life." But this moment is also a regressive move toward the mirror stage, where primordial narcissism and aggressivity prevail. The self-other relationship is infinitely crisscrossed and transmuted, rather than sharply demarcated and differentiated. It is true that from Zhang Zhenshan's point of view sex is little more than the assertion of his inner self-image and aggressiveness. He tells Guo Su'e:

Woman, you don't understand anything. You only want man.
But a man like me is not so simple. I've been rotten inside
out since I was a child, and I can't change myself now. I'm
afraid I'll never change. I want to keep experimenting. I don't
want to lose myself. This is a wicked idea! Deplorable! . . .
Well, maybe that' not true; I'm always myself—that's my
mold. . . . But if I played some tricks in front of you, I feel I'm
not Zhang Zhenshan any more, but only an ordinary man, I
hate this! It bothers me! I always defend myself, like a
vicious dog! [84]

In Zhang Zhenshan's hysterical self-reflection on the fearful
yet tempting sexual relation with women, he tries to legitimize
himself by claiming individualistic experimentation and the
preservation of self-identify. But his illogical and discordant utterances betray a deeper anxiety about the social and transindividual
values of the wickedness and dishonesty of illicit sexual relations
as well as antisocial behaviors. Zhang Zhenshan is torn apart by
the antithetical desire for Guo Su'e's body and awareness of the
social symbolic order. His social awareness is unequivocally manifested in antagonistic terms. He talks to himself:

I may do other things. I've been here more than two years. I
have energy and spite—but I shouldn't look down upon my
fellow workers! Now they are always crying and stupid, but
like myself, they will understand everything and no longer be
fooled around. . . . We shouldn't let ourselves get out of control. Just follow the trend. . . . But how about the personality?
How can Zhang Zhenshan be Zhang Zhenshan? No, I can't
put up with this any longer! Everybody wants to ruin us but
we don't have the slightest self-knowledge. . . . Humph! I'll
strike; I'll show them that I bear no responsibility, because
society shaped me just like this! . . . I am what I am; so to
hell with this goddamn self-reflection! . . . I want to jump and
crush, kick and kill . . . Ha, my head is full of such clouds!
[56]

The self-appointed proletarian leader is confused by his libidinal desires and his political ambition. Killing, crushing, striking,
and having sex—he understands very well their nature of violence,
but he is unable to differentiate between the revolutionary impuls-
es for proletarian liberation and the primordial desires of the body.

Unlike his numerous counterparts who come out as positive heroes in works glorifying revolution and war, Zhang Zhenshan is deeply disturbed by this awareness and acts like a restless, agitated psychotic. (In fact, most of Lu Ling's characters have a certain degree of hysterical propensity.) Sex for Guo Su'e, on the other hand, has a more affirmative impact on her psyche, although it does not necessarily make her a saner person. She and Zhang Zhenshan usually consummate their sexual desire after a fierce verbal tirade. The scene is thus often described as a savage, grotesque act:

> Zhang Zhenshan lifted Guo Su'e off the ground abruptly, and burst out with a sudden laughter. For a long while, he held the woman's voluptuous, burning body under the moonlight. His coarse, flat face was expressionless and tense. Then he carried her in his violently shaking arms, moving toward the woods. . . . His huge tongue began to smack and lick her lips and nose. In the tight grasp of the man, Guo Su'e felt transported. All her worries, sadness, fear and anguish were gone. She was awakened from the lethal silence of darkness. She burst into a repulsive, lecherous laughter. [87]

While the man comes to her out of spite and irrepressible physical desire, sex for Guo Su'e stands as a subversive self-consciousness. Guo Su'e seems to have invested her wish-fulfillment in life in sexual intercourse and its gratification. Her feminine self-consciousness is therefore registered in primarily preverbal, visual manifestations of the body:

> A foggy but ebullient sensation of ecstasy fermented inside her. It perplexed her. It then glowed, and burnt her cheeks with a tender, crimson color. Her visions blurred, and she gasped, feeling delighted.
>
> For years, Guo Su'e had become coarse and ignoble, because of hunger and poverty. For years, the woman tumbled in the treacherous waves of life defenselessly. Her life was smothered, her voice turned wild. She had hardly ever seen such a resplendent twilight, with an idyllic aura, enlightening her soul. A simple and tender music vibrated sonorously inside her heart. It drowned all the fury, brutality, and debauchery. Her body was soaked in sweat. Her soul was completely immersed in grace. A rare desire griped her heart,

compelled her. She wanted to rush out, and to tell everyone
who knew her about her humiliation. . . .
Guo Su'e was absorbed in her desires and aspirations.
Her mind hovered above this insipid, banal smoke, coming
from the kitchens of the houses. . . . She looked up at the
dark mountains beyond the village, and the purple clouds
hanging behind the mountains. She hoped that Zhang Zhenshan would come toward her in her gaze, and stretching out
his promising arms. [113–14]

The irony is that no promising arms are stretched out to her.
The hero cannot liberate or rescue her, for the hero himself knows
no path of liberation. The carnival and hysteria are dispersed only
by death and abandonment. Guo Su'e's self-consciousness of her
femininity or subjectivity is figured and refigured, in a regressive
interplay of signifiers: the music, the tender feelings, the clouds,
the mountains, and the man. In her gazes and fantasies, all the
images, figures, or signifiers are dismembered and dissolved. The
fundamental gaps between the self and its own image, self and
other, male and female, private and social, body and sublime, are
opened up.

Lu Ling's work is hardly intended to undermine the desires
and fantasies of his working-class heroes and heroines. He is, however, preoccupied with the task of recovering the primitive vitality
of the populace as a revolutionary force of resistance. In this
respect, Lu Ling's language of desire, class, and sexuality embodies
Hu Feng's "subjective fighting spirit" or a revolutionary subjectivity as the agency of opposition and resistance.[14] The "subjective
fighting spirit" is derived from lived experience, in the antagonistic terrain of the sensuous experience and bodily desires. Realist
representation is possible only through a "passionate expansion," a
spiritual embrace and penetration, of this powerful subjective
experience and feeling, into the oppressed individuals whose souls
have been subject to "thousands of years of spiritual slavery." This
tormented creative process by which authentic work of realism is
produced is named by Hu Feng as the interfusion and objectification of the subject with the object, a term synonymous with social
life itself. This interfusion of objectification, as we have seen in Lu
Ling's work, entails a fundamental disentanglement of the symbolic order and reorganization of the discourse of the unconscious. Lu
Ling's language is disruptive, and often chaotic. But the question
is: Does his language constitute a destabilizing effect on the reify-

ing, objectifying tendency of representation? Reading Lu Ling's work, I at least feel compelled to ask this question.[15]

An ambivalence concerning Lu Ling's representation of sexuality and subjectivity arises. Sexuality, or libidinous wish-fulfillment, is disruptive and threatening to the male social ethics and morality. Therefore it has to be contained by a symbolic order. But what about women's sexuality? Throughout Lu Ling's work and in this reading of it to a lesser degree, femininity and sexuality seem to mean a feminine subjectivity. So the question becomes: What is after all a feminine subjectivity which opposes or goes beyond the male symbolic order? I think Lu Ling's language of desire, sexuality, and subjectivity remains ambivalent and vague about all these questions. But to accuse Lu Ling of misrepresenting feminine subjectivity from a masculinist position is one thing; to point out the unsettling and disquieting incongruence of his style as an index of his battle with the revolutionary sublime and symbolic order is quite another thing. (In this present essay, the ambivalence of a male critic interpreting a male author's representation of femininity may also signal the difficulty of Lu Ling's battle from a different angle.)

However, both the Confucian symbolic and revolutionary sublime have to be confronted. The Confucian symbolic and revolutionary sublime that have repressed or ignored the psychic needs of men and women have to be subverted. Subjectivity and femininity as such have been equally subject to a psychic as well as discursive disorder. But this disorder cannot be properly understood without taking into account the dismembered modern Chinese history. Feminine self-consciousness, or a feminine subjectivity, if subjectivity is indeed gendered and of course must be engendered, has yet to emerge from the surface of history. It has yet to be re-embodied, re-presented, and re-invented, too.

NOTES

1. For a biographical account, see Yang Yi, *"Lu Ling zhuanlüe"* (Biographical sketch of Lu Ling) in *Xin wenxue shiliao* (Historical documents of the new literature) (Beijing: 1987.1, 193–205).

2. See Li Zehou, *"Qimeng yu jiuwang de shuangchong bianzou"* (The dual variation of enlightenment and national salvation) in *Zhongguo xiandai sixiang shi gao* (Essays on modern Chinese intellectual history) (Beijing: 1987, 7–49).

3. Jacque Lacan, *Ecrits*, especially "The Mirror stage" and "On the possible treatment of psychosis" for Lacan's famous schema L and shema R (New York: 1977, 1–7, 180–225). Also see Fredric Jameson's "Imaginary and Symbolic in Lacan," in *Yale French Studies* (New Haven: 1977, 338–95) and his *The Political Unconscious*, chapters 1 and 3 (Ithaca: 1981, 17–102, 151–85). For a feminist interpretation of Lacan, see Jane Gallop, *Reading Lacan* (Ithaca: 1985).

4. Jameson, "Imaginary and Symbolic in Lacan," *Yale French Studies* (New Haven: 1977, 345).

5. See Tonglin Lu's study of Mo Yan's visual and specular narration subversive of Maoist revolutionary realism, *"Red Sorgum: Limits of Transgression,"* in Kang Liu and Xiaobing Tang, eds., *Politics, Ideology and Literary Discourse in Modern China* (Duke University Press, forthcoming).

6. Roland Barthes, *The Pleasure of the Text* (London: 1976, 55–57).

7. For a brilliant study of modern Chinese women literature, see Meng Yue, *Fu chu lishi di biao* (Emerge from the surface of history), especially the chapter on Ding Ling and Zhang Ailing (Zhengzhou: 1989, 118–39, 245–56). Meng Yue's book offers a powerful ideological critique of the dominant patriarchal, revolutionary realist discourse and argues forcefully for a feminine self-consciousness, particularly among leftist women writers, which is entangled with, and emergent from, the political and ideological battles of modern China. See also Rey Chow's excellent study, *Women and Chinese Modernity* (Minneapolis: 1991), whose account of Ding Ling and Zhang Ailing constitute an interesting dialogue with Men Yue's.

8. Lacan, *Ecrits*, 193–99.

9. Ibid., 197.

10. For a classic account of dialogism and the relationship of the subject to the other, see Mikhail Bakhtin, *Problems of Dostoevsky's Poetics* (Minneapolis: 1984).

11. Lu Ling, *"He Shaode bei pu le"* (He Shaode is arrested) in *Qingchun de zhufu* (The blessing of the youth) (Shanghai: 1945, 58). Page references refer to this edition. All translations of Lu Ling's work are mine.

12. Mikhail Bakhtin, *Rabelais and His World* (Cambridge: 1968, 240). For a discussion of carnival, desire, and women, see Ann Jefferson, "Bodymatters: Self and Other in Bakhtin, Sartre and Barthes," in Ken Hirschkop and David Shepherd, eds., *Bakhtin and Cultural Theory* (Manchester: 1989, 152–78).

13. Lu Ling, *Ji'e de Guo Su'e* (Hungry Guo Su'e) (Shanghai: 1947). All page references pertain to this edition.

14. Hu Feng's theory of "subjective fighting spirit" is mainly contained in the essay, *"Zhi shen zai wei minzhu de douzheng limian"* (Situating ourselves in the struggle for democracy), first published in the literary journal *Xiwang* (Hope) in 1945 in Chongqing, with Hu Feng as editor. The ideas I paraphrased in the present text are taken from this essay. See Hu Feng, *Niliu de rizi* (The days of adverse tides) (Shanghai: 1947). Also see Hu Feng, *Lun xianshi zhuyi de lu* (On the path of realism) (Beijing: 1951).

15. Gayatri Spivak, among others, alerts us on many occasions of the danger of objectification and fetishization of the discourse of sexual difference, or woman as the other, in Western academic feminist criticism (see Tonglin Lu's introduction to this collection). I think the question arising from reading Lu Ling's work also points to a need of dialogic criticism in order to avoid the pitfalls of commodifying the objectives of feminism in the intellectual market of the West. We may grasp the writings of Lu Ling, Xiao Hong, and Mo Yan as essentially a dialogic and oppositional discursive practice in a historic moment of revolution, not as merely a discourse or counterdiscourse of a certain ahistorical "male myth." Of course, to do so entails a radical self-scrutiny of our own biases and institutional conditions under which we work.

4

Liu Heng's *Fuxi Fuxi:*
What about Nüwa?

Fuxi Fuxi[1] is the novel on which is loosely based the internationally acclaimed film *"Judou."* Both works reinforce gender difference, but with completely opposite effects. Briefly, *"Judou."*
overexposes the female character, while *Fuxi Fuxi* trivializes her.
They yield representations of men in their relationship with
woman. Both works are created from a male perspective, the novel
by Liu Heng[2] and the film by Zhang Yimou. Zhang's work operates
with a Hollywoodian benevolent attitude toward women. Liu's
work, on the other hand, is an ironical celebration of androcentrism, in Chinese style.

My paper aims to show the different levels of male domination exposed in the novel. It is my belief that Liu's work can be
read as a phallic critique, that his concern solely for masculinity
can be read as consciousness of the continuing, endless supremacy
of patriarchy in contemporary China. I will read into Liu Heng's
Fuxi Fuxi traces of the Fuxi/Nüwa myth and analyze the implica-

tions of the use of this particular myth, as well as of myth in general.

In my opinion, Liu Heng equates myth (*shenhua*) with imaginary ramblings (*guihua*) and extends this definition to history at large. *Fuxi Fuxi* does not recognize historical evolution and can be read as a critique of patriarchy, in all its Chinese institutions— namely, mythology, history, and language. Nothing, since the time of the great patriarch Fuxi, has changed. The history of the Chinese people is filled with human lies, from their construction of Nüwa down to the Cultural Revolution heroines. Not only has matriarchy never existed, but there are no traces of any approximation of the idea. Fuxi and Nüwa never were the supreme patriarch and matriarch figures, but Fuxi with its counterpart, Fuxi, travestied as Nüwa. This hom(m)osexual[3] reality can be traced into the Chinese language as well as in Liu Heng's work.

The results of my textual investigation are consistent: the obliteration of women (their exclusion from any form of power), the persistent subsumation of this sex, by the logic of the other. Julia Kristeva, in her 1974 imaginary ramblings about the persistence of matriarchal structures in contemporary China, never was so utterly wrong.[4]

LIU HENG'S TELLING OF THE FUXI NÜWA MYTH

Opening Clues

To many a reader of *Fuxi Fuxi*, an attempt to read into it the Fuxi/Nüwa myth must sound like pure fantasy. Fuxi is the title of the novel but is not a character in the novel; moreover, he is not even alluded to. As for Nüwa, even her name has been replaced by Fuxi, yielding the reduplicated name. I, however, believe that there are uncoverable traces of this creation myth in the novel and that they serve an ironical function.

The most undisputable reference is the representation of Tianqing and Judou when they make love as "two big pythons intertwining and becoming one" (*liangzhi damang raocheng le jiaocuo de yituan*) (117).[5] The couple Fuxi and Nüwa has since Han times been iconically represented as a couple whose bodies end in a serpent knot. This reenactment immediately has an ironical twist: Judou and Tianqing are not the initiators of sound customs like their mythological pairing. Indeed, the full iconic representation of the couple includes Fuxi, the *yang* archetype holding in his left hand, either after an exchange of hierogamic attributes, the *yin* element, the set-square *ju*, or holding the *yang* element, the sun; and Nüwa, the *yin* archetype, holding in her right hand either the *yang* element, the compass *gui*, or the *yin* element, the earth. Marcel Granet notes that this couple's invention of marriage and their representation with compass *gui* and set-square *ju* have made these terms *guiju* the equivalent of *bonnes moeurs*.[6] Here, the couple is committing incest.

Here are a few more undeniable markers allowing one to like the novel to the myth, but once again in a perverted way. The story is set in a town called Hongshuiyu, Flood Valley. *Hongshui* are precisely the terms used in the classics to designate the deluge of which Fuxi and Nüwa would have been the sole survivors. *Fuxi Fuxi* contains many images associated man with mud, recalling Nüwa's use of mud to create humankind: Tianqing and Jinshan are walking in mud (80); Jinshan's first wife died with her mouth full of mud. All of Tianqing's family perished in a flood, buried in mud (85). "Unburnt clay brick" (*pizi*) is one term used for Tianqing (96).

In a reversal of roles, Tianqing repairs the mud wall in which there was a hole through which he would look at Judou. Liu Heng has purposely divested Nüwa of her creative powers, by giving her agency to Tianqing for the wall's repair: it is an allusion to Nüwa's repairing of the celestial dome. But what a change: the fissured wall in *Fuxi Fuxi* separated Tianqing's room with the family privy; Tianqing used it to great profit for his voyeuristic "study" of Judou. He can now seal it, because he has fully exploited his object of desire. Liu Heng thus uses bits and pieces of the myth in a provocatively down-to-earth fashion. He desacralizes the fairy tale quality of it by bringing the lofty characters down into a primitive mise-en-scene where they are realistically portrayed as peasants.

The story starts on an exceptionally rainy, delugelike day. The couple, Jinshan and Judou, hide out in a cave, Toadmouth (*Hamazui*), which is another *clin d'oeil* at the myth because the character *wa* in Nüwa is sometimes written as *wa*, frog.[7] That is where the newlyweds first engage in intercourse. Another hideout, this time for Tianqing and Judou, is also a cave: a crevice opening somewhere between her native place and Hongshuiyu (154ff.). A hole just big enough for two people, it actually is the lair of wild beasts. Another cave to which they resort in a last instance is the vegetable cellar, a place where a chicken died because of the fermenting fumes of the vegetables (161).

The Metaphoric Chain: Devalorizing the Yang

Although the story takes place in the twentieth century (from 1944 to the present), the primitive elements which can be found in the characters' lives reaches much further back into time, creating an impression of primitive life. In their mountain cave hideout, Judou and Tianqing are called the "two cave dwellers" (*liang ge xuejuren*, 156). Frequently, the characters are not mentioned by their name but by their gender: "he and she" (*Ta shi tade. Tade!* [She was his. His!], 121) or called "woman and man" (*nanren he nüren*, 150) and even by "male and female" (*ci/xiong*, 141; *mu he gong*), or by "one coarse and one delicate" (*yicu yinen*, 131), "one moving one not" (*yidong yijing*, 148). That Liu Heng makes generalized use of opposites and generic terms is significant in what I conceive of as his overall plan to point to archetypes, to irreducible gender differences, for a negation of the harmoniously interpenetrating yin/yang motion, represented by, notably, Fuxi and Nüwa.

Liu Heng's novel gives the appearance of a master narrative. It is structured like a tale. It starts and ends with *Huashuo* (80, 168), "the story goes as follows" (in autumn of the thirty-third year of the republic, on a rainy day . . .) and is punctuated by "no matter from which side you speak, that was a day to be remembered" (*zhe shi yige zhide jinian de rizi*, 85, 165). The edge between make-believe and faithful reporting—*as if* it were for real—is maintained throughout the novel. I will return to this simulacrum of realism later. For the moment, let us delve into Liu Heng's tropes and metaphors which bind the male characters together while remaining for them Fuxi's alleged mythical characteristics.

Wood is the male element, which is also Fuxi's attribute. The clan name is Yang (with the wood radical). The main protagonist Tianqing is especially endowed with wood metaphors: he does not speak (*muran*, stupefied; *dai*, dull, slow-witted; *yumu*, dumb; *mune dehen*, simple-minded; *mudaidai de lianmian*, with a wooden face). His habitual posture, when there is a problem (for example, when Jinshan dies), is to squat down by a tree. When very upset, he eats tree bark (109) or munches his reed mat (119).

Jinshan is called a "tree rotten to the core" (*xiude buxing de mu*). He is said to be, in his old age, "apathetic" (*mamu buren*). Tianbai, Tianqing's son, also shares some of his father's wooden attributes. Tianqing thinks of him as this seed of his growing into a big tree (153). When Tianqing dies, his son goes to sit outside on a wood pile, and soon starts chopping it down completely (167).

Tianbai had formerly thought of killing his father with a kitchen knife (161). At some point or other, all men consider the other as a tree to be chopped down: Tianqing thrusts a sickle in the column outside Jinshan's bedroom (104); he dreams of clearing Jinshan with an ax (111); Tianqing chases his mother's tormentor, Tianguo, also brandishing an ax (158).

Yet the patriarch Fuxi's mythological representation by the wood element is motivated by much nobler reasons: Fuxi is credited with having brought civilization to humankind. He taught them how to make a fire; how to cook; sometimes he is said to be the god of medicine, of aphrodisiacs (I will come back to this feature later); he also taught people how to split the wood of the *tong* tree, and so on. Liu Heng is thus recycling Fuxi's attributes for his descendants, but the paradigms he uses end up as derogatory remarks concerning their bestiality. Stepping out of the mythological frame into a general vision, it is definitely clear that Liu Heng does not think highly of the yang counterpart. Civilization, as brought by Fuxi, is a catachretic term, a word for which there is no adequate referent to be found.

Judou's configuration is not, however, as clear. She oscillates between the water, fire, and wood elements. Upon entering the Yang family, she is "a juicy, tender vegetable" (*yi ke shuiwang-wang de nencai*, 80); after heavy beatings from Jinshan, she is "dried up" (*kuwei*, 86). Yet, for Tianqing, she assuredly pertains to fire: "a fire is burning red-hot on his back, it must be, he thinks, that her swollen red eyes are set on him" (109). As a sexual object, she is related to the earth element, be it for Jinshan: "She was his land. To be ploughed, to be planted" (86) or for Tianqing who would "thrust his ploughshare in the earth his uncle had so often ploughed, and sow his seeds with an ardour and efficaciousness his uncle had never been able to equal" (116). In fact, she has no fixed element, she is what men make of her.

Interestingly, in ancient legends, Nüwa is, like Fuxi, of the wood element (she is subsumed under his element). The displacement Liu Heng makes here in the attributions is significant, in that it implies that woman simply has no intrinsic qualities; that she is whatever one makes of her. Woman in mythology would have no proper designation; the same is true in his novel. It is another way of ignoring woman's specificity. She lies in the man's shadow. The *yin* female part therefore refers to darkness, in all its negative aspects: invisible, absent, the forgettable part of the sunny side of things. Judou is definitely associated to the *yin* element. She is of the night; the only interior monologue conceded to her is during the night and ends as the "gloomy" (*yinsensen*) sun rises (146).

All men, like Fuxi, thrive with the sun, another *yang*, therefore another connection with their clan name Yang. All men are, at some point or other, tanning themselves in the sun, from the old paralyzed Jinshan down to the little boys. Taking in the "old yang" (*lao yangr*, 107) reinstates them in their masculinity. For example, at the end of the novel, before the postscript, the little boys are naked and sizing each other's sex:

> The older boys walk in assurance, their sex beating away like a sturdy little hammer. Whenever their bladder is full, they stand on the side of the rock, a white rope-like urine catches the seven colors of the sun, hits upon wild flowers on the stream bank, scaring away the flitting butterflies. [169]

As for Tianqing, the sun accompanies his deeds. When he finally decides to make a move toward Judou, "the majestic (*xiongzhuang*), steaming hot (*retengteng de*) sun slowly rises" (106). All through the blissful period of Judou and Tianqing's affair, the sun appears during their lovemaking (115, 117). When things start worsening, accordingly, the sun pales (151).

LIU HENG'S CONFLATION OF
MYTH AND HISTORY: INCEST AS SYMPTOM

The Omnipresence of Myth

In *Fuxi Fuxi*, Fuxi is neither a character nor alluded to. He does not exist, but his descendants do. As for Nüwa, she is also not part of the diegesis in any way, *and* she does not have a model either. In other words, Fuxi as an ideal lives on. He is, however, no less a lie than the imaginary Nüwa. It would seem that Liu Heng is telling his (Chinese) readers that Chinese civilization is based on impossible narratives. I see his endeavor as a deconstruction of the Fuxi/Nüwa myth *and* also of historiography at large. If, as Robert Couffignal affirms, "putting a myth in narrative terms is, above all, to tell the drama of human heroes, of the difference between man and woman,"[8] then Liu Heng is showing us the inconsequences of myth in general and its persistence, and its close ties to history, as well as to concrete reality.

Reactualizing myth in the People's Republic of China is not a standard procedure. Mao Zedong himself spurned myth for its lack of historicity and of dialectical value.[9] In fact, long before the founding of the People's Republic of China, myths and legends were scorned by the literati, or else recovered by them for exemplary purposes. According to Jean-Pierre Diény,[10] this explains the absence of a unified collection of Chinese myths and legends in China. Edward H. Schafer, in his study of goddesses during Tang times, emphasizes their degradation by the Confucian elite. As concerning Nüwa, he states that she "fares best in folktales . . . rather than (like the Luo River goddess) . . . in elegant prose fiction," that Nüwa is "closer to rustic belief."[11]

It comes as no surprise, then, that the Fuxi/Nüwa myth has since then thrived outside the cities, of civilization, and mainly in non-Han communities. Rémi Mathieu, a specialist of Chinese mythology, claims there are at least fifty-four versions of the myth.[12] Together, Fuxi and Nüwa are the siblings and/or spouses who have established the institution of marriage as exchange, *lipi*, and, as a consequence of their union, have created humankind. The question of interest in this outline is the "or" of the couple's union: marriage or incest. The idea of their incest did not, according to mythologists, arise before late Tang times and spread among non-Han communities. According to the Miao people, for example, the siblings Fuxi and Nüwa were the only survivors of a flood, and so, hidden in a cave in the Kunlun mountains, or some say a *hula* gourd, they copulated to (re)create humanity. It is easy to understand why all the pieces do not fit at the same time. If this man and this woman were the initiators of humanity, should their sexual act then be labeled incest? How could they transgress and institutionalize at the same time? There does not seem to have been any interest in China's past to assemble the pieces, to tell their full, rather lurid story. As A. Plaks states:

> The Chinese literary tradition [was] interested more in the abstract relation of harmonious dual union than in the narrative depiction of the potentially dramatic causes or the precise circumstances of their conjugal conjunction.

He claims the Fuxi/Nüwa marriage must be interpreted as a metaphysical one.[13] In the same vein, Marcel Granet says: "Chinese thought is interested not in opposites, but in contrasts, alternations, correlations, hierogamic exchange of attributes."[14] Liu Heng shows with *Fuxi Fuxi* that the "literary tradition" has changed and that "Chinese thought" is not what it is presumed to be. Myth is entangled with history and with objective reality; a criticism of one affects the other.

Liu Heng's Offhanded Manner

I find that incest in the novel is treated in a very mild, humorous manner. The incest perpetrated by the nephew and his paternal aunt is one of nominal kinship, within a patrilinear system. In his study of taboo among primitive tribes, Freud has demonstrated that belonging to a clan automatically makes every member consanguineous.[15] Although the novel deals with China, which is not usually considered a "primitive" culture, the incest taboo works in the same manner: the taboo is linked to the clan's totem, which is indistinguishable from its name, in this case Yang, with its male connotations as pointed out earlier. Liu Heng shows us the active workings of the name-related taboo in the Judou-Tianqing affair while suggesting that it should be obsolete and is definitely ludicrous. He designates them by their "generic" status as "nephew" (*zhizi*), and "uncle's wife" (*shenzi*), and, as the story develops, as "bachelor" (*guanggunr*) and "widow" (*guafu*). But Tianqing and Judou are not of a different generation: they are of the same age. The marriage of Judou to the old man is an unnatural act, not theirs. The narrator scoffs at this naming game. For example, a very amusing linguistic muddle ensues, when the young couple first make love:

> "Aunt! Aunt! . . ." That was the initial silly sentence. "Judou! My dear, dear Judou. . . ." Halfway, he finally got it right (*rugang*): "My dear, dear, little pigeon, oh!!" [117]

The interspersed comments, the points of suspension, and the final double exclamation mark the excessive ridicule of the nominal taboo.

The absurdity of this *zhengming*, orthodoxy of names, is further enhanced upon Jinshan's death where not only Tianqing fully realizes that he is what the name implies, a full-fledged bachelor (*mingfu qishi de guanggunr* p. 153), but that now Judou is a widow (*guafu*) and therefore condemned to absolute continency. Here again, however, the couples pay no heed to such restriction and, although they must act even more secretly, they still meet. The town's reaction to the news of another birth by this bachelor and this widow is expressed in a light and funny manner:

> Bewildered, enlightened, then angry, then happy, then compassionate, and then . . . nothing at all (*huangran dawu, jier danu, jier dakuai, jier dabei, jier . . . jiu shenme ye meiyou le*) [167]

Common Sense and the Common Man as an Alternative?

Obviously, morality standards among peasants are not the same as for the elite. Bearing children is the most natural phenomenon, so is sexual activity, regardless of interdictions. I believe Liu Heng places himself as an apologist for the proletariat, for their easy, uncomplicated *weltanschauung*. His displacement of the myth and of the act of incest into a peasant environment is telling: there are (at least) two sorts of morality intermingled in Chinese society. The hypocritical Confucian one—represented in the novel by the old Yang clan members—and the popular, carnavalesque uninhibited one—the townsfolk. Liu Heng thus suggests that official history has always been underwritten by the latter (and thank heaven for that). This position is strengthened by the second postscript to the novel where a *juren*, scholar, is made fun of by a peasant woman for his ignorance of both sex and framing. But I shall return to this point later. To use Albert Brie's witty comment, Liu Heng, as a proletarian critic, is a *tireur d'élite*.[16]

That Liu does not, however, support the peasant's sexist attitude is not too easily extracted from the novel, since authorial comments are sparse and few. For example, at the very beginning of the novel, the narrator is content with simply reiterating what the people say. "They sighed at the thought that she would be violated by Yang Jinshan." One expects some compassionate thought, but to no avail. In fact, the next sentence is: "It wasn't that they thought he [Jinshan] wasn't a good match, but rather that he was just too lucky" (80). Throughout the novel, one need constantly read between the lines.

A Utopian Interlude: Incest as Subversion

Freud has claimed that the contact prohibited in taboo is not solely of a sexual kind. "What is prohibited, is the possibility to affirm, impose, to make one's own person to be acknowledged."[17] This is the case here. Judou and Tianqing decide to have intercourse despite the taboo. Potentially, they represent true freedom and anarchy, which they eventually renounce. Incest creates equality, anarchy, and implies individualism. Tianqing and Judou perform "adoration ceremonies" (*mobai yishi*, 92; *chaobai yishi*, 117) to each other. They are bonded because of equivalent victimization by Jinshan. From the beginning, they feel they have "the same miserable destiny" (*tongming xianglian de beimin*, 86), that their union was determined in a former life (*yuanfen*, 90), and that they have "a secret pact" (*moqi*, 84). Not only do they not want procreation, but they also attempt to assume themselves by taking their own lives. In the cellar where a chicken died because of heavy fumes, they intend to mark their revolt "in a free, unbridled yet dark manner" (*hei'an de fangzong de fankang*, 161). They prefer the hidings of animals or the vegetables cellars to the human—man-made—world. They have established for themselves a way of living which is absolutely equal, including sufferings, such as the anointment of their sexual organs with the nun's concoctions (his sex has turned white, hers is rotten to the core, 143). It is said that:

> Universal siblinghood . . . suggests an association of men and women that recognizes essentially only one tribe of human beings *with no essential intergenerational or intragenerational differences and no essential gender differences, an association that is universalist, equalitarian, and gender neutral.* [italics added][18]

It is significant that before Liu Heng some twentieth-century novelists thematized incest as an aggressive (albeit useless) attack on patriarchal society.[19] Recognized offspring from the incestuous couple would have turned the clan name register into zigzags, rather than straight vertical lines. The filiation would have no longer been patriarchal, Judou being the link between Jinshan, Tianqing, Tianbai, and Tianhuang: an impossible genealogical tree in Chinese patriarchal society.

FUXI FUXI AS A REALISTIC
NOVEL: ONLY EVENTS TAKE PLACE

Causality is Not Divine

The incest, the adultery, along with Judou and Tianqing's mutual love are simply erased following a slow descent into realistic horror. The jarring contrast between their initial cosmic lovemaking and their ultimate fondling in the vegetable cellar fully divests myth of its fairytale quality. Their first lovemaking is phrased as an elaboration on the poetic cliché *yunyu* (clouds and rain), found in almost all classical novels and used for romantic love between noble humans. In *Fuxi Fuxi*, however, it has an odd resonance: reference to the cosmic union of Fuxi and Nüwa used for illicit sex taking place between two peasants, who happen to be nephew and aunt. Before their "dance in which the heavens and mountains collide, the hard and soft sunrays converge, and the cold and hot waves mix" (115), Judou, with her broken teeth (knocked off by Jinshan) bites into the phallic-shaped turnip Tianqing is eating. Reporting the event, the narrator, in a tongue-in-cheek manner, says: "Their appetite had already moved to other parts of their bodies" (112). The reader feels the immense gap between "high literature" with its refined characters like, say, those in *Dream of the Red Pavilion*, and this twentieth-century story. Baoyu with Daiyu and Baochai (incidentally, they are cousins too) speak the poetic language of love, make poems, drink tea and sometimes refined alcohol, but certainly do not, except in their dreams, have overt erotic "conversation."

The edge between fiction and down-to-earth reality is here thinned out, conflated. Events *take place*.[20] Causality bears fruits. There are very real consequences of the characters' deeds. The illicit sexual activity in which Judou and Tianqing engage must not entail tangible proofs. They spend most of their time together trying to prevent pregnancy. In order to avoid it, they successively put soap, pepper, and vinegar in their sexual organs. All these horrifying scenes are reported in a matter-of-fact, thus chilling, tone. An ironic difference is maintained with Fuxi's great deeds, namely the invention of aphrodisiacs, of medicine, and of course, with Nüwa, of mankind.

The Female Subaltern

Let us now give some space to Nüwa, alias Judou, who is the bearer of the offspring. In ancient legends, Nüwa is not only the repairer of the heavens with multi-colored stones, but the creatrix of humanity (by modeling mud and, either because this process was too tedious or because she was pressed by time, also dipping a rope into the mud then trailing it about so that drops fell off and formed humankind). In *Fuxi Fuxi* she is the needed accessory for reproduction. She acquits herself well of the task, since she bears two children. However, these two, both male, are slightly monstrous. They have a great libido and are inconsiderate for women. Nevertheless, Judou cares for them and, once they have children of their own, she also nurtures their offspring, thereby earning this cynical attribution of "old hen" (*lao muji*, 169). Fundamentally trivialized, her role is a subservient one and thus opposite to the mythological role of manager of the universe.

The Male Subaltern

Fuxi, alias Tianqing, fares no better. The children are given names *as if* they were Jinshan's progeny, and as if they were Tianqing's cousins. Tianqing waives his claim to paternity, but also to his own individuality. He refuses to elope with Judou who proposes it twice, arguing that there will be no means of subsistence away from the land. Economic and territorial ties are real signifiers, not blood ties (and not ethics either).

Tianqing, in the end, has no recriminations; all is fair. He has finally returned to the existing order. He refrains from killing Jinshan because "this father of Tianbai is carrying on his back the other father of Tianbai, and is being observed by his own parents" (129). When Tianqing becomes conscious of his crime of incest, he feels he has not only betrayed Jinshan, but also his own father and mother (119).

The sole solution is committing suicide, which Tianqing does choose. He renounces purposeless sex, "stealing" licentious pleasures, *tou yin*—the term for out-of-wedlock sex, also used in the novel. He renounces himself, in favor of the clan. As a result, his act proves sociologist Sun Longji's claim that a Chinese person, in order to become "a good person," must kill one's self: *shashen chengren*.[21] Even by means of his death, he pays respect to the Yang clan. Tianqing chooses a way of dying that saves face for his clan, by making believe that he suffered from a heart attack. Ultimately, *Fuxi Fuxi* is a tale of submission, not of transgression. It is a description of Chinese patriarchal society, where even some men, for lacking (economic) power, have no space.

The Chinese Mode of (Re)Production

What remains is the clan. "Reproduction" is said to be the vital thing, the "unadulterated principle," as the narrator claims: "Humans are made up of men and women; animals, of male and female, it is the logic of heavens and earth to give birth to, and to raise, offspring." (*ren you nan nü, xu you gong mu, shengyang shi tianjing diyi de shi*, 121). The narrator's words are echoed in the third postscript to the novel: although they have self-deprecating ideas about themselves and their sexuality, "the Chinese are a race which excels at reproduction" (171).

The societal complex appears as an inhuman machine, which keeps working thanks to the transmission unit, namely, (written) words. In *Fuxi Fuxi*, the ceremonial of marriage is a fine illustration of the power of words. It is performed by the fifty-year-old Yang Jinshan from Hongshuiyu who, following the rules (*guiju*) of exchange (*lipi*), weds Wang Judou from Nanling, by trading with her family twenty of his thirty some *mu* of land for her, one *mu* for every *sui* (year) of the girl, a huge sum. His motivation in marriage corresponds precisely to what is recorded in the *Liji*:

> To make a union between two persons of different families, the object of which is to serve, on the one hand, the ancestors, in the temple, and to perpetuate, on the other hand, the coming generation.[22]

Jinshan, as an individual, fails, since he did not impregnate Judou, but his union with her achieves its goals: two male children, Tianbai and Tianhuang, are added in the Yang clan register. The filiation is uninterrupted (although these children are avowedly not the impotent Jinshan's). Jinshan gave land in exchange for Judou, and she gives him offspring, in exchange. No one loses, no one wins. It is the "correct," orthodox way, the *bonnes moeurs* earlier mentioned. We, as modern readers, cannot but take it as an ironical comment, considering the ill match the impotent Jinshan makes with the young, lively Judou.

THE CHINESE MODE OF COMMEMORATION

Amnesia for the Invisible

At the end of the novel, the two male figures, Tianqing and Jinshan, have died, the old one peacefully, with a stupid smile on his face, the young one, by suicide, with his penis dangling. An old hag of a Nüwa—she is almost seventy at the end—outlives the story. She is not only not granted the nobility of death, but is ridiculed: "She goes to the Yang family graveyard and sits between Jinshan's and Tianqing's graves, *not knowing which is which . . .*

and she cries for the two men she has waited upon" (168) (italics added). She is reduced to an anonymous function, that of (sexless) motherhood:

> Were the guy (*na Hanzi*) [Tianqing] alive today, he would probably be deeply hurt to see that his little dove [Judou] is no longer a little dove, nor an eagle, but an old hen which has lost its feathers. There's nothing wrong with an old hen. The old hen is taking care of her chicks, and of her chicks' chicks. *A hen after all is a hen*, hens forever possess something that cocks can't replace nor imitate. Tianqing can rest in peace. [169] [italics added]

Women assure continuity, wait upon men, remain invisible, unnamed in the family lineage. One can reflect upon the phallic representation of the word for ancestor, *zu*, which is made up of a stelelike or totemic form. The term *zu*, apart from meaning ancestors, also refers to the tablet on which were written the names of the clan. In this patriarchal society, the law belongs to the father and to the husband, in control of the woman, who does not have any voice, any presence, or any memory.

Only in one sequence are we given access to Judou's psyche: she stays awake all night, half in turmoil, half in dream, caressing her son. But she is awakened from her reverie by the smell of Jinshan's excrement (146). "Fragrant, stinky, liquid, dry, all those, the woman had to wait upon" (136).

At the onset of the Judou-Tianqing love affair, Judou is shown as the initiator, the one who is willing to transgress. She is the one who engages in sexual intercourse with Tianqing. "Are you made of wood?" she asks him, inciting him, and adds: "Do you think I'm a wolf" (111). She is his teacher; she is the one who, at nightfall, leaves her bedroom to go to his. In European retelling of myths, there is, according to Claude-Gilbert Dubois, a displacement in the importance of roles: the essential role tends to be given to the agents and the female roles become more important than the male ones.[23] (One can refer to Salome as an example.) This is obviously not the case here. Judou remains instrumental through the novel.

The Stuff Heroes are Made of

Death, however, makes heroes out of men. Sun Longji claims that Chinese civilization has always catered not only to the elders, but also to the dead and is consequently a "youth-killing civilization" (*shazi wenhua*). This statement is verified in *Fuxi Fuxi*. An amplification of such an attitude enables youth to be recognized posthumously, to be recuperated once they are dead. Upon his death, Tianqing is turned into a hero.

The words *jinian de rizi*, "a day to commemorate," which had sprung up at the very beginning of the novel, are used to refer to the day of his suicide (165). Similar terms such as a "moment [worthy] of erecting a stele" (*shu jinianbei de shike*) had been used to describe Tianqing and Judou's first lovemaking (112). However, the reader realizes that real stelae and commemorations are for males only. When the female Judou is mentioned, it is *par la force des choses*, because she is a necessary instrument for the event to be commemorated. She, per se, does not deserve a stele.

At another instance, the townspeople had found the image of Tianqing's washing his uncle so endearing that they could have erected a stele to him (135). Monuments are indeed only for (male) heroes. The term *yingxiong*, hero, is created with the term male, *xiong*—the character *xiong* opposed to *ci*, female. The Chinese language requires an added woman, *nü*, to designate a heroine. In the text, the term *xiong* (majestic) also refers to the sun, as has formerly been pointed out, and to Tianqing's sex, described by Jinshan as *xiongda qiguan*, "a great organ," "astonishingly still erect" (*baochi le jingren de tingba*, 134).

The townsfolk, also impressed by Tianqing's virility, posthumously declared Tianqing a love hero (*aiqing yingxiong*, 167). One also remembers the narrator terming him the warrior (*yongshi*, 144) for contraception. One will here again acknowledge the written character for valiant, *yong*: it comprises the character for man (*nan*) as opposed to woman (*nü*). At the very end of the novel, Tianqing has become a legend (*chuanqi*): "The children had not known Tianqing during his life, nor seen him at his death, but they knew about his immortal legend (*buxiu de chuanqi*). Tianqing, the loner, the bachelor would forever retain a part in the annals of Hongshuiyu" (170).

This elevation to the heroic status stems from what the townsfolk saw (and did not see):

> Yang Tianqing is presenting the people with his pointed naked buttocks and his two thick legs with his bursting veins, which seem to salute the onlookers. His rag-like thing and his turnip-like thing are hanging where they ought to be,

looking at the same time romantic and solemn. The male adults are surprised at the cleanliness of his arse, and wonder if their own, which they usually don't think much about, is that white. The young ones are squeezing tight their crotch, thinking worriedly of the sweet troubles that sooner or later they'll be confronted with. The women, absent, who've never seen this, send off their young kids to report; the kids come running back thrusting out their little cocks, comparing them, the women redden with shame and send them off with a slap. . . . Tianbai is stunned. . . . He is fascinated by its beautiful and ugly materiality. He examines its properties . . . he's figured out the narrow road he took eighteen years ago, and the mysterious original place which formerly nurtured him. [166–67]

The way each age and sex group reacts to Tianqing's naked lower body hanging out of the vat indicates the gap between the sexes, but also the importance of the visible. The peasants base their admiration (of Tianqing, the male) on what they see; conversely, there is no admiration for what is invisible—namely, a woman's sex. This comes close to typical psychoanalytic observation and conclusion: the invisible has no value; conversely, the all too visible is a kind of surplus value.

A FINAL INVESTIGATION OF WORDS

Fuxi's Floating Rod in the Body of the Novel

The novel, along with the postscripts and as announced by the title, is undoubtedly dedicated to the male sex, and at the end of the novel, more specifically to the male's sexual organ. In some ancient accounts, Fuxi would have been conceived by a floating rod. The myth of male autoreproduction seems to be at work. Does not Tianbai, while investigating his father's penis, say:

He is fascinated by its beautiful and ugly materiality. He examines its properties . . . he's figured out the narrow road he took eighteen years ago, *and the mysterious original place which formerly nurtured him.* [166–67]

The narration is filled with evolving images of the male sex organ as a stick, a rod, log, and the like. And the woman is the earth, which one works on, with "tools" (sickle, ploughshare). Her name, Chrysanthemum bean (Judou), strikingly differs from the higher names such as gold (*jin*) in Jinshan, or heaven (*Tian*) in Tianqing, Tianbai, Tianhuang. She is edible, to be assimilated. The only character in the novel who has a similar low name is Tianguo, where *Tian* means earth. He is the fool who takes a big stick used for marinating turnips (the most down-to-earth phallic image often evoked in this novel), and thrusts it up his rectum, perforating and infecting himself. This small unrelated event is preceded by a laconic narratorial comment: "Everyone has something in his life which isn't exactly going right" (*Renren dou huode you xie bu xing*, 159).

One insistent term, which, not surprisingly, designates Tian-qing, is that of *guanggunr*, bachelor, or literally shining or naked rod. It is said:

> If the bachelor isn't melancholic, then who can be? He is melancholic, because his smooth and shining rod has nothing to engage itself with! (*Guanggunr buchou shui chou? Chou de jiushi wucong faluo de guangliur de gunzi li!*) [153]

The penis becomes more and more central to the novel as it ends. The children, commemorating in their own way Tianqing's great sex, call it the *benr benr*, root—another reduplicated word. *Benr benr* is not a term for penis, although other words translated in English as root are. A few pages later, in the second postscript, it is used once more. There it refers both to a strange cereal, a rice sprout maybe, which is abnormally big, and also to the male sex. It is said to be the "foundation of life" (*benzhe ren zhi ben*, and to be one with food (*shi se bing tuo yiwu*, 170). Sex, food, and reproduction are interrelated.

Fuxi's Floating Rod on the Margins

Liu Heng's impersonal narration leaves very little space for guiding the reading. Yet, the title, *Fuxi Fuxi*, and also the postscript described as "three quotations with no link: in lieu of postscript and also as a critical investigation on a name" (*Wuguan yulu sanze: daiba jian dui yige mingci de kaozheng*, 170) are determining clues. The name under investigation is sex and refers to both the male organ and also to the activity. The quotations are far from being with no link. These three are, in successive order, the Pillar of Life (with the phallic imagery fully intended), by a Polish academician which gives sex as the foundation of life. The second is entitled "Notes on the Western Mountain," by a Qing dynasty *juren*: it is a hilarious account about this man's consciousness-raising by a peasant woman on questions of sex. As for the third postscript allegedly written by a Japanese doctor, it is quite harsh vis-à-vis the Chinese. Entitled "The Backwardness of a Race," this quotations first states how different races have different attitudes toward sex. This doctor terms the Chinese people's (once again we must read "Chinese men") sexual practice as atrophied (*tuisuo*); he claims that this atrophy has contaminated the race's overall complexion, *quanmian tuisuo* (177).

Liu's choice of experts (and omission of any living compatriot) definitely points to another make-believe, another imaginary rambling (*guihua*) concocted by Liu himself. Liu even winks at us quite a few times: in the second postscript, the name of the place, Shuang qingyan, echoes the name of the nunnery where Judou went to get painful and useless contraceptives; and the neologism *benr benr* mentioned earlier surfaces again. Moreover, using quotations (*yulu*) as an authority after the Cultural Revolution's excessive use of them, smacks of parody.

A tension is created between the novel and these final scientific texts, once again hinting at the impossibility of taking anything, any document, as truth for something; and anyone, as bearer of truth. I am grateful for Liu Heng's consummate skepticism and refusal of responsibility (of assuming any form of agency, any authorial stance). The nonwritten text of this novel is as crucial as the title and the final investigations on a word for its reading. The absence of the female, of Judou as such, of all that pertains to women, speaks for itself. There is no insight into Judou, while Jinshan and Tianqing are allowed interior monologues. At the beginning of the story, the reader does not know that Judou is also part of the scene. We only know of two men walking under the rain and, all of a sudden, we read:

> Had his fool of a nephew not been there, he [Jinshan] would have gotten off his mule and fallen like a vulture on the female who was on the small donkey. [81]

We are given to read the intensity of Tianqing's sexual desire and also of Jinshan's procreative desire, but not that of Judou. Any images of willfulness, independence, and determining agency for the female protagonist are totally absent. This omission can definitely be read as an incapacity, in such a male-dominated world, to let the females speak, or take up space. Ultimately, Judou—and her mythical model, Nüwa—are relegated to the image of womb, of matrix: a far cry from that of creatrix. Bereft of production, Judou also has no claim to reproduction.

The Chinese mode of (re)production in *Fuxi Fuxi* is sarcastically decried. *Fuxi Fuxi* is certainly no feminist appeal to the equality of the sexes. It is definitely a male-biased tale, but a mocking celebration of his androcentrism, where the narrativization of the Fuxi/Nüwa Fuxi's and again, Fuxi's story, into a hom(m)osexual organization perhaps particular to China. It tells the myth of the yin/yang union, regardless of the perfect balance and exchange between them illustrated in myths and legends, and also in fiction and nonfiction of present-day China.

CONCLUSION: MORE ABOUT ROOTS

Sun Longji, whose controversial work, *The deep structure of Chinese culture*, has become a best-seller among Chinese readers, claims that there are no fundamental gender or political differences between Chinese people, whether they—men or women—be living in mainland China, in Hong Kong, in Taiwan, or in the diaspora. Sun says Chinese people are sexless (*wu xing*), live and have lived in a sexless culture which infantilizes (*ertonghua*) or gerontocizes (*laonianhua*) everyone.

Without recalling his full argument—I am deeply critical of his penchant for the North American way of life and of his indifference to gender—I fundamentally agree with his thesis that survival is the basis for the Chinese way of life, and it creates dependence on the group, and consequently curbs individuality. That is especially correct when dealing with lower-class people, such as the peasants in *Fuxi Fuxi*: Tianqing refused to leave with Judou, because they would not have survived. Liu Heng perhaps drew his examples from the peasants because he believes they are representatives of fundamental, untainted culture. They hold its positive, yet also its negative, values. In a very respectful way, Liu Heng—as a proponent of searching-for-roots literature—gave them, in *Fuxi Fuxi*, space to speak. Liu made their way of life visible. He acknowledged their language and ways as the collective language of men, in other words, as a construction of a patriarchy whose referent is nowhere to be found (it floats somewhere), but which is still very much active: just try to imagine Judou or Nüwa!

In conclusion, I would like to allude to Gayatri Spivak's attitude on root-searching as a reminder to the reading of my reading of *Fuxi Fuxi*: Searching for roots is in order to grow rutabagas.[24] Or, in other words, the only empirical thing is the novel.

NOTES

I would like to thank my husband Joël and my friend Lu Chuan for the lively discussions I had prior to the writing of this paper. I would also like to thank Paula Varsano and Carolynn Rafman-Lisser for their linguistic advice for the first draft of this paper.

1. All references to the novel *Fuxi Fuxi* by Liu Heng are from *Zhongguo xiaoshuo 1988*, Huang and Li, eds. (Hong Kong: Sanlian shudian, 1989), pp. 80–171. Translations are mine.

2. Liu Heng, pen name of Liu Guanjun, was born in 1954 in Beijing, where he still lives. He works for magazines and also is scriptwriter for films based on his fiction. He has been writing short stories and novellas since the mid-1980s.

3. Luce Irigaray's term used especially in *Spéculum de l'autre femme* (Paris: Minuit, 1974).

4. Julia Kristeva, *Des Chinoises* (Paris: Ed. des Femmes, 1974).

5. The following works are sources I used for information on the Fuxi/Nüwa myth: Anthony Christie, *Chinese Mythology* (Middlesex: Hamlyn Publ. Group, 1968). Rémi Mathieu, *Anthologie des mythes et légendes de la Chine ancienne* (Paris: Gallimard, 1989). Martin Palmer, ed., *T'ung Shu: The Ancient Chinese Almanac* (Boston: Shambhala Publ., 1986). Andrew Plaks, "The marriage of Nü-kua and Fu-hsi," *Archetype and Allegory in the Dream of the Red Chamber* (Princeton: Princeton University Press, 1976). E. T. C. Werner, *Myths and Legends of China* (Singapore: Graham Brash, 1922). C. A. S. Williams, *Outlines of Chinese Symbolism and Art Motives* (New York: Dover, 1976, 3rd revised ed.). Yuan Ke, ed., *Zhongguo shenhua chuanshuo cidian* (Shanghai: Shanghai cishu chubanshe, 1985).

6. Marcel Granet, *La pensée chinoise* (Paris: Albin Michel, 1968), 298–99.

7. Edward H. Schafer, *The Divine Woman: Dragon Ladies and Rain Maidens* (San Francisco: North Point Press, c. 1973, 1980), 226.

8. Robert Couffignal, *Le drame de l'Eden: le récit de la Genèse et sa fortune littéraire* (Toulouse: Pub. de l'Université de Toulouse, Le Mirail, série A, tome 46, 1980), 145 (my translation).

9. Mao Zedong, *Maodun lun* (On Contradiction), 1937.

10. Jean-Pierre Diény, "Mythologie et sinologie," *Études chinoises,* vol. 9, no. 1, printemps 1990, 131–32.

11. Edward H. Schafer, *Divine Woman,* 90.

12. Rémi Mathieu, author of *Anthologie des mythes et légendes de la Chine ancienne,* mentioned this in a conference he gave at the Centre d'Études de l'Asie de l'Est of the University of Montreal in December 1990.

13. Andrew Plaks, "The marriage of Nü-kua and Fu-hsi," *Archetype and Allegory in the Dream of the Red Chamber* (Princeton: Princeton University Press, 1976), 35, 39.

14. Marcel Granet, *La pensée chinoise* (Paris: Albin Michel, 1968), 299.

15. All references to Sigmund Freud are to his work *Totem et tabou: Interprétation par la psychoanalyse de la vie sociale des peuples primitifs* (Paris: Payot, 1973).

16. Albert Brie writes aphorisms in the Montreal daily newspaper *Le Devoir.* This particular one is from November 25, 1991.

17. Sigmund Freud, *Totem et tabou,* 87, my translation.

18. Marc Shell, *The End of Kinship: "Measure for Measure," Incest and the Ideal of the Universal Siblinghood* (Stanford: Stanford University Press, 1988), 184.

19. Julia Kristeva mentions this phenomenon about Cao Yu in his play "Thunderstorm," in *Chinoises,* 106.

20. Stephen Heath, in the chapter "Narrative Space," in *Questions of Cinema* (Bloomington: Indiana University Press, 1983), discusses the materiality of events as they take place.

21. Sun Longji, *Zhongguo wenhua de shenceng jiegou* (Taipei: Tang lucong 2, 1983, 1990), 17.

22. James Legge, *Li Ki* (Taipei: Culture Book Co., 1973), pt. IV, 264–65.

23. Claude-Gilbert Dubois, *Une mythologie de l'inceste: Les transgressions familiales et leurs métamorphoses mythiques dans la famille des Hérodes* (Bordeaux: Eidolon Université de Bordeaux, octobre 1986), 206.

24. Gayatri C. Spivak, *The Post-Colonial Critic* (New York and London: Routledge, 1990), 93.

5

Rape as Castration as Spectacle: *The Price of Frenzy's* Politics of Confusion

The 1987 film, *The Price of Frenzy*,[1] directed by Zhou Xiaowen, portrays the social climate of contemporary China as one of inequality and mistrust between men and women. In the film, the rape of a young girl is depicted as a symptom of a troubled society in which gender divisions are at the same time rigid and unstable. Yet the film itself is wildly unstable in its attitude toward gender, veering from empathy with its embattled female protagonist to virulent condemnation. The film purports to question the construction of a gender hierarchy in society even as it establishes its own hierarchy by and in the act of looking. In this essay I will take the initial questioning to its logical conclusion by subjecting the film's own gender system to scrutiny.

In *The Price of Frenzy*, social power is overtly linked to the ability to manipulate the gaze. Women are powerless precisely because they lack this ability to see, and thus to control. Knowledge and power are associated not only with vision, but with cameras, binoculars, and by extension, the cinematic apparatus. Yet women's attempts to acquire power using these tools are characterized as paranoid and hysterical. The film denounces the "lawlessness" of rape, but withholds from women the means to resist, and in establishing the female gaze as pathology, denies its own complicity with the existing patriarchal power structure. Furthermore, its initial criticism of patriarchy are gradually displaced by a generic drama of criminality and punishment whose seeming transcendence of gender allows it to function as a ritual exorcism of sexual differences.

In the following pages I will trace the process by which this exorcism is achieved. I will also argue that the film's contradictory politics are not simply an example of cinema's universal tendency to objectify women and uphold a patriarchal status quo, but in fact reflect a particular post-Cultural Revolution sensibility which arose out of concrete historical circumstances, and is thereby open to revision and change.

The film begins in an enclosed, feminine space: a public bathhouse, in which the film's protagonists, Qingqing and her younger sister Lanlan, are bathing. Lanlan, it is discovered, has just begun menstruating, an event to which Qingqing reacts with sisterly pride. The stylized, dreamlike construction of this scene separates it from the rest of the film. Shot in soft focus through a curtain of steam, it conveys a feeling of total innocence, an Edenic world in which nakedness does not imply shame. This women's realm appears self-contained, inviolable.

Yet this idyllic world is violated immediately by the male gaze. A dissolve reveals the presence of a voyeur, who watches the women through his binoculars. In stark contrast to the misty, soft sequence in the women's bath, the watcher is shown in close up, in sharp focus, with his binoculars in the center of the frame. He is clearly a powerful and aggressive figure, even before we are made aware of his identity. Although his gaze from the tower may or may not literally apprehend the women's bath (which in keeping with its status as dream-state is not given a physical location anywhere in the film), the abrupt transition from the bath to his voyeuristic look sets him up as an intruder—*before* we learn that he is in fact a rapist.

The gaze is thus associated with destructive power from the opening sequence. After Lanlan is raped, the narrative follows the attempt of Qingqing to seize the power of the gaze for herself, in order to defend Lanlan and bring the rapist to justice. But because the gaze here is inseparable from other, predetermined kinds of power (the rapist's physical strength, the policemen's legal jurisdiction), it is beyond Qingqing's grasp. Her attempt to possess it is a transgression which necessarily ends in disaster. Indeed, the film overtly compares the extent of her transgression to the original act of rape; the "obsession" or "frenzy" of the title describes not only the violent child abuser, as one might expect, but also the woman who goes too far in seeking vengeance.

The relations of power established early on are soon acted out in the rape of the younger sister by the binoculars' owner, whom we continue to watch afterwards as he and his older brother struggle with the consequences of his crime. The two sibling pairs in fact become each others' reverse image: as the older brother tries to protect the rapist from being found out, the older sister tries in various ways to find and punish him. The rape has the effect of revealing to Qingqing everyday instances in which women are discriminated against and violated. Ordinary reality is no longer that; instead, it is a sinister theater in which patriarchy blatantly displays itself. Shortly after the rape, the older sister goes to meet her boyfriend's sister at the film studio where she works. As Qingqing enters, the friend is recording sound for a film, matching her own piercing scream to the visual image of a naked woman in a bathtub. Seeing this, Qingqing is appalled. She departs visibly shaken by what she perceives as her friend's insensitivity.

After that, Qingqing is walking toward her boyfriend's bookstore (which on its outdoor table displays, among other things, pornographic magazines). As she approaches she becomes aware (in a series of point of view shots) of the objectified images of women on the colorful posters and magazines. Flying into a rage, she attacks the display, tearing up the magazines and frightening or annoying the customers. Later she apologizes and offers to pay for the damage, but instead her boyfriend agrees to close down the objectionable part of the bookstore.

In her own work as an obstetrician she also begins to notice signs of gender inequality. The mothers who do not want daughters, who are happy if their fetus miscarries because they wanted a son anyway, begin to get on her nerves, and she is increasingly unable to perform her duties. Her overreactions are coded in the film as signs of an impending nervous breakdown. However, it is also possible to view her behavior in a different light—that of awakening consciousness.

Sandra Lee Bartky has described feminist consciousness as "consciousness of victimization":

> To apprehend oneself as a victim is to be aware of an alien and hostile force which is responsible for the blatantly unjust treatment of women and for a stifling and oppressive system of sex roles; it is to be aware, too, that this victimization, in no way earned or deserved, is an *offense*. [26]

This oppressive "force" not only manifests itself in acts of outright discrimination or violence, but also appears in all sorts of seemingly innocent, neutral situations, such as casual conversations, in movies or television, or ordinary social life. Writes Bartky, "to apprehend myself as a victim in a sexist society is to know that there are few places where I can hide, that I can be attacked anywhere, at any time, by virtually anyone" (28). This heightened awareness is a necessary prelude to or component of positive social change, but it is painful, and characterized by a feeling of continual wariness verging on paranoia.

Bartky's analysis is based on her own experience as a woman in the United States. In the case of contemporary China, what might be called feminist consciousness is subsumed under an official doctrine of gender equality, a situation that makes feelings of oppression more difficult to express. While institutionalized "difference" naturalizes the oppression of women as women, institutionalized "equality" denies women's specific claims—denies, in fact, the possibility of oppression existing (except as the archaic residue of "feudal tradition"), and therefore the possibility of its being resisted or changed.

In such an environment, the likelihood of paranoia—due to being unable to name one's feelings—multiplies. In *The Price of Frenzy* the filmmakers choose to highlight this paranoiac aspect and ignore the potential for positive action it brings into being. But it is exactly this unnamed/unnameable consciousness of victimization, as well as concern for her sister, that motivates Qingqing's actions. Her "obsession" with the rapist is an expression of her rage against a society in which "at every stage of her life, a Chinese woman was vulnerable to violence precisely because she was a woman" (Honig and Hershatter, 273). The more she comes up against societal indifference, the more determined she is to act on her rage and not let the problem disappear. In a patriarchal society, such determination inevitably invokes castration anxiety, and must be distorted (made murderous) and then punished. But although according to the terms set by the film Qingqing's acts are irrational, the feelings that motivate her actions are an understandable response to an oppressive social reality.

At the same time, Lanlan is suffering emotionally from the rape. She is hardly able to articulate her feelings, but her pain is obvious. The special treatment she receives, while well intentioned, separates her from the other children and makes her unable to forget that she is a victim. After the assault, crowds stare at her everywhere. She is unable to return to normal life, but neither is her exact experience directly addressed. Unable to put it behind her, she endlessly relives the rape in her mind, perversely taking on the characteristics of the rapist (chewing gum, reading "improper" books).

The silent horror Lanlan feels is gradually transferred from the rapist to her increasingly obsessive sister, as is much of the responsibility for the rape itself and its violent aftermath. It is indicative of the film's desire to deflect attention from the social fact of rape to the psychopathic obsession of the older sister that it does not suggest any way in which the rape victim's situation might be made easier. It does not condemn the environment in which being raped stigmatizes the victim. Instead, it implies that if she were left alone, Lanlan could recover from the rape, and that it is her older sister's behavior, and not the residual trauma of the incident and lack of social support, that prolongs and aggravates her suffering.

Nevertheless, the sisters' initial response to the rape is portrayed in a way that is subtle and haunting. After Lanlan's physical recovery, the two walk hand in hand along the streets of the city, looking for the criminal. Their task is overwhelming; there are so many men in cars that the likelihood of their seeing the man in question (whom they wrongly assume is a driver) is impossibly small. In a montage sequence set on the beach, they walk fully dressed among a crowd of sunbathers in swimsuits. In each shot they are surrounded by people, mostly men, who stare at them as if wondering (or sensing) their purpose. The shots dissolve into one another, and in the final shot, the camera zooms back to reveal a huge, endless beach completely filled with people—any of whom could be the rapist.

This shot not only illustrates the difficulty of their search, but also conveys the real horror of rape: that any one of these hundreds of men could be the rapist. Lanlan, of course, can identify the man, but Qingqing cannot, and so must project the image of a rapist onto *every* man. An anonymous assailant becomes a universalized, ubiquitous threat; every unknown man seems equally responsible.

This powerful sequence might have the effect of contextualizing the rape as an endemic social problem rather than one man's criminal act, if the rest of the film did not work so effectively to negate the implications of the sequence. A little while later, Lanlan sees the rapist again, but is afraid to react, so he gets away. When she tells her sister this, Qingqing slaps her. Her insensitivity to the girl's feelings is revealed; the hunt for the rapist seems to have taken on a meaning of its own.

A turning point comes when Qingqing acquires a camera. It is significantly in this moment, at the time she attempts to co-opt the power of the gaze, that we begin to see her behavior as truly obsessive. For the camera is clearly coded as male (her boyfriend must explain its operation to her) and invested with phallic authority. In a display of women's legendary mechanical ineptitude and discomfort with technology, she handles the camera with extreme clumsiness, as if she were handling a gun. And indeed, as the term "phallic authority" suggests, the camera is a weapon: when Qingqing seizes it and immediately points it at her friend, he recoils threatened.

The next scene shows her back on the street, "armed." In contrast to the scenes described earlier, she seems self-assured, unafraid to walk in the road among the cars. In a series of shots that again dissolve into one another, we see her turn the camera calmly and efficiently upon driver after driver. At this point, she actually encounters the rapist, in the passenger seat of a car his brother is driving, and succeeds in snapping his picture. Her use of the camera appears to be a successful appropriation of power, but unfortunately, feminine ineptitude interferes. She has taken all the pictures with the lens cap on, and as a result, the developed roll of film is completely blank. (As if to graphically illustrate the proper role of the female gaze—that is, the narcissistic look—the boyfriend hands her a set of prints that are all portraits of her.) Having seen the rapist, she is unable to either recognize him or preserve his image for identification—her gaze, it turns out, is impotent.

To emphasize this point, the scene of her receiving the blank roll of film is immediately followed by shots of both sisters separately looking at themselves in mirrors. Such scenes recall Mary Ann Doane's observation:

"Woman's films" as a group appear to make a detour around or deflect the issue of spectacle and the women's position (an obsession of the dominant cinema addressed to the male spectator), and hence avoid the problem of feminine narcissism. Yet this narcissism returns and infiltrates [the text] by means of a paranoia which is linked to an obsession with the specular. [83]

The Price of Frenzy, like *Caught* and *Rebecca* in Doane's analysis, constructs a nonnarcissistic female gaze only to demonstrate its impossibility: the female gaze, it seems, can only reflect back on itself.

Qingqing's shift from victim (insofar as she is identified with her sister) to transgressor is formalized in a scene at her workplace. Already suffering mentally and physically from the weight of her "obsession," she is suddenly attacked by an angry family, who blame their daughter's miscarriage on her, and in an act reminiscent of feudal tradition, attempt to punish her. Qingqing stands passively while the family members beat her, until finally the hospital personnel are able to pull them off her and send them away. As if in a trance, Qingqing goes into the bathroom and looks at herself in the mirror. The angry voices of the family become weird, abstract sounds in the background. A trickle of blood runs down her lip from her nose. Staring at her own image, she smears the blood with her finger into horizontal stripes on either side of her nose.

This inscription of violence onto her body is a revealing act of signification. The injury inflicted by the family attests to her alienation from society, but in accepting it, she makes it an act of choice. The mask she creates in blood tells us she has committed herself to combat at the expense of all other values. Her previous roles as loving sister, capable daughter, doctor, and friend are sacrificed to this desire for vengeance.

The rape itself no longer matters; nor does the sister whom she has ostensibly set out to protect. Her obsession has affected her to such an extent that Lanlan (who senses the change, even though she is not present at this secret ritual) is afraid to stay with her, and runs to the boyfriend's house for protection. Even though the violence of the family is crude and offensive, Qingqing's response to it irretrievably distances her from those around her, as well as from most viewers. She is no longer a rational person reacting to sexist oppression with justified anger; by abandoning reason and absorbing society's violence into herself, she has crossed the limits of the acceptable, and become monstrous.

The fear this shift evokes, it seems, requires violent exorcism, and so the rest of the film abandons social analysis and concentrates on bringing its linear narrative to a close. To counteract the frightening image of the avenging, castrating woman, the film becomes an increasingly Hollywood-like spectacle, complete with overwrought car chase, suspenseful showdown in a picturesque tower location, hostages, gunmen, and police intervention. Finally there is the dramatic murder of the rapist, whom Qingqing actually kicks off the tower to his death. While satisfying the requirements of a formulaic adventure or suspense story, the latter part of the film limits the likelihood of provoking any serious critical reflection on the problem of rape, offering instead a closure marked by spectacular death, loss, and finally a nostalgic return to the quasi-imaginary world of the bath—which now seems like more of a memory than a real possibility.

The utopian return to the bath at the end would seem to indicate that there is no room for women in society apart from this dreamlike, enclosed space. The world outside the bathhouse is violent and unsafe, and women are powerless to change this. Women's inability to resist violence is linked to their inability to control the gaze. For even when Qingqing masters the camera, none of her hundreds of pictures capture the rapist's image. He, on the other hand, has seen her through his window, figured out that she is looking for him, and learned to stay out of her reach. Thus while she thinks she is looking for him, she is already caught in his gaze.

It is the old policeman who is finally able to connect the rapist to the light in the tower. Throughout the movie, images of the tower either precede or follow images of the policeman, as if to associate him with omniscient power and knowledge even before he has actually discovered the light and decided to investigate. It is the policeman who is able to return the rapist's look on equal terms—that is, through his own set of binoculars. The look that meets the rapist's own is the first challenge to his power. He has been seen before, and recognized, but this is the first time that recognition poses any threat. The threat does not come from the victim or her avenging sister, but from a representative of the law. The policeman represents the law literally and also symbolically in his role as father figure for the sisters and perhaps for society at large. It is he who confronts the gaze of the rapist with his own, for it is the law of the father that must oppose the revolt of the son. Women, who cannot return the gaze, are the terrain on which the oedipal battle is fought. Qingqing's transgression is not in wanting to punish the rapist (clearly he must be punished), but in daring to assume an authority—the right to punish—that is not hers, but rightfully belongs to the law. Her adoption of violence is shown to be a threat not so much to the social order (which is the *implied* threat the film needs to negate) as to herself, in that it costs her Lanlan's trust and her boyfriend's life. Her revenge is accomplished at a considerable price, which would not have been the case if the rape had remained a crime between men—the rapist and his *rightful* judge, the policeman. The difficult question of women taking independent action against rape is thus foreclosed.

I have attempted to show that *The Price of Frenzy* opens an inquiry into the nature and effects of rape only to shut down its own investigation by censoring and punishing the investigator. Throughout, I have been using terminology and concepts borrowed from Western feminist theory, but the film must ultimately be replaced and understood in its proper historical and cultural context as part of a debate about gender and violence going on in China during the 1980s. According to Honig and Hershatter, violence against women received unprecedented media attention during that decade. Though statistics were not made available, it seemed likely that crimes such as female infanticide, kidnapping, and rape were increasing. In the press, attempts to understand the reasons for the increase were clearly constructed along ideological lines. For the most part:

> Gender violence was decried as a form of lawlessness and explained as a product of Cultural Revolution chaos or, alternatively, of the rapid influx of Western ideas into China in the 1980s. Except in the case of infanticide, violence against women was not linked in a systematic way to the subordinate position of women in society. [274]

The explanations of rape presented by the Chinese press are expressed also in *The Price of Frenzy*, although in China the film (as popular entertainment) would not necessarily be recognized as a participant in this discourse. For instance, "Western influence" is manifest in the slick pornographic magazines that are associated with the rapist. There are condemned by women cadres for being immoral, and linked to rape by Qingqing.[2] The film's use of the magazines reflects the official view that reading pornography (which can mean almost any sexually suggestive or explicit text) will lead one down a slippery slope toward degenerate sexual behavior and (for men) eventually into committing crimes such as rape (Honig and Hershatter, 59–62 and 285). The rapist is in fact characterized as oversexed in the scene where he admits the crime to his brother. When asked why he would want to attack a child when he could easily have any woman he chose, the rapist answers, "you can't stop [girls] from whoring," implying that in his view Lanlan had "asked for it," and that he was not responsible.

But more than the alleged influence of pornography, the film attributes the crime to a general collapse in the social order. Clearly there is a power vacuum in Chinese society, creating a climate in which acts such as the rape of a child inevitably occur. The breakdown of the traditional family has left children virtually parentless and forced to care for each other. Both of the sibling pairs are in this situation. In the sisters' case, the absence of the parents (and their ineffectuality when they are there) leaves Lanlan vulnerable, since Qingqing alone cannot adequately protect her. In the case of the two brothers, the older is clearly not willful or strong enough to keep the younger from engaging in antisocial activities, and is himself involved in crime. For both sibling pairs, the absence of social control precipitates a forceful return of the repressed—an instinctual violence—that must be controlled through the reimposition of law. But in the 1980s, the law has become impotent, perhaps swollen with bureaucracy; the policeman is able to capture the rapist only after his retirement (that is, when he is no longer bound by procedural regulations).

In such a context, the rebellious course taken by the older sister is not so much a "feminist outcry" as—along *with* the rape—a symptom of this social breakdown. Resolution must come through the strengthening of law and the restoration of (the symbolic) order, not through the independent actions of social empowerment of women. The "frenzy" of the title, first (literally) imposed on the image of the rapist with his binoculars, then progressively transferred to Qingqing, ends by referring to neither of them, but instead to the disturbed, anarchic environment they share, of which their acts are only symptoms. Yet we should not forget that this exposé of the post-Cultural Revolution social (dis)order is carried out on the field of a young girl's body. By using her rape as a critique of something else, the film becomes a participant in a discourse that condemns rape as "lawlessness" while ignoring its root cause—that is, the subordinate position of women *within* the social order itself.

By relying so heavily on possession of the gaze as an index of power, the film identifies itself with masculine authority—the cinematic apparatus being none other than the ultimate controller of the gaze. The filmmakers acknowledge this by using diegetic cameras and binoculars that blatantly allude to the movie camera, and by including the scene in the film studio, in which a woman's scream is produced to fit another woman's eroticized screen image, both voice and body becoming commodities used to glamorize an assault that in the "real life" of the diegesis is neither glamorous nor erotic.

However, this explicit reference to the production apparatus becomes an occasion to connect the image of Qingqing with that of the rapist. Through clever editing, we see first the studio woman screaming, then a shot of the woman on screen (matched in scale, as if that movie were the one we are watching), followed by a false eyeline match: when the victim looks up and screams, the cut that ought to reveal what she is reacting to instead shows Qingqing entering the studio, in a perfect shot/countershot construction. Thus cinema itself is displaced as an object of critical reflection. Clearly the threat of castration that Qingqing signifies is an alibi, used to hide the guilt of the filmmakers themselves, to prevent them from being implicated in the "frenzy" the same way the magazines and the film-within-the-film are implicated. That the threat she represents is in fact castration is concealed by the film's persistent effort to equate her with the rapist and with male violence.

This double concealment leaves most questions unasked, unless the spectator happens to be consciously assuming a critical feminist stance. This is probably why the Chinese government censors, who so thoroughly scrubbed Yu Luojin's description of marital rape clean of any political connotation in *A Chinese Winter's Tale* (Yu Luojin, 200–208), only felt the need to make one small cut in *The Price of Frenzy*, taking a few seconds off the opening shot of the bathing women. This act of censorship—the judgment it contains—in itself reaffirms women's inferior status. Strangely, it takes for granted what the film does not—that is, that the perception of women not only as objects of the gaze but of the viewer's desire is inevitable.

The censors, like the film itself, ignore the political meaning of women's response to violence, and deny them the possibility of political agency (unlike Yu Luojin's story, where the politicizing of sexual violence was perceived as a threat to the dominant ideology). The Chinese critic Li Tou, on the other hand, does see the film as political, but sees Qingqing as "authoritarian" representative of the political order which is being critiqued. Blind to the issue of sexual violence, he is unable to relate the film to the real situation of Chinese women. Clearly the film's basic lack of coherence reflects contradictions present in Chinese society, which this film does very little to resolve.

Nevertheless, *The Price of Frenzy* is an important film from a feminist standpoint, insofar as it challenges official dogma regarding gender equality and provides provocative material around which questions about gender and violence can be raised. It thus paves the way for a more useful political critique. Whether or not this challenge will be taken up, either within cinema or elsewhere, remains to be seen.

NOTES

The writer wishes to thank Professor Tonglin Lu for her extensive comments on the various drafts of this paper.

1. *Fenkuang de daijia* or *The Price of Frenzy* was released in this country as *Obsession*. I chose to refer to the film by its original title rather than that of the English translation because it is more descriptive and better reflects original intent. I use both terms, "frenzy" and "obsession," in this essay.

2. These magazines are Asian in origin, but their proliferation in recent years is held to be the result of corruption by the West. This explanation allows officials to avoid confronting attitudes toward sexuality in their own society.

WORKS CITED

Bartky, Sandra Lee. "Towards a Phenomenology of Feminist Consciousness." *Feminism and Philosophy.* Mary Vetterling-Brassin et al., eds. Totowa, N.J.: Littlefield, Adams, 1977, 22–35.

Doane, Mary Ann. *"Caught* and *Rebecca:* The Inscription of Femininity as Absence."*Enclitic* 5/6.1/2 (1981/2): 75–89.

Honig, Emily, and Gail Hershatter. *Personal Voices: Chinese Women in the 1980's.* Stanford, Calif.: Stanford University Press, 1988.

Li, Tou. Lecture. University of Iowa, 4 Oct. 1990.

Yu, Luojin. *A Chinese Winter's Tale* (excerpt and commentary). *Seeds of Fire.* Geremie Barme and John Minford, eds. New York: Noonday Press, 1989.

6

A Brave New World? On the Construction of "Masculinity" and "Femininity" in *The Red Sorghum Family*

Since the 1970s, in the relatively tolerant atmosphere of the post-Mao era, there has emerged in China a tendency toward "independence of literature"[1] from the service of immediate party politics, culminating in a new "literary revolution"[2] by a younger generation of writers. Prominent among the latter is a group of what has since been labeled the "root-searching" writers (*xungen zuozhe*).

As these writers see it, ages of totalitarian repression in China by feudal and communist rule have reduced the Chinese people to a state of powerless, "paralytic submission," and alienated them from their roots, whether the roots are conceived of as some lost cultural forms or as some kind of primordial human nature. Hence in their works, these writers attempt to look outside the existing mainstream culture to locate the roots whose retrieval, they feel, might provide some kind of answer or message for an emasculated nation. Based on the assumption of an absence of effective agency, or to use the sexual metaphor, of a loss of virility among the people resulting from political, cultural oppression, many root-searching writers are particularly interested in constructing some kind of masculinity and the ideal masculine subject (*nanzi han*). Among them is Mo Yan, the author of *The Red Sorghum Family*.

As a text, Mo Yan's *The Red Sorghum Family* is not monological. It is instead the site of different serious as well as parodic discourses whose conflicts and interplays deserve detailed discussions of their own. Seen from the perspective of power and gender, the novel revolves largely around the construction of a kind of semiprimitive, masculine ethos, and an ideal male subject who embodies such an ethos. From a discursive, ideological point of view, masculinity is the "nodal point"[3] in the signifying practice of the novel. As a fictive-ideological formation, the novel exists in an oppositional relation to the dominant state ideology (communist and feudalist) insofar as it attempts to create the resistant subject, reversing in the process the established good-evil, hero-villain dichotomies in feudal and communist culture, and celebrating love and sexuality. On the other hand, the subversion is diffused to no small degree not only by the very simplistic logic of reversion underlying the novel's attempt at creating resistant subjecthood but also by (1) Mo's return to a patriarchal, feudalistic, and even misogynistic ideology and discourse in his depiction of the male-female relationship and (2) his fetishizing of sadistic killing and violence as the mark of masculinity.

Ultimately, the construction of heroism or masculinity of the protagonist is made possible in the novel only in relation to a constructed femininity of women characters and through the victimization, and the eventual killing off, not only of women but also of the lesser male characters. If the fictive, ideal world of the red sorghum glories in blood, in crude masculine power, it also perishes by them, as the narrative development of the novel consciously or unconsciously shows.

Like many of its contemporaries, *The Red Sorghum Family* finds its locus in a remote and semiprimitive setting in the past. As is highlighted toward the end of the novel, the narrator, who is an author like Mo Yan, sees a dichotomy between "my" world— that is, the world of culture and urban civilization—and the world of the red sorghum (450–53).[4] Whereas the former is characterized by ugly distortion and pretense, contaminated by "green poison," the latter is a pure world of black, primordial soil, muddy, brownish river, and vast landscapes covered with dark red sorghum the color of blood (453). It represents for him as well as for Mo a kind of "permanently longed-for" perfection—"pure humanity and pure beauty" (453).

With the erect stalks of red sorghum and blood as its dominant symbols, this world of pure humanity and pure beauty is saturated, supposedly, with a natural masculine ethos or heroism. At the plot level, such unspoiled masculinity embodies itself in uninhibited sexuality as well as profuse blood-spilling. At the level of characterization, the same masculine quality is epitomized in the character of Yu Zhan'ao, the narrator's grandfather, although other characters are also depicted as partaking of the masculine spirit. Apparently, for the author, if the land of the red sorghum stands for a free and virile world outside the repressive forces of the dominant culture, the daring and merciless character Yu represents the masculine subject par excellence.

In the creation of the character Yu, Mo Yan is evidently trying to reverse or undermine the dichotomy of good and evil firmly established in the official Chinese literary tradition. Instead of a character embodying such virtues as loyalty (to the party, the court, or the state) or righteousness, Mo glorifies as a hero a blood-thirsty gang leader who defies the interpellation of the existing social-economic order and forces his way into a masculine subject position by taking the law into his own hands. Likewise, Mo's heroine, the narrator's grandmother, is one who deviates from traditional feminine virtues in pursuing personal happiness—an adulteress who would have been censured within both feudal or communist ideologies for moral depravity.

A significant part of the author's effort to create resistant subjecthood lies in his celebration of love and sexuality. In defiance of a long feudal tradition where sexuality in itself, because of its potential threat to state interest or the masculine code of heroism,[5] is seen as evil and dangerous, Mo celebrates the illegitimate love between Yu and Dai, the narrator's grandmother, as beautiful, rejuvenating—"a stroke of pink" in the history of the place (82). Especially worth mentioning is Mo's attempt at confronting the suppression of female sexuality in official Chinese literary and cultural tradition. In Dai, as well as Lian'er, the second grandmother, the author wishes to create female characters who, presumably because of their affinity to a fertile nature symbolized by the dark soil and the red sorghum, are passionate in their sexual desire. Thus Mo attempts to represent female sexuality, glorifies Dai as "a pioneer for sexual liberation," a "heroine," and also directly challenges, through Dai's mouth, the feudal moral codes which have served to deny and suppress female sexuality:

> Heaven, what is chastity? What is the right way? what is good? what is evil? You have never told me. I can only act according to what I know. I love joy, I love force. My body is my own. I am responsible for myself. I'm not afraid of damnation or punishment. I'm not afraid of hell. I've done what I ought to do. [83]

Had he been more consistent and thoroughgoing in questioning the traditional patriarchal values, Mo could have been called a radical feminist. However, such rebellious or subversive stance is undermined by Mo's own adoption of a surprisingly feudal, patriarchal discourse in his overall depiction of the male-female relationship. Along with and in spite of the novel's subversive aspects, its celebration of sexuality and female desire is made to reflect the glory of a grand male conquest by Yu in the patriarchal market of exchange of women. In one sense, the love story between Yu and Dai is one in which Yu the pauper is able to win out and possess the woman with supposedly higher exchange value—through violent means.

In the character of Yu, Mo attempts to create an ideal manly man *(nanzihan)*. Within the signifying formation of the novel, the narrator identifies Yu, his grandfather, with the signifier of power and masculinity. He is depicted as the bearer, first of all, of natural male potency—a kind of crude male sexual power, aggressive and irresistible to the female sex. The episode in which grandmother first sees Yu, for example, demonstrates this irresistible potency. While being carried to her wedding at her husband-to-be's house, grandmother finds herself strongly attracted to the muscular body of Yu who is carrying her sedan-chair. If the grandmother is represented as having her female desire, it is the masculine power of the grandfather that has aroused her and held her in thrall. She is subject to his superior power even in desiring. The signifier of masculine power dominates and defines that of female desires. Thus when later Yu waylays and rapes her, his potent power is said to captivate her completely. She is "soft and limp like noodles, squinting her lamb-like eyes" (81). Her sexual desire having been aroused by his male sexual power, his "strong and forceful movements" (81), she submits to the man with great pleasure.

Later on, as the narrator describes for us, even though Dai tries to keep Yu away from her for some superficial reason of morality, she simply cannot resist him and longs to prostrate herself in front of his sexual potency. Even upon hearing his voice she would be unable to control herself. Therefore, one day, while she is inspecting the wine-making process, not having acknowledged Yu publicly, the man bares his penis at her and urinates into a jar of wine, flaunting his sexual power. She is rendered powerless by his act:

> Grandma was all flushed; she stood there motionless. He got hold of her in his arms and kissed her on the face. Grandma turned pale instantly; her legs gave in and she collapsed onto a stool. [174]

Completely subjugated by his powerful masculinity, she publicly acknowledges him. When he asks her in front of the winery workers whether the child in her is his, she says while weeping, "If you claim it is yours, it is yours" (174). She is, of course, also saying: if you claim I am yours, I am yours. And when Liu Luohan, the confused manager of the winery, shows his bewilderment over Yu's claim that he can make the wine better, she simply whimpers "Let him have his way, I don't care" (175). The man's urine in the jar is said actually to improve the wine quality greatly, another proof of his natural phallic potency.

Thus, while the novel challenges the repressive moralistic tradition of feudal and communist China by openly representing and celebrating female sexuality, the latter reflects back a supreme masculine power in the signifying space of the text. For all the sensuality and rebellious courage allowed to the grandmother by the narrator, in relation to Yu's irresistible virile power, Dai is identified with a kind of (desirable) femininity, which consists of, among other things, both passivity and a willingness to subordinate to male power. To borrow from the language of the French feminist Luce Irigaray, the author wittingly or unwittingly resorts to the patriarchal practice of "specularizing"[6] his female character(s) in order to construct a desired manhood. For it is precisely the supposed femininity of the woman, her passivity and willingness to submit herself to his power, that makes the masculine potency possible. The constructed femininity and masculinity exist in an opposition-structural relationship; the latter would collapse if not for the former, and vice versa.

Even within Mo Yan's own story frame, Yu's sexual conquest is no mere victory of natural phallic power, but a forced entry into a subject position from which he could exercise the same kind of patriarchal power over women as his social superiors. Seen in this way, the subversion effected against the patriarchal institutions by their union becomes a problem of male rivalry. It is, in Irigaray's words, "hom(m)osexual"[7] in nature. Clearly, by killing off the grandmother's husband and his father, he has undermined the normal exchange of women in a feudal hierarchical system where men's purchasing power is determined by their own social, economic positions. In terms of class articulation, his forced entry into the subject position whose legitimate occupant is the woman's husband is indeed a victory scored against the feudal system.

However, the victory or subversion is significant mostly in the realm of the male-male relationship. For from the way Mo Yan characterizes Dai in connection with the two men, she is objectified equally in relation to both, in spite of all the convenient difference Yu is supposed to have made in her life (such as getting rid of a leprous husband and sexual enjoyment). Her identity or desirability is defined in very similar terms in both relationships—that is, as culturally determined exchange value before marriage (cohabitation) and as use value after marriage.

In her analysis of the objectification of woman in patriarchal societies, Irigaray points out that as commodities, women are two things at once: usefulness and exchange value.[8] As usefulness, women function to reproduce their husbands in the (male) children. As exchange value, the natural women are given prices by the patriarchy in accordance with certain cultural-economic standards reflecting male desires, whether in terms of gold, of the degree of voyeuristic pleasure they offer to the male gaze or something else. In their exchange value, the women's natural bodies are marked by the male phalluses[9] and reduced to a "plus or minus quality" (175) accordingly. Thus alienated from their natural selves, women become "a mirror of value of and for man" (177). Irigaray's analysis here seems to explain very clearly the ideological standpoint of *The Red Sorghum Family* in its creation of femininity. From a male perspective, the ideal woman is not only defined as essential passivity in a binary relation to an all-powerful male aggressivity but also eroticized into a visual object for male contemplation.

Thus the grandmother is often portrayed as the picture of passive beauty. Although she has rosy cheeks, bright eyes, she is inanimate "as if made of wood" (97). On another occasion she is said to look like "a beauty sculpted out of wax" (138). Indeed, when Mo Yan depicts Dai as having a full face, long eyes, thick black hair, gracefully long neck, a slightly sad, but tranquil goddesslike expression (138), he could have been rendering into language a painting of a classic Chinese beauty (*shinü*). And the expression he uses most often to praise the grandmother's appearance is none other than a clichéd expression (ab)used widely in traditional Chinese culture: "having the looks of a flower and the moon" (*huarong yuemao*, 12, 63, for example). To top it all, despite its perfunctory criticism of foot-binding, the novel, to a rather surprising degree, endorses the feudalistic valorization of women's bound feet as quintessential femininity.

In feudal China, as if it were a test of their capacity to bear subordination and oppression by their male masters—that is, their fathers, husbands, and sons—women are subject to a long and excruciating process of foot-binding whereby their feet are permanently stunted and distorted into "three-inch golden lotuses" (a term of praise for tiny feet). The bound feet are made to signify female beauty or femininity: the smaller, the better. The size of a woman's feet is thus turned into the currency whereby her exchange value is set.

It is to a large extent according to such currency that the grandmother in *The Red Sorghum Family* is presented as a desirable object, an object of high exchange value in the market. The narrator tells us that the grandmother starts binding her feet at the age of six. After long years of pain, she is finally able to come out with "the smallest feet of the village" (13). More than once does the narrator refer with fondness to her tiny feet as "tips of bamboo-shoots" (15), "little golden fish," or "golden lotus petals" (49). With something akin to admiration, he speaks of the men that have been attracted to her bound feet:

> What first attracted Shan Tingxiu [her father-in-law to be] about her is this pair of tiny feet. What has first aroused lust in Yu Zhan'ao is also her feet. Grandma is proud of her feet. So long as one has such a pair of feet, one does not have to

worry about not being able to get a husband even if one's face is pock-marked. [101]

Thus it is her bound feet that have endowed her with a particularly high exchange value that has made her attractive both to her husband's family and to Yu. And after Yu has laid his claim on her, the author also makes her realize her use value as a woman by bearing Yu's son, just as she would have born her husband's son had he been a normal person. Moreover, as the use value of a married woman entails the monopolized control of her sexuality by the man who owns her, so is Yu the guardian of Dai's sexuality.

In this respect, the feudalistic ideology and model underlying Mo's representation becomes especially clear. While Yu as the patriarch indulges in what amounts to polygamous sex by keeping two women—grandma and Lian'er or second grandma—he embodies the male control of female sexuality. He begins by killing the lover of his own widowed mother because of their love affair, which leads to the suicide of his mother. He smashes the robber who was going to rape Dai on her way to her husband's home and rapes her himself several days later. And then, as if by deflowering her, Yu has established his claim over her sexuality and being, he forces her into accepting him as her husband substitute, from which position he jealously guards her sexuality. Thus after the gang leader nicknamed "spotty neck" kidnapped her for a ransom, the first thing that seems to concern him is whether the other man has been impertinent to her. After her return, he simply blurts out this urgent question: "Has he *ruined* you?" (emphasis mine). Even though he has not "ruined" her but has only touched her breasts, Yu retaliates by eventually killing the offender and potential rival.

What is related to Yu's role here but even more interesting is what appears to be the author's attempt to guard his heroine's chastity through his narrative arrangement. Parallel to what is represented as her desirability or high exchange value is her inaccessibility to men other than Yu. Not only is she kept safe from the robber early on in the story, but neither her husband nor her father-in-law are able to touch her. The "spotty neck" does not rape her because he believes she has slept with her leprous husband. She is even able to escape from the attempted rapes by Japanese soldiers by pretending madness.

In general, although men other than Yu are made to contribute to the impression of her desirability by, for instance, voiding their desire for her through bawdy jokes (those who work in the winery and those who fight in Yu's gang), most of those who try their hands on her fall victims to Yu's killing (the robber, the Shan father and son, the "spotty neck"). It is true that for a brief time Dai runs away with another man, but that is only an act of jealousy as well as a ruse against Yu who has gone off with another woman. Necessarily, the aberrant affair is short-lived. Grandma comes back to Yu after some bitter name-calling, once again capitulating before him even though he persists in his polygamous practice. Otherwise, despite some tantalizing suggestions about Grandma's possible promiscuity in the narrator's commentary, the narrative makes sure she keeps her respectability and chastity.

As a desirable but chaste woman, the grandmother is presented as the polar opposite of another female character in the novel, Lian'er, or second grandmother. Both women are related to Yu, supposedly in their unorthodox sexual involvement with him: while the grandmother serves the role of an unofficial wife, Lian'er is made to fill the role of an unofficial concubine. They are characterized in radically different lights otherwise.

In the patriarchal traditions of both Chinese and Western literatures, there has always been a dichotomization in the characterization of women into two stereotypes: the refined, beautiful but domesticated woman, and the alluring but terrible seductress. They are, respectively, the angelic and the monstrous women[10] in Western literature and the "gentle lady" (*shunü*) and the "fox spirit" (*hulijing*) in Chinese literature.[11] In their study of such phenomena, Western feminists have pointed out that the two opposite images are actually obverses of each other. If the angelic woman or the gentle lady is an idealization reflecting male desire, the monstrous or the "fox spirit" fear of femininity—the fear that the woman, her sexuality in particular, might exceed male control.

In Mo Yan's novel, if the character of Dai, with her delicate beauty, her exchange as well as use value to her man, is close to the angelic or gentle lady stereotype, that of Lian'er is closer to the stereotype of the fox spirit. Different from the grandma with her passive charm, Lian'er is depicted as alluring in a wild and aggressive manner. Instead of small feet, small statute, slanting eyes, and skin "smooth like white jade" (5), Lian'er is said to have a strong body, extremely dark complexion, big feet, and "two fat, sexy lips" (338). In Mo Yan's representation of Lian'er, what is merely tentatively and evasively suggested about the grandmother—that is, lustfulness—becomes fully embodied. In general, if the image of the grandmother represents both desirability and control, that of the second grandma or Lian'er represents wild or primitive sensuality and lust.

On the one hand, the author is fascinated by what he sees is the mysterious depth of wild female sexuality represented by Lian'er. Thus Lian'er is depicted as so irresistibly sexy that Yu cannot help but falling captive to her magic charm. On the other hand, this sexual power of hers is characterized as excessive, threatening to Yu as a male subject, because it could deprive him of his control over himself and her, thus feminizing him. When they first start their amorous relation, after Yu has given in to Lian'er's seductive wiles, "they madly made love for three days and nights" (347), till at the beginning of the fourth day, Yu wakes up to find both of them half-dead. But when he wakes up Lian'er, her eyes are said to be again aglow with the seductive blue sparks. Yu has to run into the courtyard literally to escape her power (349). In fact the language used to depict her sexuality is such as to suggest both the bestial and the devilish. While her shiny black skin is like "the skin of the black donkey," her body "exudes golden flames" and her eyes are permanently afire with lustful blue sparks (358). She wallows in sex and drives Yu, the hero, crazy with longing for her. So insatiable is her "black body" (359) that it would disgust the man. As if all this were not enough to suggest the sexual animal in her, the narrator explicitly attributes "hysteria and madness" (*diankuang*) to the woman even while apparently glorifying her sexuality (385). In a rather crude manner, she is portrayed as having been "bewitched" by the evil spirit of a yellow weasel. The bewitchment supposedly takes place in the sorghum field one evening when a devilish yellow weasel beckons to her and hits her with its tail. Instantly enchanted, the girl would laugh, cry, talk, and scream in a horrible voice. Every time she comes under the effect of the evil spirit of the yellow weasel, she sinks into a "mud pond of lust and death" from which she experiences both pain and a kind of orgasmic pleasure (400).

Perhaps nowhere is the novel's hidden fear of excessive female sexuality and its accompanying misogyny more pronounced than in the destiny it allots to Lian'er. In the novel, Dai, as the embodiment of desirable but controlled female sexuality, is prevented from "being contaminated" (409) by the Japanese, whereas Lian'er the lustful woman is subjected to the fate of being gang raped brutally by a group of Japanese soldiers. As if by being excessive sexually, she called for such a fate, she is finally subjugated, her sexual power crushed by being reduced to a bloody lump of inanimate flesh. The narrator explicitly tells us that Lian'er's own madness is partly responsible for her torture by the Japanese, since in a fit of outburst of the evil spirit in her, she is said to have screamed horribly, which both angers and arouses the bestiality in the soldiers (407). And as if gang rape were not enough to strike home the point, the author has Lian'er killed twice, both times in highly symbolic manners. The violent rape by the soldiers leaves her dying slowly. Yet in the last days of her life, she becomes completely possessed by the evil spirit again. Screaming and cursing, she refuses to breathe her last breath. And it takes the esoteric magic of a certain wizard with his magic sword to finally conquer the evil spirit in her and end her life.

After all, it is only logical that if for the sake of his master-signifier—masculinity—and the masculine subject, the author needs to have femininity as the structurally different and opposite signifier, constructed narcissistically according to his culturally written desire in a feudalistic language, any perceived excess that cannot be contained in his ideal femininity, and hence might threaten the royal position of the male subject or the male psyche, no matter how alluring it is, has to be wiped out with a vengeance.

What is even more disturbing is that, under Mo Yan's pen, not only Lian'er but virtually every other female in the novel is killed off, in one way or another, the only exception being the girl who is yet to become the mother of Yu's grandson, the narrator. Not even Lian'er's little daughter is spared death by bayonet, whereas the grandmother is shot to death by the Japanese, not to mention the other deaths. In the killing and fights between the people of the red sorghum land and the Japanese soldiers as well as between rival gangs, the only important characters that have survived are Yu and his son. They are left to kill, although not for long. The heroic or masculine spirit embodied by them is made possible not only through specularization but also through their extermination.

Such misogynistic treatment of the female sex is not new in Chinese literature. It is in fact consistent with what critics have labeled as a kind of misogynistic sadism in such classic Chinese works as *The Water Margin*[13] where the hatred for woman derives from the male fear that female sexual power might deprive man of his manhood. And in such works, the misogyny in *The Red Sorghum Family* is also accompanied by a general "delight in violence and sadism,"[14] all in the name of heroism or manhood. To a large degree the so-called heroic spirit of the red sorghum world also takes the form of ample blood-spilling. Yu the masculine subject par excellence is none other than the greatest killer in the novel. As if he were the incarnation of some primitive wildness and some vengeful spirit, Yu kills man after man ranging from the lover of his own mother, the Shan father and son, "spotty neck," and many a Japanese soldier and rival gang member. The novel as a whole is filled with gruesome killing and often graphic details of torture and mutilation. Those who fall victim to what appears to be the immanent violence principle of the fictional space are not only women but numerous lesser men. Ultimately, however, this principle of violence proves self-destructive. In the very process of wreaking violence on its structural opposites, a constructed masculinity consumes itself. At the more concrete level of narration, as killing and violence are carried on under different pretexts in the novel, so does the heroic spirit of the male subject peter out. When almost all men and women of the red sorghum world are consigned to death, Yu and his son seem to have little justification for existence as masculine subjects. Thus the author arranges for their removal from the scene by having them defeated by the authority, followed eventually by their capture by the Japanese.

There is little doubt that Mo Yan's very attempt to construct a kind of raw masculinity and a subject (subjects) of power in the presumably acultural, semiutopian setting of the red sorghum field bespeaks of a deep disillusion with the official Chinese ideology and cultural legacy, be it Confucian or communist. No less clearly reflected from Mo's endeavor is the reverse of what the author tries to construct in his fictional world, the sense of lack and of powerlessness discussed at the beginning of the chapter. With regard to its construction of a masculine ethos, the narrative development of *The Red Sorghum Family* follows a downward curve. As with his construction of femininity, if Mo Yan's creation of an imaginary masculine subject and masculinity is driven by his ideologically coded desire, his final eradication of them perhaps tells of his fear of the anarchic and violent principle underlying his creation. It could also be an indication of his recognition of the fantastic nature, the impossibility of his fictional construct. It could be read, in addition, as a reaffirmation of his subjecthood within the existing dominant culture, whether the gesture be sincere or playful.

Finally, what is perhaps an important question raised by *The Red Sorghum Family* is, given, the agelong rule by totalitarianism in China, where does one turn for a meaningful master-signifier and what discourses can one use to formulate a new subjectivity, fictional or otherwise? It is a very difficult question. But it is perhaps not too much to expect that the answer should mean less misogyny and a more meaningful connection with reality than the killing orgies of Mo Yan's protagonist.

NOTES

1. Pan Yuan and Pan Jie, "The Non-official Magazine of *Today* and the Younger Generation's Ideals for a New Literature," 194, *After Mao: Chinese Literature and Society, 1978–1981*, Jeffrey C. Kindley, ed. (Cambridge: Harvard University Press, 1985), 193–219.

2. It refers to the aggressive pursuit of new ideas and modernist techniques (many of which of Western origin) in the literary field by a young generation of writers.

3. Zizek uses the concept of nodal-point (*point de capiton*) from the psychoanalytic tradition to refer to the crucial element in a discourse that serves to totalize it, and through which all the other signifying elements take on meaning. Zizek, 87–88.

4. Mo Yan, *Hong guoliang jiazu* (*The Red Sorghum Family*) (Beijing: jiefangjun wenyi chuban she, 1987).

5. C. T. Hsia in his analysis of *The Water Margin* defines the traditional Chinese code of heroism as consisting of honor, filial piety, loyalty to the emperor, friendship, and indifference to sexual temptation. See Hsia, "The Water Margin," 86–88, *The Classical Chinese Novel: A Critical Introduction*, C. T. Hsia, ed. (Bloomington: Indiana University Press, 1980), 75–114.

6. Here I am borrowing Luce Irigaray's concept of specularization. According to Irigaray's analysis, the feminine as such is repressed in the Western patriarchal culture. The patriarchal representation of woman is specular in nature—that is, it serves to reflect the male psyche, his desire, fear, and the like. The feminine thus depicted is often no more than a mirror in which the male subject could "reduplicate itself, to reflect itself by itself." See Luce Irigaray, *This Sex Which Is Not One* (Ithaca: Cornell University Press, 1985), chapter 4.

7. As Irigaray sees it, what is at stake in the exchange of women in a patriarchal system is the relationship between men. Women, reduced to objects of exchange, are functional only for the realization and regulation of man-man—that is, hom(m)o-sexual relationships. See Irigaray, *This Sex*, chapter 8.

8. Ibid., 175–76.

9. Here I am using the word "phallus" in a Lacanian—that is, symbolic sense—to refer to patriarchal power in a cultural system.

10. See Toril Moi, *Sexual/Textual Politics* (New York: Routledge, 1988), 58.

11. See Cai Xiang, "Qing yu yu de duili," *Wenxue pinglun* 3 (1988), where the author discusses what he sees as an oppositional model in Chinese culture which dichotomizes love and lust and the relation it bears to the characterization of women in literature. "Fox spirit" is a cliché expression for seductive and evil woman.

12. Moi, *Sexual/Textual*, 58.

13. Hsia, *Classical Chinese Novel*, 38.

14. Ibid., 39.

7

Femininity as Imprisonment: Subjectivity, Agency, and Criminality in Ai Bei's Fiction

In a tongue-in-cheek preface to the collection which includes her novella *Red Ivy*, Ai Bei states: "A woman is a thing like a novel; you read one sentence, and probably can't stop yourself from reading to the end in one breath."[1] In the novella itself, the narrator exclaims: "Such unfathomable little animals women are!" (197/134). Given Confucius's claim that women are equivalent to "inferior men" (*xiaoren*), these comments raise the apparently facetious question of whether or not it is a sign of progress to view Chinese women instead as "novels" (*xiaoshuo*, literally "small talk") and "little animals" (*xiao dongwu*) Evidently, the repeated appearance of the qualifying diminutive (*xiao*) in the three terms suggests a continued be-"little"-ment of women: in the moral-philosophical terms of Confucian patriarchy, she is inferior; as a *thing* written by another hand and held against certain political, social, and esthetic rules, her existence is secondary; and as an *ani-*

mal, she is obedient to certain natural laws. In all cases woman is subject to standards or laws; she is created and reduced by them. Doubling this perception of women's subordination, *Red Ivy* is about women in prison, women with reduced legal status, women visibly, as well as invisibly, enclosed and diminished by law.

In selecting a women's prison as the setting for a fictional work, Ai Bei is obviously engaging in a different project from that carried out by Michel Foucault in his historical and philosophical consideration of the development of the prison in the West. Nonetheless, some reference to Foucault's reflections can be useful to our reading of Ai Bei's text. Both writers begin from the immediate significance of the prison as image par excellence of confinement imposed by sets of rules. Foucault, however, proceeds from here to interpret the historical phenomenon of the prison as evidence of subtle and insidious relations between the state and the individual, relations which he finds duplicated and proliferated by other institutions and discourses. Of central interest in his work is how the interplay of knowledge and techniques of power culminate in people's acceptance of the power to punish, their tolerance of punishment, and implicit in this, their acceptance of norms or standards of behavior set for them.[2] Foucault is concerned with an agonizing question basic to Western Marxist critics of capitalism and totalitarianism: "Why submit to the power which belabors you?"[3]

Ai Bei, on the other hand, makes a fictional journey *into* the institution of the women's prison. From the inside, she seems more interested in the significance, or more exactly, the emotional impact of a women's prison as a metaphor for feminine subjectivity. To think and feel as a woman is to experience imprisonment, whether inside or outside prison walls. Ai Bei's question is not *why* women submit or even how they come to submit, but rather what submission is as experience, how it feels. This is not to say that she neglects gender-specific social and political relationship. In fact, the oppressive, authoritarian relationship Foucault describes between state and individual is useful to keep in mind when reading *Red Ivy* precisely because the author seems to take the same for granted. She proceeds from a clear sense of Chinese women's socially constructed inferiority. The reader finds no sign, no reminder of the earlier stereotypical woman from the People's Republic of China, the woman who presumes, or even desires to "hold up half the sky" or to be man's equal.

Foucault's reading of the prison institution as a threatening form of architecture on the political landscape, signaling and producing relationships between the state and the individual, allows him to analyze mechanisms of power created by ideological institutions and envision their extensive, homogeneous imposition on and internalization by the individual. Ai Bei, by contrast, enters a nation-specific and gender-specific prison to view an interior landscape. From here she makes us understand that to speak of "women prisoners" is tautological. Their inner condition is that of a prison: they are confined by a subjectivity created by an intricate configuration of the state, patriarchal norms, and also personal history, desires, and emotions, and even their own bodies. While Foucault asks how the state creates docile bodies, Ai Bei is concerned with the experience of a particular kind of docile body: that of Chinese women.

The idea of feminine subjectivity as imprisonment is, of course, disturbing, and *Red Ivy* offers little to mitigate this depressing perception. It does, however, complicate it by formal shifts which raise certain questions. The texts examines feminine subjectivity not, as it might have, through one character's oppressively closed-in inner world, but rather through glimpses of nine different women's lives. These women are not all inmates of the women's prison; some are guards and some merely relatives of one of the guards. In presenting these characters, narrative voice shifts continuously between first person and omniscient third, from the inner world of one character to that of another, and from inside the prison to outside it. Do these textual shifts and corresponding shifts in subject perspective suggest a continuity, a collective feminine subjectivity, or reveal weakness in the prison walls of such a continuum? Even as it confines it, the structure of prison walls also signals the residence within of a variety of lawbreakers, a term which in itself suggests at least successful instances of freedom from the restraint of law. By this logic, are the actual prisoners perhaps freer than their guards or women outside prison? Or is women's existence somehow by definition lawbreaking even as it is imprisoned? In other words, does being a woman immediately imply infractions of laws which are invisible? Is she necessarily an outlaw even when not in prison. And is an awareness of feminine subjectivity as a women's prison possibly a first step toward escaping that structure?

This series of questions hinges on the problem of feminine agency, a possibility or reality of resistance to confinement, which the narrative shifts in *Red Ivy* may or may not affirm. Certainly such resistance is not affirmed at the level of content or theme. Here Ai Bei seems a kindred soul with Foucault, intent on searching out the insidious ways in which an individual is brought to acquiesce and even assist in the functioning of a structure which oppresses her.[4] The obverse side of being a lawbreaker is that a term of imprisonment distinguishes one as such. A prisoner by definition experiences herself as criminal because she is excluded, isolated, and deprived on the one hand, and assigned to a specified group or community on the other. Her perception of her confinement through her definition insures feelings of loss, guilt, and self-condemnation, the emotional components of the docile body. Resistance is precisely what these feelings call upon her to suppress; it is exactly her criminality.

These, then, are the interrelated issues which I will be tracing through Ai Bei's text: feminine subjectivity as prison, the possibility of agency, and the experience of criminality.

FEMININE SUBJECTIVITY AS PRISON

According to Amy Tan, Ai Bei writes about "the self in conflict with both society and the self that society has created." Tan raises "questions about the odds for or against existence and survival of the individual."[5] While questions of the self are central to the story *Red Ivy*, the text shows Tan's comments to be problematic both in terms of the implied possibility of an individual self separate from and able to struggle against its social construction and in their reductive generality. *Red Ivy* is not an allegory of the individual pitted against society; it is insistently about the self as a complex subjectivity which is sexed, gendered, and historically located. This is evident in the story's symbolic consideration of the physical construct of a *women's* prison and its juxtaposition of the lives of nine different women characters, some within and some without that prison. It is further explicit in the character of Ji Li, who begins the story as first-person narrator. Ji Li's persona expresses a desire to know and analyze the feminine self in the questions she frames, as part of her job as guard, and through her integrative role in the narrative as the observer of and only connection between all the women presented in the story.

As Ji Li approached the women's prison, enters it to begin work, and meets her first prisoner, she internally voices a series of questions and reflections:

In that prison world where there were no freedom and no male companionship, were they like women everywhere, arguing over petty matters and becoming enraged with jealousy when they saw younger, prettier women? [97–98/61] Did these criminals destroy the beauty of society and create flaws in it, or were they the products of a flawed society? In life, with all its yardsticks, anyone whose desires exceed the norm or who momentarily loses control over her emotions may be judged wanting by these yardsticks and become one of society's criminals. And once you are labeled a "criminal," you become a subhuman, stripped of your liberty and your dignity. [100/63] Was this five-foot-tall woman, so frail that a breeze could knock her over, a murderess? [101/63] What if her original conviction had been a mistake? [102/64]

These reflections are highly suggestive and I want to draw out their implications here, particularly as they reveal the complexity of Ji Li's motivations and assert the symbolic nature of the text.

Her first question is not the expression of a vague or innocent curiosity, an unspecified desire to know if these women criminals are the same in all respects with other women, but rather specifically to know if women separated from men are still petty and jealous. Are they different in these terms from those Ji Li distinguishes as the "spoiled young maidens and beloved wives, innocent souls used to affection" who pass by imagining "dirt and chaos" behind those walls? (97/61). Has the suffering of their lives made them more knowing and raised them above certain attitudes generally considered common afflictions of women? Has their separation from men made them more human, or better yet more feminine? Can women perhaps be more themselves when not sexually defined by their relation to men as maidens or wives? Ji Li's thoughts suggest she is drawn to these socially condemned women by a profound disillusionment with women existing in innocence, women who purportedly have the status of being human and ostensibly retain their dignity and liberty. She suspects the innocence and humanity granted them and so equally doubts society's labeling of the imprisoned women as criminal and questions its yardsticks. She even lacks faith in society's ability to make factual judgments, as when she asks, Did this woman really murder someone?

Given Ji Li's attitudes, her questions regarding responsibility, whether these women have destroyed the beauty of society, or are the results of flaws in that society must be read ironically. The question occurs in the context of a conception of women as arbitrarily delimited by oppressive social standards, the subject of dominating ideologies. When so defined, societal beauty depends on the successful control of desires and emotions, conformity to a normative behavior, not on some independent and just standard. Regardless of how one answers the question, whether it is by social judgment or social flaws, it is still society that determines how a woman may behave and conversely creates the criminality of women.

Consequently Ji Li identifies sympathetically with these women judged as criminals, women imprisoned by yardsticks reified into reinforced concrete. To her, and hence to the reader, this women's prison is immediately a metaphor for women's social existence with the ambiguous advantage that the walls are visible, the judgments part of official records. Her desire is to observe and discover what remains, locate the self left within when women are physically separated from society, the source of ideological determinations, even as it surrounds them.

Ji Li's privileged position as guard, as inside and outside this material prison, is an immediate indicator of the problematic nature of this sympathetic identification with and desire to know woman's self, herself through observing these women. With both her occupation and preoccupation, she stands in the position of enforcer of yardsticks, is in effect one of their reifications as guard and as observing, judging mind. During her first moments inside the prison, the text repeatedly asserts Ji Li's consciousness of the complication created by her privileged difference through abrupt changes in her emotions and discordance between her perceptions and those of the women in prison. When the warning line is pointed out to her, immediately the sympathetic feelings of oppression she has been experienced are replaced by curiosity. Reflecting that she was "after all as person come to guard these criminals," she steps deliberately on "this line separating freedom and non-freedom" (100/63). After expressing concern about the quality of food in the dining hall, she notes with cynical bemusement the women prisoners' eagerness to "kiss up" to the guards by lying about their satisfaction with prison conditions to visitors. As she watches a prisoner rehearsing alone her half of a dramatic dialogue between a husband and wife, she is disturbed by the evidence of deprivation also inherent in the women's forced separation from men. "How can there be any emotional exchange? What's the purpose?" she asks (105/66). Subsequently she watches uncomfortably as the prisoners perform an incongruously crude, sensuous dance set to a modernized rendition of an aria from one of the model operas of the Cultural Revolution. These operas and sexual attitudes generally promoted during the Cultural Revolution were insistently puritanical, yet these women prisoners seem entirely unaware of the disharmonious combination of their suggestive movements and the music. Ji Li has to stop herself from laughing when she learns the dance is entitled "The Party is My Mother."

While Ji Li is aware of a distance between herself and the women prisoners compromising her sympathy and making suspect the possibility that she can discover here women's true self, the desire to locate and identify with a shared feminine selfhood remains. In the final scene of this introductory section of the story, the poignant grief Ji Li feels as she watched a condemned woman about to die is disrupted by the sound of the dining hall bell. In an almost Pavlovian reaction she and the supervising guard begin stealing glances at their watches and Ji Li bitterly reassesses her earlier feelings as "petty bourgeois sentimentality" (112/71). However, a further narrative twist undermines this labeling of the truth about her emotions as ultimately inferior to her animal appetite. Preoccupied with her self-judgment, Ji Li turns to leave and almost collides with the armed guards who have come to escort the condemned prisoner to her execution. At this moment, a more profound identification seems to take place. Ji Li suddenly sees not from the analytic position of observer but from what seems the impressionistic, emotionally reactive one of condemned subject: "white uniforms, white caps, white gloves, two enormous white objects flashing past my eyes . . . my heart contracted, and I was having trouble breathing" (112/71). Caught off-guard, Ji Li is not simply feeling sympathy for this other woman, but identifying in a profound, unmediated fashion with the suffocating sense of being condemned. In this instant, her conscious desire to know woman's self is temporarily put to death by its realization, the fleeting revelatory experience of the feminine self as condemned subject in the moment before execution.

As if the idea of ideological institutions, social and political yardsticks, which confine and define women were not oppressive enough, subsequent sections of the novella toy with the role of equally relentless biological factors. The issue is first raised in an argument about equality of the sexes between two women outside the prison, Ji Li's paternally related cousin and maternally related aunt. Assuming a traditional stance on the issue, the aunt explains women's dominated status as arising from a relative physical weakness: "Except for when she's going through the physical and emotional trials of pregnancy, lactation, lying in, menstrual interruptions, or menopause, the average woman spends seven years of her life menstruating! If you add all those years together, when a woman's body is unbalanced and her moods keep fluctuating, you can imagine the incredible toll it takes on her strength and health, and all this during the most precious years of her life" (125/82). As a result of her relative physical weakness, woman becomes naturally subordinate to man. This evolutionary argument leads the aunt to claim, as a matter of survival, women's need to be "obedient, conciliatory, self-deprecating, and ingratiating" (125/82). Integrating this natural inferiority with woman's subordinate social status, the aunt asserts that "the standards by which women are judged are determined by men, based upon their sense of beauty, their interests, and their needs" (125/82). These standards form women's psychic inheritance, specifically her inclination to judge herself according to masculine yardsticks.

The cousin argues vehemently that the situation can be changed and, indeed, is changing, but the aunt silences her by moving the argument to a personal level. She informs the cousin that she had heard the younger woman was living with a man. The cousin vehemently denies this as shameless rumor, and the aunt inquires with affected innocence, "What good would spreading rumors like that do him?" "They don't do him any good," the cousin responds, "but what they do to me. . . ." (127/84). At this point, she realizes she has been tricked into assisting the aunt's argument regarding woman's unchanging lot. She stops abruptly.

While the aunt invokes the claim that anatomy is destiny and, for women, a poor one at that, the text ultimately adopts a more ambiguous position on women's biology. At a point just when *Red Ivy* seems to be most insistent about the oppressive nature of women's physiology, the evidence is complicated. In this scene one woman prisoner is having a particularly difficult time with menopause and experience "a ringing in her ears, light-headedness, palpitations, and night sweats, so she was moody and easily irritated" (200/136).

A second prisoner, scheduled to take a technician's exam, is unable to do so because of debilitating menstrual cramps. The text is apparently substantiating the aunt's thesis on women as victims of nature. In almost impish fashion, then the text focuses on a third prisoner, Chen Dehao, "the hulking and impetuous kid-naper" of young women for brides (158/106), a criminal occupation which in itself seems rather unnatural for a woman. Chen Dehao is 23-years-old, accused by the menopausal prisoner of being a fake woman because of her flat chest, Adam's apple, and sexual attraction to other women. The authorities' interest is aroused by the accusation. They discover Chen Dehao has never had a menstrual period and send her for a physical examination. As a result, "she was diagnosed as being of indeterminate sex. Was she a man? A woman? That could only be determined by opening her up to see if she had ovaries or testicles. If it was found that she had both, or neither, formative surgery would be performed to make her either a man or a woman, based upon what society considered her to be, her own preferences, the degree of malformation, and what was surgically possible" (199–200/135–36). Upon learning this news, Chen's cellmates suddenly find her presence frightening, as if a man had been discovered in disguise in the women's quarters, and she is totally humiliated at the pronouncement that she is not a real woman. The changes this knowledge causes in the women's relationships and the physically violent and socially motivated nature of the surgical intrusion ordered for the prisoner aggressively challenge the dubious recourse to physical facts in the social construction of gender and even of sex.

WOMEN AS LAWBREAKERS:
POSSIBILITIES FOR FEMININE AGENCY

Given Ai Bei's unrelenting presentation here of an ideologically and biologically overdetermined feminine subjectivity, the text would seem to discourage any possibility of resistance or agency. To the reader, *Red Ivy* may even seem indifferent to the problem altogether. Nonetheless, through its critical portrayal of feminine subjectivity as prison, *Red Ivy* does suggest itself as a kind of literary resistance. It remains possible and appropriate therefore to consider what comment *Red Ivy* makes regarding feminine agency by looking at moments within the text where resistance seems to be denied or affirmed.

The two microhistories of prisoners which are detailed in the text offer little encouragement regarding the notion of agency. One woman, Huang Li, is a peasant convicted, on rather vague evidence, of the murder of a child. Her conviction is the result of a series of breech births which had left Huang Li both childless and incontinent. Her lack of control over her bodily reproductive and excretory functions, is not only a physical metaphor for her powerlessness, but also the cause of her husband's abandonment of her. Alone and without the right to claim a portion of food from the communal dining hall since she cannot work in the fields, she struggles against starvation during the famine years of the early 1960s. She steals raw wheat from the fields during the night and is suspected of adultery as another means to obtain food. After being charged with and brutally whipped for adultery by the men of her village, she retreats to her home and does not reemerge. She is discovered there one day with the corpse of a child in her arms. The text reveals only that the child, already bloated from starvation, had curled up on Huang Li's doorstep, and intimates that Huang Li had brought in the dying girl as company in her own lonely wait for death. Ironically, however, Huang Li is convicted of murder and avoids death herself through incarceration. Not only does she receive adequate food in prison, but also medical treatment which cures her incontinence. In prison she gratefully remains a quiet, timid, and obedient figure, a trustee to the guards and vulnerable to bullying by fellow prisoners.

The other prisoner whose past is related in the text is Li Zhenzi, a doctor who saves her husband's life during the Cultural Revolution by agreeing to sleep with the leader of the dictatorship of the proletariat team. She is driven to this action by a sense of guilt as much as love, for, as her husband tells her, his being targeted and beaten is not for any wrong he has done but rather because of her. Before their marriage, she had rejected the proposal of this same leader of the dictatorship of the proletariat team, thereby creating in him the desire to revenge himself on her husband. After the husband is able to return home and she tells him what she has done, he reacts with a complex mixture of guilt and repugnance. Viewing her action as a tremendous personal sacrifice on this behalf, he refuses to divorce her but at the same time withdraws emotionally and physically from her. Unable to endure this circumstance of nominal forgiveness, Li Zhenzi develops a morphine addiction which ultimately is the cause of a patient's death and her consequent incarceration. Like Huang Li, Li Zhenzi keeps generally silent, and in their silence resides an acceptance of their shamefulness, their guilt, their criminality.[6]

The reader, of course, recognizes in these personal histories the implicit claim of innocence of the women, the culturally determined character of their sense of shame in connection with

sexuality. How and why can they be held responsible for everything from famine, breech births, and medical complications, the
Cultural Revolution, and contradictory patriarchal demands
regarding sexual behavior? The internalization process through
which Huang Li and Li Zhenzi acquiesce in their pronouncement
as guilty is aptly described by Rey Chow in another context:
"Putting the blame on herself, [a woman] becomes an accomplice
to the invisible social demands whose power lies precisely in their
ability to solicit the woman emotionally *from within* to assist in
her own destruction."[7] The self-destruction enacted by these
women is materially evidenced in the story through Li Zhenzi's
addiction and Huang Li's physical appearance—the latter's face is
so flaccid and wrinkled that her eyes, windows of the soul, are
nearly invisible.

Turning for the moment to less acquiescent characters who
seem to show clear evidence of resistant behavior, let us consider
Ji Li's outspoken cousin who energetically rejected the traditional
posture of Ji Li's aunt regarding women's equality. Her blatant
rejection of conventionally defined feminine behavior is revealed
not only in her nonfeminine aggressiveness, but also in her tight
blue jeans, open discussion of sex, actual sexual behavior, familiarity with foreign thinkers, and living alone and apart from her family. These forms of resistance, however, carry with them in the text
another interpretation as a kind of superficial modern posturing.
The cousin's modern behavior contains a suspect quality, not only
to the less modern characters around her, but also to Ji Li and consequently the reader.

Ji Li reflects cynically at one point that "whenever a woman
is considered 'modern,' it means she's either immoral or has psychological problems" (107/68). While her comment suggests that
she rejects this common attitude, her perceptions of her cousin
ultimately recall both judgments. The cousin's three sexual affairs
and a suggested fourth with Ji Li's uncle do not of themselves necessarily indicate immorality in this text. It is Ji Li's reaction to
another act and the inconsistency of this act with the cousin's pur-
ported values and beliefs, which impugns the cousin's moral and,
considered in combination with the affairs, psychological integri-
ty. The cousin meets and becomes involved with a male graduate
student, four years younger than she. When the opportunity arises
for him to go abroad to study, she declares her support of this step
in his career, but secretly she tries to enlist Ji Li's assistance in
preventing it. She asks Ji Li to copy an anonymous letter she has

drafted, which would ruin the possibility of his obtaining the necessary official permission to go. Shocked, Ji Li regards her cousin: "I suddenly realized the incredible amount of torment that had forced her into such demeaning conduct. She seemed so pitiful, so tragic, that I wanted to console her, but I just couldn't bring myself to say anything to someone who could stoop so low" (173–74/117). She challenges the cousin's claim that love is driving her to this extreme, saying it is not the cousin's love, but her *need* for *his love* that motivates her. Ji Li continues in a fashion typical for her in this narrative, uttering a conventional truism. "The sun would rise in the west before you got any true happiness out of sharing your life with a man you had to trap to get into your bed." "You're so juvenile!" the cousin tosses back (174/117).

While, as we will see later, there is other justification and support in the text for the cousin's evaluation of Ji Li, nevertheless, it is clearly the cousin whose esteem suffers most here. The independent quality of her rebellious behavior as resistance to externally (or internally) constructed determinations of her as woman is called into question. The young graduate student arrives on the scene, and Ji Li watches with disenchantment and even disgust as the cousin suddenly becomes a different person. "It was astonishing to see my cousin standing there as if nothing had happened. But she was staring at him like a hungry cat that's spotted a fish. She hung on his every word, a sweet smile on her face, even if what he said wasn't funny" (174/118). In other words, she is behaving with conventional femininity, revealing her dependence on male favor for her own happiness.

Significantly, the cousin is left out as a physical presence in the text from this point on. She is mentioned only later in a conversation between Ji Li and her aunt, when it is implied that, since the graduate student's departure, the cousin has begun an affair with the uncle. Not only has the cousin been disempowered by Ji Li's revelation regarding her emotional dependence on men and by her textual distancing from the reader, but the aunt further dissipates the cousin's strength here by suppressing her own jealous suspicions and suggesting to her husband that they keep the younger woman for dinner when she comes by. The cousin's unconventional behavior now assumes the shape of the pitiable and desperate actions of a needy woman. She transforms from an independently powerful, controlling personality into a 37-year-old spinster who uses whatever tactics possible, including a flirtatious gloss of modernity, to obtain the protection of men. The psychic inheritance of women described earlier by the aunt has manifested itself with an ironic vengeance in the modern cousin.

Logically, as Ji Li is the one who sees through her cousin, who expresses doubt regarding social yardsticks for women, and who assumes the voice of first person narrator four times in the story, one might expect her to evidence the greatest possibility of agency, of ability to resist. She is the observer, the controlling mind through which we read other characters' appearances, words, and behavior for nearly half the text. For the remainder of the text, however, either her thoughts are presented in third person, she occupies a supporting role, or she is absent. This alternation of voice and subjective focus obviously complicates any urge the reader might have to identify with Ji Li by periodically placing us in different relation to her. We are inside her thoughts, outside her thoughts, seeing her physically from the outside, or not seeing and forgetting her. These relationship changes, which repeat those between Ji Li and the other women in the text, effectively subvert whatever preliminary claim Ji Li makes as guiding intellect, morality, or emotion in our reading.

Given the opportunity afforded by these different angles of presentation, do we observe resistance in Ji Li? Certainly she shows an attitude of resistance, but also repeated instances of failure in this regard. As already noted above, Ji Li periodically resorts to the use of conventional wisdom as she monitors both other women and herself. Just after Li Zhenzi has explained to her why she became an addict, Ji Li is emotionally overwhelmed and on the verge of tears. She reflects: "It wouldn't be seemly for a guard to cry in front of one of her prisoners. Her prestige would suffer. She coughed a time or two to stop the tears from flowing, calmed her emotions as best she could, and gave the standard speech of encouragement: 'Don't give up. No matter how bad things get, you must live out your life as best you can.'" (165/111).

Later, when dealing with a particularly truculent prisoner, Ji Li refers to that woman's use of makeup and informs the other prisoners: "There's what you call bad habits. . . . That's what immorality does to you!" (189/129). As they specifically occur in the context of the prison, these bits of ready-made wisdom in fact are part of a plot development that shows Ji Li increasingly turning into a guard, assuming the conventionally established position set for her. Although she approached the prison ready to identify with these women prisoners, and although Li Zhenzi in particular does make substantial claim on her sympathies, nonetheless, Ji Li increasingly utilizes the tried and true tactics of her superior, group leader Liu, in dealing with the prisoners.

Group leader Liu and Ji Li are positioned in apparent antagonism from the beginning. Ji Li's antipathy to Liu is revealed in first impressions of her as "unscrupulous," a "proper, *sexless* woman," whose "spirit was like a towel that had been wrung dry" (98/61, italics added). Liu is alert to Ji Li's unspoken aversion to her and her attitude toward the prisoners, and a competition of methods develops between these two guards, the one representing a harsh, punitive stance and the other a sympathetic, caring one.[8]

When Li Zhenzi reveals to Ji Li her hiding place for drugs, information that in a prison marks a triumph for a guard, group leader Liu in her direct fashion states: "I know you're better at ideological work than I am, and you can rest assured I'm not jealous. . . . But don't forget, softhearted people have no place here" (166–67/112). Soon after this, Ji Li is confronted with a fight in her team which results in one prisoner feigning a seizure. Not recognizing this as manipulative behavior, Ji Li sends another prisoner for the doctor. This prisoner, judging Ji Li incompetent, reports to Liu instead. Liu arrives and gets things under control with a few threats and orders. Then she turns and says to Ji Li: "Come get me if they give you any more trouble. Heh-heh, you're not jealous of the prestige I carry around here, are you?" (184–85/125).

Ji Li denies the jealousy she does feel and becomes anxious about the blow to her prestige that the incident must represent in the eyes of the prisoners. Her first effort to resolve this is to take part herself in the team's physical labor. She does so not as a sympathetic gesture or as any effort to identify with the women, but as a consciously manipulative move, to "make them feel guilty and grateful for her sacrifice" (186/127). In other words, she is playing upon their separately defined roles as guilty criminals and caring guard or guarding. The maneuver is mostly successful, but the prisoner who had run for Liu during the fight remains contemptuous of Ji Li's authority.

Almost immediately, Ji Li is afforded an opportunity to bring this woman into line as well. This is the woman whom Ji Li soon afterwards accuses of immorality for using makeup. The prisoner is enraged by the insult and threatens to dash her own head against the wall and commit suicide. While all the other prisoners are frantically trying to restrain the woman, Ji Li steps up and adopts group leader Liu's voice and tactics. She orders the other prisoners to release their hold and calls the woman's bluff: "Okay, Jiang

Hong, we're waiting! Do it!" (190/129). Jiang Hong collapses in tears and team leader "Ji, now looking cool and collected, said in a relaxed tone, 'Jiang Hong, write a report of what happened and bring it to my office at noon.' She turned and swaggered off" (190/129).

Abruptly, however, the text informs us that Ji Li is "distressed to realize that she'd turned into a rough, unyielding woman" (190/130). As happens throughout much of Ai Bei's text, this statement works ironically. While Ji Li is distressed by her apparently becoming unyielding, becoming something like the sexless, proper woman that she identifies in Liu, the reader instead observes her submitting, *yielding* progressively to Liu's model and prisoners' expectations of guard behavior. What distresses Ji Li is not that she is unyielding, but rather that she has yielded.[9]

Ji Li resists Liu's authority and prison discipline in one other way which asserts itself as of particular interest to those of us who make a career through literature. She reads while on the job. On her first day Ji Li observed another guard on duty reading a book. Liu knocked the book out of her hand and warned her she could have her pay docked for this breach of discipline. Unintimidated, the guard aggressively responded: "Instead of bossing us around, why don't you get a cat and abuse it for a change" (108/68). Subsequently in the text, Ji Li is twice described as reading while at work. She is not so boldly impudent as this other guard and slips her novel into a drawer when Liu appears.

For this text to present reading as a defiant act encourages readers to view its reading in turn as an act of resistance within an external structure conceived by analogy as oppressively authoritarian. Again, however, Ai Bei puts a disturbing curve on this pitch for reading as resistance. When Liu interrupts Ji Li in her surreptitious reading, she has come from a meeting where she successfully negotiated, among other things, a conjugal visit for the addict Li Zhenzi. Ji Li is taken aback by this news. She restrains from expressing anger she feels at another guard's suggestive remark and quotes another bit of ready-made wisdom from an instructional book on foreign penal institutions: "Conjugal visits can be considered on an individual basis" (203/139). Considering Ji Li's familiarity with the individual circumstances, the profound estrangement, of this particular couple, the comment is painfully ironic and inadequate. In this same scene where reading is an act of defiance, it is also a source of the conventional wisdom to which Ji Li periodically resorts. Consequently, in this instance, while reading first appears as resistance, it also demonstrates the potential for slipping into the category of compliance.

WOMEN AS CRIMINALS:
EXCLUSION, UNITY, AND COLLUSION

Ji Li's interest in locating a shared, resistant sense of self with these women prisoners is seriously reduced by her becoming a guard. The text, however, continues to explore the question of a collective feminine subjectivity and possible collective resistance by looking at the nature of connections between women presented in *Red Ivy*. I am guided in my discussion here by an offhand, witty comment of Ji Li's cousin.

When the narrative first introduces Ji Li's cousin, the reader learns that she is an aspiring writer working in a guesthouse, cleaning spittoons and toilets. She claims that she prefers this easier, freer lifestyle over the toils of academia, and expresses scorn for such toils by summing them up as "useless research on the birthplace of one of China's famous novelists or determining the semantic difference between 'unity' (*tuanjie*) and 'collusion' (*goujie*)" (114/73). Provocatively for us, the phrase brings together the feminine self as someone separated (and defined) by a personal history from others with positive and negative notions of a collective identity. We have already seen in Ji Li a playing out of the dynamics implied here. The personal details of her life (details which include a distinguishing fame as the niece of a provincial party secretary and her role as guard) divide her from others; she desires a unity with the prisoners as a way to uncover and confirm her sense of a feminine self; and, within this potential arena for unity, she colludes progressively with the collectively predetermined sense of her role as prison guard, a role which interferes with any shared identity. This collusion is thus both a unification with conventional assumptions regarding relations, and paradoxically an act of exclusion. Let us look further now into how the text depicts or interrupts connections between women.

There are many things to interfere with connections between women in *Red Ivy*, several of them alluded to above. There are the separate categories of prisoners, guards, and women outside the prison institution. Inside and out of the prison, older women are jealous of younger, and different pairs compete for the affections or loyalty of others. Cousin and aunt, for instance, compete for the uncle's benevolent attentions; Ji Li and Liu compete for the prisoners' obedient loyalty. Beyond this, even physical differences divide, or are evidence of divisions between, the women. The case of the hermaphroditic prisoner is the most obvious example of this, but the relationship between specific physical appearances and gender or sexual identity is also highlighted by descriptions of the different women's bodies. Team leader Liu, the sexless, privileged figure of authority, is appropriately fleshy, "wonderfully soft and springy," with "a flat, incredibly broad rump" (98–99/61–62). The complexity of the modern cousin or 37-year-old spinster, is revealed in her "slightly drooping buttocks," clothed in tight blue jeans, and accentuating "her typically Chinese figure with its long waist and short legs" (121/79). When dressed only in underwear, she further exposes "a scrawny, flat chest," without "a hint of maturity," giving the impression not "so much that her femininity had wasted away as [that] she'd never had any to begin with" (171/115). Jiang Hong, the truculent, makeup-wearing prisoner, and sometime prostitute, has "soft white shoulders, dazzling and quite remarkable. Her rounded breasts, which jiggled slightly with each breath she took, were taut and soft at the same time; they inspired envy and jealousy in women and nearly uncontrollable passion in men" (176–77/119). In their bodily appearance, then, the women seem simultaneously to reflect and require the social definitions which divide them and confine them to individual types, without making them "individuals."[10]

However, the desire for a more basic unity, first expressed through Ji Li's desire to identify with these criminal women, remains despite the emphasis on difference. This desire also continues to be problematic, now in the terms suggested by the semantic *similarity* between the words unity and collusion. The final few scenes of the novella present this complicated relationship between the desire to ignore difference and both the collusion and exclusion this creates. Guards are excluded here, and in these scenes the prisoners of Ji Li's team come together outside the prison walls. It is the morning of the lunar new year and Li Zhenzi's predictably agonizing conjugal visit has concluded with her husband leaving, probably forever, while she was still asleep. She awakes feeling cold, depressed, lonely, and frightened. The text tells us that "suddenly she had an overpowering desire to return to her cell, where she could talk with her cellmates for as long as they'd listen and enjoy a wonderful day with them" (209/143). This desire is all the more remarkable since up until this point the

reader's image of Li Zhenzi has always been of her standing silently and at a distance from her cellmates.

Li Zhenzi dresses and opens the door of the apartment set up
for her conjugal visit to find her cellmates waiting quietly outside
with armfuls of food. She is emotionally overwhelmed by this
demonstration of group solidarity. "As though she were waking
from a dream, Li Zhenzi felt a surge of warmth coursing through
her body" (210/144). The text further enhances this euphoric sense
of mutual caring and understanding by informing us that none of
the women ask where Li Zhenzi's husband has gone. "Li Zhenzi
was deeply touched. By not asking, they showed that they understood. Maybe the lifelong trials of being a woman had made suffering commonplace to them" (211/144). On the surface and at a corresponding emotional level, the text identifies a collective
subjectivity for women here in the common experience of suffering. On reflection, however, suffering as a motive for drawing
together primarily affirms their inferior, imprisoned status. They
are here to comfort and be comforted, not to resist. Significantly,
then, Li Zhenzi proposes to the women, now her friends, that they
all go back together to the cell block and everyone readily agrees.

The women's prison is their home, where their internalized
sense of criminality, primary component to their sense of self, is
made visible. Their feeling of comfort there is described earlier in
the text when a recidivist prisoner returning to the sanctuary of
niangjia, her mother's home, where who she is already established
(176/119). Whereas outside prison this woman is burdened by an
anxiety at having to hide evidence of her criminality and fear of
being caught, back in prison she can relax. With typical perversity
the text takes women's last refuge for a positive, collective feminine subjectivity, their oneness in suffering. It implicates it as an
acquiescence to this self defined as criminal and a collaboration
with the institutions which confine and oppress them.

The complexity of the text does not end here. There is a final
scene providing further shifts in interpretation. On their way back,
the women run into a group of children having a snowball fight.
The children, apparently not realizing that the women are criminals, pelt these aunties with snowballs:

> [The women] stood there like dummies, just watching the
> snowballs smash against them, sending powdery snow flying.
> After the first barrage the children stopped and stared at the

snow-splattered figures in front of them, growing suddenly fearful. One or two had already retreated a few steps.

"Attack! Why don't we attack?" Jiang Hong's voice broke the silence. She scooped up a handful of snow and threw it at the children.

"Attack!" Her fellow prisoners, having snapped out of their confusion, rushed forward, shouting and scooping up ammunition. The children were quickly routed. Caught up in the frenzied joy of battle, some of the women grabbed the children and jumped about with them, some picked them up and kissed them, some hugged them and rolled in the snow.

The children screamed in fright and fought to run away. Huang Li alone knelt in the snow in the middle of the yard, like a snowman, covered in silvery white and completely motionless. [212/145]

Again, the passage tantalizes with a picture of a united group of women, this time defending themselves, actually taking the offensive and routing their attackers. However, both victory and unity are compromised here. First and obviously because these attackers are children, not figures of authority, and because the child-murderer, Huang Li, is excluded from this battle through the emotional complications of her personal history. The children's terror, because they realize these women are convicts or because the women's behavior is unexpectedly aggressive, or for both reasons, further disturbs our sense of the joy of this battle and victory. The three verbs indicating physical contact between prisoners and children—grabbing (*zhuazhu*), picking up (*baoqi*), and hugging (*louqi*)—also function to remind the reader that these women are all deprived of children, of the possible biological, emotional, and social role of mother. With this reminder, the text reasserts not only their deprivation but also the implied criminality of the women. They become different from other women in this socially imposed exclusion from child-rearing, in the denial of what is conventionally considered a fundamental and natural desire and right of women.[11]

If we resume, then, our metaphoric reading of femininity as imprisonment, the way in which the confinement of these women doubles social constructions of femininity, the configuration of women's relationship to children is transformed here. The children through their fear recall authority and the conviction that women by definition are dangerous. Despite biological and emotional bonds to children, somehow women must be excluded from child-rearing, from precisely that arena where authority continually reproduces itself.

In the context of trying to see if Chinese women have succeeded in changing their status as inferior men, this text and its generally perverse consideration of women further imprisoned as fiction or animal, imprisoned several times over, is disturbing. What unifies women, what provides them with a feminine subjectivity, at best, is dialectic here, but even that in a rather depressing fashion. Gender and sexual determinations are portrayed as inclusive and shifting, at times overdetermining and at times indeterminable, with cultural or ideological factors constantly in complex relation to physical ones. The possibility for agency, an assertion of selfness and of resistance to a multitude of oppressive constructions for women, seems always compromised, either by women's acquiescence, an internalized sense of criminality and inferiority, or by the cooption of actions originally conceived of as resistant by existing power relations. And, in relation to this, any appearance or even experience of a shared sense of the feminine self or possible collective resistance reaffirms an only shared sense of condemnation. The pleasure afforded by commiseration remains suspect.

In the end it is only the perversity of the text itself that might signal resistance. There seems to be a fiendish delight behind the ironies and failures presented (the cousin transformed to spinster, Ji Li turned into a guard, the final image of Huang Li alone as the other prisoners play with the children). As readers we feel that we are being played with, even bullied. In our terror at the suffocating sense of woman as condemned subject, perhaps we do locate the first step toward escaping this experience of feminine subjectivity, the desire to escape.

NOTES

1. "Nülao," in *Nülao* (Taipei, 1990), 3. Subsequent page numbers for quotations used in this paper from Ai Bei's story will be indicated parenthetically. Unless specified, there will be two page numbers, the first from the original Chinese version and the second from the English translation in *Red Ivy Green Earth Mother: Stories by Ai Bei* (Salt Lake City: Peregrine Smith Books, 1990). For the most part I will follow Howard Goldblatt's translations with occasional minor changes.

2. *Discipline and Punish: The Birth of the Prison* (New York: Vintage Books, 1979), 303.

3. See Paul Smith's discussion of the Frankfurt school in *Discerning the Subject* (Minneapolis: University of Minnesota Press, 1988), 59.

4. See Foucault's chapter "Illegalities and Delinquency" where he discusses delinquency as "object and instrument for a police apparatus that worked both against it and with it" (283).

5. "Forward," in *Red Ivy*, xi.

6. The word *zhen* in Li Zhenzi's name means both loyalty and feminine chastity. Thus even her name acts as a constant and painfully ironic reminder of an action that was both an act of loyalty and an unchaste action.

7. *Woman and Chinese Modernity: The Politics of Reading between West and East* (Minneapolis: University of Minnesota, 1991), 119.

8. The conflict in attitudes reflects a broader dynamic which simultaneously regards authoritarianism as parental and arbitrarily dictatorial.

9. In typical contrary fashion, the text provides a different sort of explanation, almost an excuse, for why Liu is the sort of guard Ji Li appears to be becoming. When Ji Li first meets Liu and notes the tone of authority she adopts with the prisoners, Ji Li wonders: "Maybe she was abused at home, and her occupation gave her a chance to vent her frustrations" (102/64). Later in a prisoner's comments, Liu's economic and family pressures at home are indicated by the description of her rope-frame bed, rotten in spots from repeated incidents of children's bed-wetting. Thus, while Ji Li seems to be submitting to Liu's model and prisoner expectations of what a guard must be, Liu's guard style signals a transference of frustrations from other oppressive social demands.

10. Here, too, Foucault's concept of individualization can be useful in understanding this text. He conceives of individualization as a classifying and categorizing which affirms the norm rather than as the confirmation of some existential quality of freedom and coherent unity in a single person. Individuality is a confirmation of norms because it is a measuring against these norms. It is part of a process that "compares, differentiates, hierarchizes, homogenizes, excludes. In short [the process] *normalizes"* (*Discipline and Punishment*, 183).

11. Based on the text, however, the nature of motherhood is also quite strange here. The prisoners are aggressively playful with the children, not tender or nurturing, and their play "terrorizes." In addition, excepting the child-murderer, Huang Li, whose children are all dead, none of the prisoners are ever identified as having given birth to a child. Thus, it becomes unclear whether this is a deprivation of maternal nature or an absence of such that is being depicted.

8

Sisterhood? Representations of Women's Relationships in Two Contemporary Chinese Texts

Su Mi's marriage with that man did not seem to be as unbearable to her as she had imagined. But when she was visiting their bedroom, the huge mirror on the wall beside the double bed made her feel uncomfortable. Knowing that Su Mi's body was going to be ravaged and that the mirror was going to record faithfully their love-making, she felt it hard for her to be happy again. . . . It was Su Mi who helped bring about her marriage; it was the fleeting look of both loss and envy in Su Mi's eyes that made her decide to marry the young doctor assigned to her by her mother. They will never understand Su Mi. They will never understand me either. Su Mi died with her secrets, while I continue to live with mine.

Jiang Zidan

In spite of the onlookers' curious and contemptuous stares, Lao Li grabbed her arms and said, "I love you. Really, I love you." They had never used that word "love" between them, a word that has been contaminated by relationships between men and women. But she used the

word this time. Lao Wang broke into tears and
yelled, "It's too late. Too late." Lao Li also started to cry and said, "No, it's not too late. No."
Tears running down on her cheeks, Lao Wang
said, "Yes, it's too late. There are things that are
very fragile. Once you destroy them, you can
never restore them again."

Wang Anyi

The above excerpts come from the two texts that I intend to
discuss in this paper. *"Dengdai huanghun"* (Waiting for the twilight) by Jiang Zidan[1] and *"Dixiong men"* (Brothers) by Wang
Anyi.[2] The two narratives differ in structure, point of view, and
narrative strategy, but they share one thing in common: they both
explore relationships between women.

What interests me in the representations of women's relationships in these stories can be captured by two terms: relationships between and among women are represented as both close
and ambivalent. But before I address these two words, I would like
to give a brief summary of each story.

Jiang Zidan's *"Dengdai huanghun"* is told alternately by a
female first-person narrator, who is also the major character of the
narrative, and by a third-person narrator. In the story, five other
characters are related to the first-person narrator in different ways:
her mother, her husband, her ex-boyfriend, her son, and Su Mi, a
nurse from the same hospital where the narrator's mother works
as a doctor. When she is adolescent, the narrator meets Su Mi and
becomes very close to her, because Su Mi, for unknown reasons,
likes to spend time with her. When the narrator experiences her
first menstrual period, which prompts her to ask Su Mi many
questions, Su Mi exposes her to a variety of ideas concerning womanhood. They remain close to each other until Su Mi gets married.
Su Mi's marriage, however, makes the narrator unhappy, although
she herself soon meets and falls in love with a married man who is
unwilling to sacrifice his name and family for her. She finally mar-
ries a man who pleases her mother more than herself and then
becomes a mother herself. During her pregnancy, the narrator
learns that Su Mi has killed her two sons, and when found sane,
has been convicted of and executed for murder. The narrator wonders why, when she herself is about to finalize her womanhood by
becoming a mother, Su Mi chooses to renounce motherhood in
such a drastic way. When Su Mi refuses to "wait for the twilight,"

she herself does not know what her choices are as a woman but waits for her twilight to come.

Wang Anyi's *"Dixiong men"* is narrated in a more conventional way: told from a third-person point of view, the story line is developed chronologically, and the narrative structure is less fragmentary than in *"Dengdai huanghun."* It is about, first, a relationship between three married women college students at a university, and then a closer relationship between two of the three after they have graduated. When in college as students of fine arts, the three women live in the same dorm room and develop close bonds. Adopting the custom of men, the three women address each other as *Lao Da* (the oldest brother), *Lao Er* (the second brother), and *Lao San* (the third brother) according to their age. They do almost everything together: sleep in and skip classes, work like crazy for exams, and stay up very late talking. When they talk, their topics usually are relationships between men and women, individual identities for man and woman, and the difficulties of finding such an identity in contemporary China. They are excited about how much they share, and indulge themselves in their deepest concerns in conversations. But the bond among them develops in such a way that ambivalence emerges: when one of them, Lao San (the third brother), shows signs of wanting to be close to her husband during some of his visits, the other two feel betrayed.

Upon graduation, when Lao San turns down a job opportunity at the university, not desiring to live apart from her family, and decides to return to her hometown to work, the bond between the three is further undermined. They end up in different places and start building their own homes until several years later when Lao Da and Lao Er renew their friendship. They now call each other Lao Li (Lao Da) and Lao Wang (Lao Er) according to their last names, another unconventional form of address between two relatively young women. They write each other frequently and visit whenever they can and consequently grow close again. This causes some uneasiness for Lao Li's husband. When Lao Li gives birth to a child, Lao Wang goes to Shanghai to help. They remain quite close until one day when Lao Li is frightened by and reacts very strongly against Lao Wang over an accident that occurs to her child for which she blames Lao Wang. Lao Wang feels hurt and decides to leave. The last excerpt quoted at the beginning of this chapter occurs when Lao Li tries to stop Lao Wang from leaving at the railway station. Lao Wang goes back to her own city, still searching for something that she herself is not clear about.

In the two stories, the close and yet ambivalent women's relationships create a juncture where representations of women and their self-representations meet and raise questions concerning gender roles and gender relations. In this discussion, I will argue that what these women share is a desire to make sense of their own existence, to move away from certain conventional norms for women, and to find a space of their own. I will argue that it is this desire that creates a discrepancy between the existence of the desire and the lack of space for a recognition of the desire in other relationships. The discrepancy helps create a narrative space with a new level of signification within which the desire is manifested. I will also point out that it is this desire that draws these women to each other and it is the same desire that separates them. The question is how to understand the nature of such desire in its manifestation with the close and yet ambivalent women's relationships.

In "*Dengdai huanghun*," specifically, the discrepancy is dramatized around the meaning of the body, when the body is singled out both as the base and as the problematic—body as the material or physical existence as well as the site of power struggle over its control—of the interrogation. This double-edged nature of the body, which often entails ambivalence and confusion in the narrative, makes it possible both for the text to question the normal reading of the body and also for the reader to further examine the interrogation itself. In other words, by focusing on the body, the narrative manages to raise many questions, along with some confusions, in the understanding of the female body and bodily changes. If the body is the focal point of the discrepancy in "*Dengdai huanghun*," the notion of the "self" is the one in "*Dixiong men*." It is also the base and the problematic in the women characters' search for their individual self outside the realm of the norms of womanhood. The difference between focusing on the body and focusing on the self, therefore, does not necessarily entail a fundamental difference between the two texts. On the contrary, in spite of the difference in their focal points, both texts are constructed to interrogate the meaning of womanhood, with, interestingly enough, identical assumptions—possibly unquestioned about the notions of the body and the self, which may well be the very source of the ambivalence manifested in the representations of these women's relationships—an issue to which I will come back later.

The opening paragraph of *"Dengdai huanghun"* reads:

I was sick. The moment when I heard the terrible news about Su Mi, I sensed very clearly the arrival of the sickness. It got into my body like that red dragonfly. I saw the red dragonfly years ago for the first time when I was thirteen. [68]

The sickness, which is both literal and symbolic, sets the tone for all the relationships represented in this narrative, including the one between the narrator and Su Mi. The terrible news about Su Mi is that she has allegedly killed her two sons and mutilated their bodies.[3] The terrible news, the sickness, Su Mi, the red dragonfly, and the narrator's age converge to open up a narrative avenue, so to speak, for a seemingly free flow of the narrator's consciousness. They trigger her memories, since age thirteen, about her own fears and doubts as a girl turning into a woman, as a daughter, the girl-friend of ·a married man, a wife, a mother-to-be, a mother, and Su Mi's friend. As the paragraph suggests, her sickness in relation to the terrible news about Su Mi is a reiteration of the arrival of the red dragonfly, the first coming of her menstrual period, when she was told, by Su Mi, that she "has become a real woman" (70). The color red, symbolizing both woman's bodily experience of menstrual moments and giving birth, and the blood shed in Su Mi's alleged killing of her sons, introduces the question of how to interpret women's bodily experience and how it is related to the question of what it means to be a woman.

Structurally, the narrator's coming of age, symbolized by the red dragonfly, functions as a narrative thread that holds the fragments of the story together. Symbolically, it brings women's bodily changes and the reading around them together, and thus opens up a variety of questions that function to interrogate the norms of womanhood. From Su Mi, as I have mentioned, the narrator learns to read the coming of her menstrual period as the beginning of her womanhood. Meanwhile, she is warned, by Su Mi, that it also means the beginning of a life-and-death cycle—with the coming of the menstrual blood, a woman is on her way to becoming a mother. Once she has given birth to a new life, according to Su Mi, it symbolizes the beginning of her own death. What is emphasized here is the biological or the physical changes of the female body.

If we assume that any human life or human being has to go through a life-and-death cycle, what is so special about the changes in the female body if they are just part of the cycle? The narrative cannot avoid tackling this question within the context of social and cultural constructions pertaining to women's bodily changes. The powerlessness of the red dragonfly, and its death being related to a child, point directly at both the social and physical processes of a woman becoming a mother—being a woman, she has to give, along with a new life to a child, her own life. While this sounds confusing, it is caused precisely by Su Mi's own confusion in connecting a life-and-death cycle too literally to the notion of motherhood. Instead of further questioning the construct of the meaning of mother, she tries to break the cycle by destroying the lives that she gave. Her destruction of the life and body of her own sons indicates her desire, no matter how drastic and futile its expression, to escape this normal cycle. In doing so, she is punished for failing to submit her body to the norms of society and to stay inscribed by the norms of motherhood, and this is essentially what is at stake here. Su Mi's punishment comes not because she loves another woman, but because she loves herself too much—the body here is not the source of eroticism or the object of desire but the source of questioning. The question, in other words, has to do with what it means when a woman refuses to subscribe her own body to the norms of motherhood. Using the narrator's coming of age, the narrative reveals a process of struggle between the narrator's experiencing her own bodily changes and having to subscribe to the meanings around them and her witnessing the destruction of the body, when it, in the case of Su Mi, fails to subscribe to the norms of womanhood.

The notion of coming of age in the narrative, then, is a series of contradictions and paradoxes, found both within the narrator herself and within her relationship to Su Mi. When the narrator is entering the stage of womanhood with the coming of her menstrual period, Su Mi is at the peak of young womanhood—in the eye of the narrator she is the embodiment of the beauty of a female body. It is through the eye of the narrator that the reader sees the body of Su Mi:

> Undoubtedly, Su Mi took her as a close friend. Sometimes when she changed her underwear, Su Mi did not even bother to do it in a different room when she was around. When she saw Su Mi's beautiful body, her heart trembled. It was the trembling of the heart of an innocent girl who was astounded by the beauty of a mature woman. [70]

The narrator also goes on to describe the curves of her body and the smoothness of her skin and compares her body to that of a goddess; her desire expressed here is to have a similar body of her own. It is not a desire to possess another body but to transform it into her own, an underpinning desire in the representation of the relationship—the desire for the self. When she witnesses Su Mi's beautiful body and desires to have a similar one, she simultaneously introduces Su Mi as an embodiment of contradictions and thus her ambivalent relationship with her. On the one hand, Su Mi teaches the narrator the inevitability of becoming a woman and the traditional roles for which women are naturally responsible, and she herself seems to practice what she preaches. On the other hand, she undermines her teaching completely with the sense of pessimistic inevitability in her teaching and when she commits the alleged killing. Her fatalistic views about the physical changes of woman's body trivialize, to an extent, her challenge to the norms of womanhood.

It is the narrator who is represented as perceiving these contradictions. While the killing comes to the narrator as a terrible shock, her own thoughts about her experience as a mother suggest that her shock may well be of a different order from, say, that of her mother's and husband's. She recognizes Su Mi's action as a refusal to fulfill her roles as a woman with no other alternatives, and as a brave but desperate and futile gesture to terminate her assigned role with a bloody no. In reading Su Mi's body and its destruction, the narrator manages, as I have suggested repeatedly, to raise questions about the meaning of full womanhood and how they dictate women's experience and the nature of their relationships.

Meanwhile her reading also introduces a tension. While the narrator is critiquing the construction of meaning around the bodily changes in a woman, it also confuses, as I have mentioned earlier, the notion of sex with that of gender. There is a desire in both Su Mi and the narrator to maintain the authentic meaning of the female body as naturally given and therefore entitled to being free of control. As a result, there is a tendency in the narrative to romanticize the body and a failure to explain the paradox of Su Mi except as symbolizing a subversive character whose voice is silenced for pursuing a free body.

The representation of the tension between the body and the ongoing construction of the meaning of the body, however, does not stop just here. If we read the text from a slightly different angle—that is, if we read women's relationships with each other over against other relationships—one thing becomes apparent. The former can be perceived as a way employed to problematize the others. These women characters, in other words, come together and relate to each other in a rather unconventional way, making efforts to understand their roles in those other relationships.

Within this context, one of the recurring questions directly related to the construction of the meaning of the body is the notion of motherhood. Between the mother-daughter relationship of the narrator and her mother, Su Mi has an interesting role to play. Her own life experience and her relationship with the narrator are represented as both constructing and deconstructing the meaning of womanhood and motherhood, and this evokes an ambivalent feeling in the narrator. On the one hand, the narrator questions motherly love constructed according to social norms and required of every woman; on the other hand, she struggles with Su Mi's extreme action, which according to prevailing codes is either mad or criminal. The narrator tries to challenge the former, but she does not seem to have the power to relate herself to the latter.

Her challenge to motherhood, however, is my concern here; it is realized on three levels: (1) the narrator's own relationship with her mother; (2) her own experience of marriage, pregnancy, and motherhood, and (3) her relationship with Su Mi who exerts a strong impact on her coming of age.

In representing her relationship with her mother, the narrator does not celebrate her mother's motherly love. Instead, she is both cynical and ambivalent toward her mother's expressions of motherly responsibility:

> She is my life giver. She gave me flesh and soul. If she had wanted it, she could have taken back everything that belonged to her. Were you happy at that time? I asked. Of course, it was the happiest time in my life, she replied. I didn't believe her. I suspected that she said it to win more feelings from me. You should be happy. It's woman's natural responsibility to be a mother. Unless she becomes a mother, a woman is not a real woman. She continued in a voice as old as her white hair. I had nothing to say and my enthusiasm vanished. We were related by blood, but we were entirely different women. Would she be willing to sacrifice for me? I had overestimated her. She had never noticed a loss. On the contrary, she thought that my existence had fulfilled her. Her

happiness was no more than her expecting to give birth to fulfill herself. [74]

The narrator's account deconstructs the meaning of motherly happiness—by asking whether it is a selfless love, or a selfish love, or a self love—hence echoing the challenge of the sacredness of motherhood staged by Su Mi. Reporting her own experience as a mother, the narrator has these thoughts:

> I had never had a wish to be a mother. I had never wanted to create a strange new life. [71]

As a mother, instead of marveling at how exciting it is to be a mother, an experience most women are believed to report, she continues to dwell on her wish for not wanting to be a mother. As for her relationship with her child, she reports her experience, at various moments when the child is born and growing up as her son, in a very unmotherly way. Right after the child is born, she has these thoughts:

> If a mother tells others that she fears and hates her new born baby boy, it is undoubtedly a hilarious joke. . . . Because I pretended to be responsible, people thought I could be a good mother, I know if a mother does not love her son, she cannot expect to be loved by anyone else in this world. [83]

She continues to question, though secretly, the mother-child relationship after she has become a mother for several years:

> I call the little boy walking beside me my son. People had told me that he was my son, really mine. . . . Mummy, look. My son turned around toward me. Every time when he called out to me this way, I would always sense some implied meaning. It is terrible that a five or six year-old child has already learned to imply something. I'd rather that he called me by my name or didn't call me at all. But, no, he insisted on calling me mummy—to show that he was my own flesh and blood. [71]

As the child is growing up, she still is unable to give up struggling with these thoughts:

That boy was growing up rapidly to be a happy child, whose carefree and content expressions seemed to show the world that I was a good mother. We appeared to be very close and unseparable, and the past between mother and son became a big secret between the two of us. He continued to be the boss in my life, commanded me to live according to his rules, and expressed his love to me every day to prove that I was a good mother. I was so charmed by the illusion of deep love between mother and son that I indulged myself in motherly love and forgot the essential opposition between me and the child. [84]

Unlike Su Mi, the narrator has not refused to play the role of mother. Instead, she continues to fulfill her motherly responsibilities and has apparently played the role of mother quite well at least in appearance. And yet she continues to demonstrate a contempt even toward herself for playing the role so well. The challenge of motherhood carried out by Su Mi in action is carried on by the narrator in words, who is explicitly mocking herself for playing the role of good mother. While both Su Mi's action and the narrator's words seem futile—Su Mi has to be vanished from the face of the earth for taking the action and the narrator has to conform to the norms in spite of her secret defiance—the challenge is, at least, stage to question the constructed norms of womanhood through challenging the traditional discourse of motherhood.

A similar challenge is found in Wang Anyi's story, *"Dixiong men,"* in which Lao Wang or the second brother is the major character, although, as I have mentioned earlier, the questioning in this narrative is focused on the conflict between women as an individual self and the norms that they are expected to subscribe to. In the early part of the story the three "brothers" are a group that shares a common desire: they do not want to become ordinary women, even though they are all already married. They express such a desire both through their late night discussions and through practice—they do not behave according to the norms of femininity. In their endless conversations, they raise many questions about the roles of men and women, although they often end up being equally, if not more, confused than before. The desire they share and the confusion caused by the collective expressions of the desire generate a new desire to transcend the confusion. The manifestation of the desire, however, is itself already a gesture of challenge.

Let us trace the path of Lao Wang to see how the questioning is manifested. It is she and Lao Li or the eldest "brother" who find Lao San (the third brother) betraying their ideal of not becoming an ordinary woman. When Lao Wang and Lao Li renew their friendship several years after graduating from collect, it is Lao Wang who goes back and forth between Shanghai and Nanjing, demonstrating an unusual enthusiasm for continuing their friendship. It is she whose presence and talk plants an ambivalence in Lao Li's mind toward the contradiction between woman being an individual self and being a loving mother. Before the child is born, Lao Li:

asked the child in her womb silently: is it a good thing or a bad thing to give birth to you? . . . she thought from now on there was not only a man who would have to wait for her to come home for supper, there would be a child as well. Waiting would wear away so much patience and feelings. Wouldn't it be great if she was a loafer . . . She constantly repeated in her heart: my darlings, I won't abandon you! But deep in her heart, she also longed for freedom, for being a loafer wandering around the world. [18]

When the child is born, Lao Wang comes to help. Their conversations once again provoke some ambivalent thoughts in Lao Li:

[Life] is the replicate of countless people. In our body there flows the blood of countless people whom we have never met! She trembled involuntarily at the thought. . . . They turned around to look at the sleeping baby. He seemed to have become a strange thing and they couldn't recognize him. What is ourselves then? [22]

This questioning or uncertainty of motherhood echoes the challenge found in *"Dengdai huanghun."* As Lao Li and Lao Wang grow increasingly close, it is Lao Wang who gives up the friendship upon discovering the impossibility of maintaining a close relationship with a woman who also tries to be a good mother. Like Su Mi's killing of her own children, Lao Wang terminates a long treasured relationship as a rejection to complying with the norms, a seemingly less drastic but equally significant gesture. It is also Lao Wang who, having failed to find a partner in her quest for the self, continues being a childless woman and keeps moving from one job to another, hoping to find one that can make her happy. "Gradually, she herself became confused as to what she wanted" (30). While the challenge to norms of womanhood continues, however, it finally becomes an individual quest: the narrative begins with a collective effort among three women, but ends with Lao Wang continuing alone. In both stories, the bonds between and among the women characters are deteriorating, leaving their efforts at resistance behind as a detour on their way to becoming real women. To Lao Wang, the only one who seems to continue her detour, the passage is like "a boat going through the Sanmen Gorge, with extremely steep and high cliffs on both sides showing only a strip of the blue sky" (30). Her hope, the blue sky, is both remote and hard to reach.

In both narratives, while other relationships are being problematized in association with women's relationships, the latter themselves are not represented positively either. The questioning of womanhood in general is simultaneously charged with a desire for finding a real identity, either through focusing on the notion of the body or that of the self. That is to say, within women's relationships, there is a tension between looking for a different model from mother and wife, and a tendency to comply with the norms. There is also a tension between challenging the norms and looking for individual identity, a tension, in the case of "*Dixiong men*," generated from a desire on the part of women to look for the self. This brings me to another question that I raised earlier: Why, in the representations, are women's relationships not glorified or celebrated but problematized?

At the beginning of "*Dixiong men*," the narrative is charged with a desire on the part of the three characters to find their real self:

> Unlike them, most people finish their lives without having one chance to look into themselves and express themselves. Gradually, these people come to believe that their inner self resembles their appearance and there is nothing secret about it. . . . These women, however, belong to those very few ones who create opportunities to get to know themselves. What is more lucky for them is that among the vast universe of people who are coming and going, they three happen to meet at the same time and the same place. [6] For a long time in the past, they did not know who they were and spent their days just like everybody else did. Luckily they found each other

when they were almost hopeless. Now they have . . . found themselves. [8]

The bond between the three women is formed on the basis of their desire to find themselves as individuals. Ironically, of course, they search for their individuality collectively. Although Wang Anyi, the author of *Dixiong men*, recognizes the paradox of challenging conventional norms of womanhood (with attempts to do away with them) and the desire for individual identity, she only suggests that the pursuit of an individual identity is unrealistic. In many places, therefore, she uses language in such a way that one can detect a touch of sarcasm in her treatment of the women characters' pursuit of or search for their individual identity of the self.

Sometimes, for example, after their late night conversation, she describes them in this way:

> They became increasingly less clear about who they were. They then would resume a long period of eventless days filled with sleeping, eating, going to classes, handing in homework, and writing love letters to their husbands. [6]

The contrast between their serious late night conversations, which only make them more confused about themselves, and the eventless days when they continue to play different roles, is clearly very ironic. Another example can be found in her representing a conflict among the three of them. The conflict occurs when during one of the husbands' visit, Lao San wants to spend more time with him by spending the night at the school guesthouse. The other two:

> smiled sarcastically. They looked at each other with a tacit agreement, an agreement that was meant to exclude Lao San. . . . They remained awake in the dark; that unoccupied bed made them feel rather sentimental, as if one of their comrades had fallen behind. [6][4]

A comrade is "fallen behind" (*diaodui*) is a common expression found in official discourse with highly charged political connotations. It is clearly used as a parody here. Another parody, *"Lei Feng,"*[5] is found when the three resume their friendship after the incident and become excited again in their conversations on what it means to be a human being in this vast universe:

They felt they have touched the core meaning of the human being and human life, a black hole of universe. . . . This time their heart is filled with the warm feelings similar to the ones they had when they struggled to learn from Lei Feng. [7]

And

They woke up next morning and their spirits were high. Remembering the talk of the previous night, they found that they had reached one story higher [another parody] and had become a new person: we must do something positive in this declining world. Their heart was filled with the pride of a savior. Then they picked up their unwashed bowls and chopsticks and strode to the cafeteria like martyrs. [8]

Obviously the author is trying to dramatize this search for the self, and imply how unrealistic these women are to look for their real self when they are often confused as to what they are actually looking for.

What I see as being satirized here, however, is not the notion of the true self, but specifically the women's attempt to find it. The author acknowledges a desire for individual identity, but she does not do it with an awareness that such a desire is based on the myth of a rational, autonomous self. In the narrative, therefore, there is an implicit degendering tendency to recognize the issue mainly as a conflict between a collective power and a desire on the part of the individual to pursue her own identity. The idea of a true self, in other words, is not being questioned, and the narrative stops at the level of satirizing the attempt.

In representing women's struggles for an individual identity, both narratives convey a strong sympathy toward women like Su Mi, the narrator, Lao Li, and Lao Wang in their quest for self. The bond between and among women is vulnerable mainly because, according to the narratives, the tension between individual women and social norms requires women to invest their love in the right places: marriage and family. If they invest their love in a wrong place, such as in their own individual values, they get punished socially and psychologically. Meanwhile, however, the stories also suggest the double-edgedness of such a quest for the self—it can be used as a form of resistance, but it can also become problematic if it is pursued as a goal in and of itself. The representation of resistance and the almost inevitable failure of it is also what these texts endeavor to convey.

What I see at stake here is that while the women characters interrogate the meaning of being a woman, their efforts are constantly deconstructed, so to speak, by their already constituted positions in gender relations, of whose symbolic and constructed nature they have not yet been made aware. Their search for the self, then, is both a form of resistance and a blind spot where certain unquestioned assumptions converge. The same is true of the notions off the body. The question of what it means to be a woman, when asked, can function to challenge the social norms of womanhood. When pursued, however, it can also become the barrier that sets women apart when they disagree about what the answer should be. In the two narratives, their bonds fall apart when they each decide to stop at their own solution, either by complying with the social norms, or by taking extreme actions, or by continuing to question. The tension is shown in *"Dixiong men"* when Lao Da and Lao Er break up with Lao San, and when Lao Wang (Lao Er) breaks up with Lao Li (Lao Da). In *"Dengdai huanghun,"* between Su Mi and the narrator, a similar desire is shared that binds them together for some time, but the construction of the desire is such that it makes them mutually exclusive in their quest for the true meaning of being a woman: Su Mi refuses to wait for the twilight, while the narrator continues.

Within the context of Chinese culture today, the search, as I have mentioned above, represents a desire for a recognition of individual values and individual expressions by both men and women. The insistence on a nongendered real self is what is problematic. Instead of being perceived as a cultural issue, which is related to the notion of ideology, construction of subjectivity, and possibility for resistance, searching for a real self is represented as an existential issue with some ultimate truth to it. It both denies the gendered nature of the issue and deconstructs the significance of the bond among women in patriarchal culture. In other words, the notion of the self is modeled on the patriarchal myth of a free man, which creates a desire in women that is both real and problematic. What is real is that Chinese women are looking for their own individual identities; what is problematic is that when they want to do away with conventional models for women, such as *Xianqi liangmu* (subservient wife and good mother), *Malie zhuyi laotaitai* (Marxist-Leninist granny), and androgynized professionals, they are left with the notion of a free individual, which many theorists have critiqued as both patriarchal and ahistorical. The bond among women to quest for such a self, then, becomes a paradox. When women come together not only to challenge social norms but also to search for an ultimate self, their desire for such a self-identity is very often interpellated back into the patriarchy, where they may become more ready to accept their natural roles to be a real woman. And the existence of a sisterhood based on such a desire becomes too contingent to claim its ground. Hence the question mark behind the word "sisterhood" in my title.[6]

NOTES

1. Jiang Zidan, *"Dengdai huanghun"* (Waiting for the twilight), *Shou Huo* (Harvest), no. 1, 1990, 68–85. All the English translations from the two narratives in this paper are mine.

2. Wang Anyi, *"Dixiong men"* (Brothers), *Shou Huo*, no. 3, 1989, 4–30.

3. I was reminded that Su Mi does not lack her counterpart in the West: the wife of Jason of Golden Fleece fame in Greek mythology.

4. "Fallen behind" in Chinese is *diaodui*, which is a phrase commonly used in the official discourse.

5. Lei Feng is a long deceased PLA soldier who was set up by the CCP as a revolutionary model for the nation.

6. In an early draft, I raised the issue of lesbianism. My contention was that an immediate identification of these texts with lesbianism was problematic. I believe that new paradigms need to be explored and established, otherwise such immediate identification would be rather too simplistic. Due to this brief argument at the beginning of the chapter, many responses I received focused on the issue of lesbianism which was not the major part of my discussion, so I decided to take that part out of the paper. However, the nature of the responses made me realize the importance of the issue, and as a result, I would like to use this final note to present my original argument and leave it for further debate:

"How, then, does one read these Chinese texts that carry sexual implications in exploring relationships between women? Are these, to put it more bluntly, lesbian texts? The question, in other words, is: Can one read both narratives or one of them as lesbian text(s)? The sexual implications in *"Dengdai huanghun"* especially trigger such a question. For a sophisticated reader educated in the West, it is not difficult to detect such an implication and associate it with lesbianism. While there may be no simple answer to this question, I should like to argue that a simple answer is by no means compatible with the textual complexity of the narratives, nor is it compatible with the contextual complexity within which the narratives are situated. The English word *lesbian* has its own social, cultural, and political connotations or implications in the West. A lesbian literary text constructed and read within this context usually explores lesbian sexuality—an important identity and a significant distinction between representing women's relationships in general and relationships between lesbian women. In spite of the sexual implications in my two texts, however, the narratives do not focus on sexuality per se, be it heterosexuality or homosexuality. What is explored, rather, is the politics of reading the female body through, especially in the case of "*Dengdai huanghun*," one woman reading another woman's (as well as her) own body. The question, therefore, is whether we should read the two texts as lesbian texts or texts with a lesbian theme on the ground of ambiguous sexual implications represented in these women's relationships? Whether or not, contextually, such ambiguity is mainly subversive at the level of what it means to be a woman—that is to say, concerning the norms of womanhood? What is more, how to understand the ambivalence represented within the relationships between these women? Is it caused by a tension between heterosexism and lesbianism, or a tension between social norms concerning gender relations and woman's desire to challenge gender relations and the norms? Why is it that in both texts the close relationships between women are represented in such a way that the closeness gradually becomes obscured, problematized, and eventually undermined?"

9

Can Xue: What Is So Paranoid in Her Writings?

According to the Confucian concept of "rectification of name"[1] (*zhengming*), the act of correct naming or purity in language is perceived as capable of maintaining the social structure.[2] Moreover, writing or literature (*wen*) must carry the principle (*Dao*) in the Confucian tradition.[3] Despite their claimed modernity, a large number of Chinese avant-garde critics of the 1980s and 90s still unconsciously believe in this Confucian didactic view of language. This belief, however, is very likely disguised by a modernized and westernized theoretical vocabulary.[4] On the one hand, these critics have promoted experimental fiction as an open-ended and modern form. On the other hand, they have also attempted to establish a new order, which in many ways resembles the old patriarchal order it tends to replace. This self-contradictory stance is illustrated by their attempt to monopolize the position of subversive subject vis-à-vis communist ideology by debasing different literary styles and the opposite sex.[5] However modernized and westernized they may be, for these critics, to experiment with language necessarily implies a mastery of the object of subversion—language—on the part of the subversive subject. Logically speaking, from a masculinist point of view, women are supposed to be mastered by language, but not to master it.

In this context, Can Xue's writings are more interesting because they inadvertently challenge and subvert the preconceptions about language imposed by a newly established patriarchal order. By 1985, at the age of 33, Can Xue was a relatively well-recognized experimental writer in China, although she had, only shortly before, started publishing her fiction in various Chinese literary journals. Can Xue is among the very few Chinese women who enjoyed such a reputation.[6] Due to her works' shocking and puzzling effects on their readership, a large number of avant-garde critics have paid tribute to this woman writer. As a subversive voice within the supposedly subversive order, Can Xue's position becomes doubly subversive—vis-à-vis the dominant official ideology *and* the institutionalized male-centered subversive position among Chinese intellectuals. This may explain why her works both fascinate and disturb her mainland Chinese critics. In this chapter I shall attempt to pinpoint the ambiguity inherent in their comments on a woman's successful experiment with language even when measured by a heavily masculinist standard, and at the same time to approach Can Xue's works from a different perspective.

In order to overcome their uneasiness toward Can Xue's double subversion, a number of Chinese male critics have adopted a common strategy: to attribute the originality of Can Xue's texts to an imaginary madness. Interestingly, these critics can detect symptoms of her hysteria only in her works but not in her life. Tautologically, her fiction serves as both the proof and the result of her alleged insanity. However, this logic is not as puzzling as it may appear. A woman's experiment with language amounts to an attempt to master this exclusively masculine property—language. Perceived from a masculinist point of view, any attempt to disrupt the masculinist rationale is in itself maddening not necessarily for the female intruder but for the newly established male order. Consequently, Can Xue's success in such a maddening attempt cannot be explained in any other terms but by her inherent madness.

Cheng Yongxin, editor of *Selections of New Wave Fiction in China*, made the following comments:

None of Can Xue's works can avoid a fundamental undertone: the delirium of a paranoid woman, afraid of being hurt
by other people.[7]

With an apparently more sophisticated vocabulary, Cheng
Depei, a well-known critic of the literary journal *Shanghai Literature*, expresses the same opinion. In his article "The Dream Which
Tortures Can Xue," Cheng Depei describes the characters of this
woman writer as "scopophiliac" (*kuishikuang*):

The skepticism and crisis of a scopophiliac character only
prove that his/her target is very likely illusory. The dispersal
of illusion will eventually reveal that his/her target is no one
else but him/herself. As a result, hidden behind this
scopophilia is an exhibitionist with a narcissistic tendency.
The madness expressed in this form of scopophilia proves
that his/her exhibitionism has reached an uncontrollable
degree. For us, the true value of images of a mother, of a husband, or of a father in this dream is insignificant, because
dreams can never truly reflect the reality of our daily life; at
the most it can vaguely verify the reality and history of a psyche.[6]

Of these two critics, we must thank Cheng Yongxin for his
frankness. At least, he has the honesty to designate Can Xue
directly as a "paranoid woman." Interestingly, according to the
same critic, the fear which in Can Xue's works earns her the name
of "paranoid woman" can be transcended in Yu Hua's masculine
imagination. The "transcended" fear in Yu Hua's fiction "reminds
[Cheng Yongxin] of Robbe-Grillet's novels and Antonioni's films."[9]
Taking into account the fetichization of the West prevailing
among contemporary Chinese intellectuals, the names of a French
novelist and of an Italian filmmaker indicate less any tangible
quality of Yu Hua's works than an unreserved endorsement of
them. Ironically, Cheng Yongxin's endorsement of a male writer is
based on the very same element which allows him to condemn a
woman writer as insane, namely, the portrayal of an omnipresent
fear in their works.

With all his meaningless fancy psychoanalytic terms, Cheng
Depei basically tries to make a similar statement. However, contrary to his expectations, Cheng Depei's floating signifiers do not
necessarily endow his statement with more scientificity than

Cheng Yongxin's straightforward curse. At the most, this effort only reveals his fetichization of the West, as if a westernized vocabulary were all it took to prove the true value of his diagnosis of a Chinese woman writer's mental illness. In other words, like the Chinese "Adam" who published "Adam's Bewilderment,"[10] a general identification with the West helps the male critic to regain his masculinity, thus allowing him to treat women as Confucian inferior men.

Instead of analyzing her works, these critics spend most of their energy psychoanalyzing the author, as if the experimental quality of her works were derived from her mental illness. With her works framed by the symptoms of madness, the task of a complaisant literary critic[11] has been transformed into that of a condescending physician. We do not need to "understand" her works, because "dreams can never truly reflect the reality of our daily life," as Cheng Depei states. By depriving Can Xue's characters of any "true value," these critics no longer need to *understand* her works, the nonsensical nature of which becomes the legitimate proof of her madness. Ironically, by privileging the "true value" of a meaningful world over a woman writer's experimental quality, these avant-garde critics, despite their claimed modernist stance, cannot avoid falling into the old trap of socialist realism.

In fact, Cheng Depei's diagnosis that Can Xue hides exhibitionism and narcissism behind her scopophilia may be used as a weapon against himself. This fancy vocabulary may endow his passage with a simulacrum of dignity, since no one in China or in the West (probably including himself) can fully understand what he means. Except for this simulacrum of dignity, his statement does not have any true value. His painstaking effort to play the role of an observing doctor reveals his own fear of an unknown world created by Can Xue's special sensitivity to the nightmarish reality of daily life in contemporary China. This sensitivity results not only from an intent to subvert the party line, but also from her double-marginality as a woman writer in both communist ideology and its subversive partner, Chinese experimental fiction. Thanks to her first marginality, her writings recreate a world which crystallizes the absurd logic inherent in communist discourse. Thanks to her second marginality, she does not need to acknowledge or follow any particular masters, be they Western or Chinese, as is normally the case with male experimental writers.[12] In this case, her femininity among a group of male writers and critics with an implicit or explicit masculinist ideology becomes a mark of marginality which is related to, but not limited by, gender identity.[13]

The situation of Chinese women in general is complicated by their representational power used by, or against, the Communist Party. This gender situation results from a social and cultural context particular to communist China. On the one hand, the size of the minority population in China, despite its diversity, remains relatively small. Most minorities live mainly in remote border regions. Consequently, in comparison with other large countries, such as the United States and the former Soviet Union, China is a much more racially homogenous society. Furthermore, Chinese minorities usually do not offer striking physiological differences from the Han Chinese majority. On the other hand, the oppressed classes in the old society, peasants and workers, were supposed to be the components of the new leading classes in the communist regime. The communist leaders' identification with the past slaves to a large extent eliminates the possibility of taking full advantage of the slaves' absolute otherness in their representation of the oppressed. In this context, women, as inferior men in the many thousand years of Chinese history, have been endowed with a unique representational power in the composition of minority discourse in communist China. Thanks to their large number, irreducible physiological and social differences from the members of the old and new dominant orders, they can be saved repeatedly without losing their otherness vis-à-vis their saviors. To a large extent, women's inferiority and difference are the most significant materials with which the Communist Party has created the self-image of the great savior of the people.

However, the communist slogans of women's emancipation further marginalize the second sex by denying any potential subject positions to women—beatified and iconized as symbols of the party's political stance. Later on, the Chinese people's deep disillusionment with communist ideology has unfortunately been accompanied by a misogynistic discourse in contemporary Chinese society, as if women's representational power indeed identified them with the party. In this case, women are doubly marginalized by their double representation—as the object of communist salvation in the official discourse of the party and as a symbol of the Communist Party in the anticommunist discourse of the avant-garde intellectuals. Consequently, Can Xue's experimental fiction inadvertently subverts a largely institutionalized subversive position of male experimental writers predicated on the Con-

fucian misogynistic tradition implicitly reinforced by this fallacious identification of women with the party. This may partly
explain why her commentators need to downplay the effect of her
works by attributing it to their author's alleged insanity.

In this chapter, on the contrary, I argue that Can Xue's works
are interesting not because of her (or her works') madness, but
because of her (or her works') lucidity. Her writings capture the
reality of contemporary China through a "feminized" language
thanks to its marginality or "fluidity"—to borrow Luce Irigaray's
expression.[14] This reality is paranoid since the ideological vacuum
existing in post-Mao China has deeply shaken the basis for even
daily communication by depriving language of any commonly
acknowledged referentiality. The disappearance of any master signifier makes Can Xue's fluid language an excellent tool for exploring the nightmarish situation in contemporary Chinese society. I
base my argument on a textual analysis of the three following
short stories by Can Xue: "A Mei's Melancholy Thoughts on a
Sunny Day" (*A Mei zai yige taiyang tian li de chousi*),[15] "In the
Wilderness" (*kuangye li*),[16] and "What Happened to Me in That
World—To a Friend" (*Wo zai nage shijie li de shiqing—gai
youren*).[17] Each of these three stories was first published in various
literary journals in 1986. Furthermore, these stories can be said to
deal with sexual relations in three different forms: marriage as a
process in "A Mei's Melancholy Thoughts," the routine life of a
married couple in "In the Wilderness," and a strangely idealized
love in "What Happened to Me in That World."

INSANITY AND REALITY

In "A Mei's Melancholy Thoughts on a Sunny Day," the narrator, A Mei, matter-of-factly reports on her marriage. As in an
ordinary family in mainland China, after eight years of marriage, A
Mei lives with her son and her mother. The only strange circumstance is that after the birth of their son, named Big Dog (*dagou*),
her husband disappears.

The two expressions in the title of this story sound somewhat inappropriate. "Melancholy Thoughts (or Longing)" (*chousi*)
in classic Chinese may evoke a poetic or romantic image of a beautiful woman who, from a distance, longs for her lover or husband.[18]
However, A Mei's melancholy thoughts about her absent husband
cannot be more prosaic and dispassionate. Moreover, "a Sunny
Day" (*taiyang tian*) in the communist vocabulary connotes hope

and happiness in life.[19] Actually the story describes a life completely devoid of any ray of happiness. By not fulfilling the readers'
expectations formed either by classical Chinese literature or by
socialist realism, this title sets a transgressive tone for the story at
various levels: language, culture, ideology, and politics.

Ironically, the story starts with a description of the weather:

> Since last Thursday, it rained ceaselessly. This morning it
> stopped suddenly. There is a severity in the sunshine, and a
> terrible stench in the muddy courtyard. [*hdpxs*, 301]

The sunshine, after an almost week-long rain, should normally be considered especially welcome. In Can Xue's short story,
however, it becomes repulsive not only because of its smell, but
also because of its severity. The name of the narrator, "A Mei," is
a pun on mold (*mei*) or on early summer rain (*meiyu*). In the first
case, because mold will disappear in the sunshine, its severity
metaphorically threatens the existence of the narrator. In the second case, because the narrator is identified with rain, the sunshine
may be perceived as a mark of the end of her life. In both cases,
sunshine, an image commonly used as a metaphor for hope and
happiness in socialist realism, is transformed into a metaphor for
desperation and death. Furthermore, taking into account that one
of the flattering names attributed to Mao Zedong during the Cultural Revolution was "the red sun"[20] or even "the reddest and reddest sun in our hearts,"[21] the subversive implications in Can Xue's
short story become apparent. Like the unfortunate sunshine, marriage, instead of evoking happiness in a supposedly normal situation, becomes nonsensical.

Before the marriage, Old Li, the narrator's absent husband-to-
be, has a very close relationship with his future mother-in-law.
After a period of intimacy between the future mother-in-law and
son-in-law, Old Li offers to marry A Mei with whom he has barely
had any previous contact. A Mei describes this scene:

> It was very hot in July. Everywhere in the houses there were
> little insects. One day, he decided to propose marriage to me.
> That day, I went to the kitchen to fetch water. He came in by
> surprise. As I was getting ready to escape, he unexpectedly
> opened his mouth:
> Hey, you, do you have any objection to me? (. . .)

Then, he asked me whether I was willing to marry him immediately. While talking, his entire body was twitching uncomfortably. Later on, he found a stool. The stool was dark and oily, and one of its legs was already loose. He sat there shakily. Again and again, he repeated the same arguments; the most important one being that my mother owned a house. If he married me, he could live in this house and no longer needed to look for an apartment. At that moment, I tittered. He blushed immediately. With a stern look he angrily asked me: Why did you laugh?

At first, I had intended to leave and to write a letter. But I have stayed here for such a long time listening to you.

With a sense of relief, he said, Oh! I see. [*hdpxs*, 302–03]

In fact, this apparently absurd scene can be considered a concise and realistic picture of marriage in contemporary China. Most marriages are no longer arranged, but many of them are still suggested by the parents. In China parental intervention is very often still crucial in the decision of a son's or a daughter's marriage. As a result, the acceptance of a marriage proposal in some cases depends more on the satisfaction of the prospective parents-in-law with the proposing party than that of the potential spouse. Naturally, the way of pleasing a spouse's parents may vary from one case to another. Can Xue's portrayal of the implied sexual relationship between A Mei's mother and her future husband seems, on the one hand, to push this logic to its extreme, and on the other, to emphasize the absurdity inherent in this very form of marriage.

The increasing materialism in Chinese society is also expressed in marital relations. Possession of certain objects has become one of the commonly accepted preconditions for marriage. Because of the scarcity of available housing in China, a large percentage of married couples still live separately. Under these circumstances, Old Li's choice of housing as the most important motivation for marriage can easily be justified.

The expression used by Old Li to begin the conversation— "Do you have any objection to me?" (*ni duiwo you shenmo yijian*)—is certainly not unfamiliar to a reader from mainland China. Before the 1980s, this expression had been widely used in personal conversation. The word "objection" (*yijian*) originally indicates ideological criticism. The sentence supposedly expresses the speaker's desire to receive ideological criticism from his/her interlocutor in order to improve his/her political behavior in accordance with the party line.

Since any personal interests in Mao's China of the 1960s and 70s had a suspicious undertone, any personal ties constantly needed to be justified by a coverage of revolutionary interests. This process of constant camouflage has largely altered the nature of communication in both private and public life in China. If personal relationships were politicized (a woman, for example, must marry a man because of his loyalty to the revolution[22]), a large number of revolutionary slogans were also transformed into substitute for personal expressions as in the case of Old Li's question addressed to his fiancée. This constant confusion between public politics and personal privacy leads toward a trivialization of the former and an impersonalization of the latter. As a result, both political and personal language may very well resemble meaningless noise, which does not convey anything but a simulacrum of communication.

Because of the motivation (sexual implications between the future mother-in-law and son-in-law), the justification (housing), and the use of language (the personal use of politicized language), Old Li's marriage proposal indeed appears highly absurd especially to a reader accustomed to a much more romanticized or rationalized image of marriage. However, this absurdity in sexual relations which differs from Mo Yan's romanticized version of masculinism,[23] Su Tong's exploration of the dead-end in sexual relations,[24] and Yu Hua's sadism,[25] marks Can Xue's sensitivity to the nightmarish reality in contemporary China. Instead of looking for transgressive models mainly in predominantly Western previous literary works, Can Xue more consciously and lucidly manipulates materials found in contemporary Chinese society in order to subvert the existing conventions of socialist realism.

By crystallizing the logic of communist ideology in its manifestations of daily life, Can Xue succeeds in capturing the absurdity inherent in this logic. In Old Li's relationship with his future mother-in-law, a defective process of naming (to become the daughter's husband) is a cover for an unnameable reality. In his desire to obtain a room by means of marriage, Old Li reverses the relationship between a goal and its means. In his use of impersonal language, the tie between signified and signifier has been broken. Can Xue's apparently surrealist world epitomizes the logic of communist ideology in its camouflage, reversal, and fragmentation.

DISAPPEARANCE OF BOUNDARIES

Can Xue's short story "In the Wilderness" (*Kuangye li*) describes the married life of an anonymous "her" and her equally nameless husband, "him." Both of them suffer from somnambulism. The story is apparently told from her perspective, and consists of an endless and aimless hide-and-seek between her and him from the house to the wilderness. The final contact between the couple entails a fatal destruction. Although the destruction occurs mainly in the imagination, its effect is not less substantial. In Can Xue's world, the line of demarcation between dream and reality does not exist, and an imaginary death is equal to death *tout court.*

From the beginning, the relationship of the married couple is presented in an interesting light:

> In the evening, she went to bed. Suddenly she realized that she was not sleeping. Therefore, she got up. Without light she wandered around the room. As she walked, an ominous noise arose from the rotten floor. In the dark, a black lump, similar to a bear, knelt in the corner. This lump was moving, and noisily tramped on the floor.
>
> "Who is that?" Her voice was frozen in her throat.
>
> "It's me," her husband answered in a frightened voice. They were afraid of each other.
>
> Ever since then, like two ghosts through many rooms of this big house every night they wandered in darkness. During the day, she lowered her head, as if she could not remember what had happened during these nights. [*hdpxs*, 319]

On the one hand, this house does not offer any protection to its inhabitants. Both the husband and wife seem not to have the slightest sense of security which the shelter of their own house should provide. As indicated by the title, the home is turned into an extension of the wilderness. To this extent, the line of demarcation between nature and culture has disappeared. On the other hand, the lack of protection does not prevent their house from functioning as a prison. Moreover, the wilderness also becomes the extension of the prisonlike house. The wilderness, in this respect, resembles civilized society in that it forces individuals to face each other in a kind of unfriendly, even hostile atmosphere. As a result, the identification between nature and culture is tantamount to a synthesis of the worst qualities of both entities. Neither culture nor nature can provide shelter for human beings who live in a threatening world. Neither nature nor culture can offer an open space where one individual may escape from the threatening presence of the Other. An individual living in this house as an extension of the wilderness cannot avoid both a horrifying sense of an invincible loneliness and a threatening presence of the Other. On the one hand, s/he feels lonely as if s/he were lost in a wild world of nature. On the other hand, s/he feels threatened by his/her numerous neighbors who, hostile or not, are interested in each other's private life, as in a highly populated society such as China's.

The synthesis of nature and culture in its most negative features in Can Xue's story is epitomized by the apparently routine life between the married couple. It is difficult to imagine a more negative relationship between human beings than the nightmarish situation of this couple. They are both absent and present to each other; absent because any actual contact is impossible, and present because each remains an ominous force in the other's imagination. The psychological impact of this environment is so powerful that it affects human beings not only mentally—by provoking an invincible fear, but also physically—by materializing the threat through a fearful imagination. At the end of the story, in the husband's imagination, a formless hand (very likely his wife's) touches the husband's painful toe. This imaginary hand, however, finally destroys the clock, the flying gear wheel of which symbolizes the phallus, or the husband's masculinity. In this context, the line of demarcation between imagination and reality has also disappeared, since the psychological effect of fear is so intense that it becomes "real."

With these blurred lines of demarcation, a reader would like to ask: Is this story about a reality or a dream? In Can Xue's story, everything, including reality, is a dream.

The heroine of "In the Wilderness" says:

A dream, which came through that little window, follows me. It swam into the room like a shark and blew cold air behind my neck. I couldn't sleep these days. You see, my skin became wrinkled. Taken by surprise last night while trying to escape from the carnivore fish, I broke the paperweight. How long will this game of hunting and chasing last? she complains inadvertently, I can no longer distinguish dream from awakening. I raved in the office, scaring all my colleagues to death.

Who can understand this kind of thing? Some people perpetually live in similar situations all their lives. They have no other choice but to sleep while walking and talking. Perhaps we will finally become like them. [*hdpxs*, 321]

Again, similar to the narrator of "A Mei's Melancholy Thoughts,"' the female protagonist of "In the Wilderness" deliberately chooses a solipsistic language as a refusal to play a role in communicative exchange. In fact, both she and her husband recognize the impossible nature of such communication. Her husband, however, participates in this simulacrum of communication more willingly. According to him, since many people are asleep while talking, their own situation can be considered perfectly normal. In other words, the nightmarish situation created by defective communication is normalized by its repetition in the eyes of the male protagonist, whereas the normalized situation is again problematized and unmasked as nightmarish by the female protagonist's idiosyncratic language or refusal to take part in communicative discourse. In the final analysis, a kind of madness lies in this impossibility of social communication to which each participant pretends not to pay attention in order to continue the game. In this context, the female protagonist's idiosyncratic language is not necessarily a mark of her madness—as Cheng Yongxin and other critics have claimed—but a mark of lucidity which allows her to uncover the insane logic in social communication. The difference between her language and the object of its limitation, communicative discourse, is that the former acknowledges its solipsistic nature, whereas the latter's normal function depends on the ignorance of its true nature by its participants. Logically, her language which duplicates social communication by making its impossible nature explicit is necessarily delirious—or at least idiosyncratic. Consequently, it does not surprise us that the female narrator shocks her colleagues in the office by her ranting, because her language does not aim to address anyone but herself. However, her monologue is actually an acting-out of communicative discourse the true nature of which people must ignore in order to keep functioning in such a system.

With the intention to unmask this impossible nature of social communication in Chinese society, Can Xue's writings tend to deconstruct most boundaries which are normally taken for granted, such as those between signified and signifier, dream and reality, life and death. As a result, Can Xue in her fiction captures the absurd essence of the world of post-Mao China, where any well-defined value system has been dismantled, discredited, and dissimulated.

In this world, even dream itself is no longer spontaneous and becomes the fruit of an imaginary will. As the husband protested loudly:

> This is merely a dream, a dream I myself wanted,—he was frightened by her footsteps which approached.
>
> The footsteps stopped near him, but no one was there. In this wilderness there was no one. Those footsteps were only the product of his imagination. The imaginary footsteps stopped near him.
>
> An invisible hand deliberately touched his painful toe. Despite himself he could not avoid it. His frozen body hair stood up—like numerous pins.
>
> After the last ring, the wall clock broke. The gear wheel, like a little bird, flew to the sky. The distorted rubber tube stuck tightly to the dirty wall.
>
> A pool of dark blood oozed on the floor. [*hdpxs*, 323]

By claiming that the dream originates from his will—"a dream I myself wanted" (*wo ziji yuanyi de meng*)—the husband perceives dreams as products of rationalization and will. Interestingly, this is the only point where the male protagonist invokes the notion of will. Will is indispensable in constructing a rational society and provides a man with potential power, since it is an important means to exercise control over the subject of will and other people. In the story, the will of the male protagonist may also be considered the only mark of masculinity, without which man cannot exercise his power. Ironically, this will is not only equal to dream, but is also powerless within the dream. The husband mentions his will precisely because the dream escapes from his control and threatens his life. Finally, this dream as a product of the masculine will ends in the destruction of the clock, the gear wheel of which flies away like a little bird. The Chinese character for bird (*niao*) can also be read as (*diao*) which indicates the male sex. In other words, the final picture of this product of masculine will symbolizes the destruction of the phallus. The mark of masculinity in this case is turned into that of the castration complex. The husband asserts his will because he is afraid of losing his masculine power over a dreamlike world. But his dream is substantialized by means of his will, which is in the final analysis merely another form of an invincible fear. The dream supposedly engendered by his own will finally destroys him.

In this world where will is confused with dream, and dream with reality, the dream as a product of the imagination oppresses the subject of will to the point of destroying him. The subject is oppressed and finally destroyed by the production of his own imagination. At the same time, this destruction is supposedly accomplished by an imaginary her, a gendered other—the product of his invincible fear. In this case, sexual relationship becomes imaginary. However, because the imagination is largely motivated by fear, it becomes aggressive, violent, destructive, and self-destructive. Consequently, this imaginary nature of sexual relationship is precisely the source of mutual and self-destruction. In addition, both the fish, as a metaphor for her haunting dream, and the bird, as a metaphor for his clock—which is smashed at the end of the story—remind us of the image of the phallus, respectively from the female and male perspectives. The fish, which comes through a small window and follows the woman, suggests rape. The character for bird *(niao)* in Chinese can be read as *(diao)*, the destruction of which can be interpreted as an image of castration.

By transforming marriage into a daily practice of rape and castration, the story presents the most legitimate form of sexual relationship, marriage, in a most destructive light. Since referent and referee can no longer be distinguished from each other, language has lost its function of differentiation. As a result, the distinction between legal and criminal sexuality has also disappeared. Furthermore, because the house is an extension of the wilderness, culture becomes nature. At the same time, nature resembles culture by restricting the freedom of human beings. Even the wilderness can offer only limited space, where the runaway husband must encounter his castrating wife.

FLUID, ICE, AND SOLID GROUND

Usually, Can Xue's world is submerged in a darkness generated by fear, hatred, and death. This darkness, however, is not absolute. In her short story—"What Happened to Me in That World—To a Friend" *(Wo zai nage shijie li de shiqing—gai youren)*—a strange light breaks into the usual darkness. Unlike the repulsive sunshine in "A Mei's Melancholy Thoughts on a Sunny Day," this pure and immaculate light originates from icebergs and icicles floating on the sea. The world of ice may be considered a limitless mirror, which not only reflects the narrator's image, but also extends her subjective world to infinity. Both this mirror and the narrator's body are equally fluid and shapeless.

However, even in this particular story, love and light exist only in "that world"—the imaginary world—where the memory of a remote past is reflected on an icy surface. In contrast to that world, this world—the "real" world—is also submerged in darkness. In "What Happened to Me in That World," the overwhelming presence of darkness in this world subtends the transparent and icy light of that world. Similar to Can Xue's other stories, in this "real" world, strange and revolting individuals constantly wage wars in order either to destroy each other or to conspire against the narrator. In opposition to this world crowded with mysterious individuals, that pure and transparent world of ice includes only two human beings, you and me, or more precisely only myself alone, waiting for your arrival. As Can Xue describes:

> I close my eyes, and withdraw into a corner. Friend, I am thinking about that iceberg. I believe that, as soon as the ocean unfreezes the iceberg will start moving. I lift my head from the water, watching the iceberg moving like a solemn meditating white whale. Icicles under the sky drip down, "pitter patter, pitter patter." "Crack," a sky-high icicle breaks. Pieces of broken ice glitter with a blue luster and swiftly draw arcs, which disappear at a glance. The brilliance of icicles is external and dazzling. Friend, have you ever had a similar experience? When your chest is open and your head becomes a reflector, thousands and thousands of stars suddenly darken. Even the sun becomes puzzled, alternately brightening and darkening. I lift my head from the water, shake little pieces of broken ice from my hair, and narrow my eyes. Frost drips from the sky. Softly I say to myself: One morning, I will say "This is how it is." Then, everything will start again. The earth again becomes a unified entity. Under the immense and hairy carpet, vague desires and strange emotions grow. Plants gradually are drenched in lascivious green. But I cannot start again, I have already entered this world. The brilliance of icicles is eternal and dazzling. Frightened comets fall on the ground, turning into ugly stones. The silent iceberg is luminous. I stubbornly stay in this world.

Friend, I am growing in order to become one of these numerous sky-high icicles. While the glimmering reflection shines, my body is itching all over, just as if numerous sprouting leaves were on the verge of exploding from the inside. I shake my head and hear the cool breeze whistle in between the leaves. Abundant fluid floats out of my armpits. [*zgxcxsx*, 367–68]

In this passage, there is a recurrent pattern: actions, which require more mental than physical effort, such as thinking and speaking, are *mise en abyme*. That world appears only after she directs her sight inwardly to an imaginary image, the icy ocean and the meditating white whale as a metaphor for the iceberg. In this context, that world may be perceived mainly as the product of her thinking. At the beginning, she is "thinking" (*xiang*) about the iceberg," which "moves forward, like a solemn meditating (*chensi*) white whale." In the middle of the passage, the narrator "says to herself softly: 'I say [this is how it is.]' " (*wo qingqing de dui ziji shuo: "wo shuo: 'jiu zheyang' "*). The *mise-en-abymes* of the actions of thinking and speaking emphasize the subjective aspect of the imaginary world, since both actions are doubly self-reflexive. In the first instance, the white whale as a metaphor for the iceberg also represents the narrator's body. Both, equally submerged in the icy ocean, move slowly while thinking. At the same time, the iceberg as well as the icy world originates from the narrator's act of thinking. Thinking engenders itself in this boundless ocean. The second instance is even more striking. The narrator tells herself that she is pronouncing a sentence. Furthermore, this sentence is also an imaginary point of birth for a new world. However, since the narrator whose imagination gives birth to the new world has "already entered the world," this imaginary birth is virtually impossible.

Whiteness, transparency, silence, cold, and loneliness suggest a world of negation and of nothingness. To a large extent, that world, purified by these unusually colorless images, serves as a negation of reality. In Can Xue's story reality is represented by this world. Negation is also a process of poetization by means of which images and words are purified. In this process of poetization, since imagination, sensation, emotion, and vision are no longer separated from one another, the subject and the object of observation very often merge into a single unit. Due to the interchangeability and constant merging between the subject and the object, that world is tantamount to her subjective world in which the act of observation itself becomes narcissistic. While closing her eyes, the narrator imagines herself watching the mirror image of her body moving in the icy ocean. Like the young Parque in Valéry's poem,[26] she accomplishes an endless cycle of seeing herself seeing.

In this icy and taciturn subjective world, one can only hear the lifeless sound of dripping water and breaking ice. For the narrator, however, this peace merely indicates a state of waiting—waiting for a man, who will share her experience. In other words, the narrator would like to merge not only with the imaginary iceberg, a symbol of the objective world, but also with an equally imaginary male friend—a specifically gendered other. In the latter case, the act of merging bears a strongly sexual undertone. Even though she appears to be the only living being in that icy world, when she speaks, the narrator constantly addresses her friend rather than herself. Moreover, the story's subtitle "To a Friend" (*gai youren*) suggests that it is written in epistolary form. The masochistic image of opening the chest has both sentimental and erotic implications, since the chest is metaphysically the source of passion and physically a female erogenous zone.[27] The head, usually containing the faculty of reason, turns into a reflector. As a result, the source of rationality becomes simply a mirror of nature in its coldness, colorlessness, randomness, and transparency. The imaginary merging with her male friend is unusually luminous so that in front of their (erotic) union both stars and the sun lose their glamor. At the same time, since the "you" in this dialogue remains silent and unresponsive, the luminous merging is only a mirage and does not affect the narcissistic nature of that world. Finally, turning into an echo of her own voice by absolute solitude, the narrator has no other choice but to talk to herself. Even the masochistic gestures, which are potentially liberating, such as opening the chest and turning the head into a reflector, cannot help her substantiate the intensely desired imaginary merging. As a result, the failure of communication in that world makes sexual union impossible.

Nevertheless, the highly sensual language used in this narrator's monologue expresses a boundless desire for union and for love. This desire, according to the narrator, can apparently be realized only through the birth of a new world. At the same time, the idea of this birth is already conditioned by the imaginary existence of that world as the point of departure from which the narrator can imagine this birth. The multi-layered imagination in Can Xue's story accentuates the fictionality of that world. The story, despite its apparently epistolary form, is only a monologue, succinctly illustrated by the following sentence: "I say to myself: 'I say.' "

The friend exists in the story mainly as a symbol of masculinity—with his "body smelling of cigarettes"—and of otherness—as a silent listener. Functioning as a mirror and as the focus of her intense desire, the friend is shapeless and without any fixed identity. In this love story unique in Can Xue's fictional works, the abstract nature of the friend epitomizes the impossible relationship of love between man and woman. Love is expressed not in the form of dialogue but in the form of monologue, since the only possible lover is a silent mirror of the narrator's subjective world. Since this narcissistic love lacks any warm feeling which could potentially bind two individuals together, passion can only exist in the lifeless world of ice.

> Friend, now is the time. Listen! Burning hailstones fall like a torrential rain. Large transparent trees wave their spotlessly white canopies. The water of the ocean ripples sensually. You and I, hand in hand, emerge from the sea. Bathed in the light and flames of ice, we narrow our eyes. We sing "Mother's Shoes" with voices deep inside our chests. [zgxcxsx, 370]

Both burning hailstones (*ranshao de bingpao*) as well as the light and flames of ice (*bing de guangyan*) are oxymorons. The combinations of ice and fire suggests the incompatibility of love and reality. The language Can Xue uses to describe this romance unique among her works is characterized by a large number of oxymorons. Apparently disconnected or contradictory images are combined in order to convey an uneasy sense of discontinuity, fragmentation, and nonsensicality. Throughout the story, this sense is so persistent that it finally establishes its own continuity and coherence. Like the water of the ocean, this language which "ripples" is highly sensual. Rationality, metonymically indicated by the head which is transformed into a reflector, ceases to function and cedes its voice to the body. In "What Happened to Me in That World," the language of the body is expressed by the images of the white whale, of the open chest, and finally, of the two lovers, hand in hand, emerging from the ocean. This essentially imaginary and figurative language poeticizes the body as both the subject and the object of love:

When the ocean wriggles slightly, my back emerges from the surface of the water. A burning intense light expands my heart. Turning back, I look for the mirror, and with a quick glance discover that my eyes have been transformed into two violets. The white whale's meditation will never be interrupted. At a distance, pieces of broken ice run into one another. The icy world does not distinguish day and night. I raise my head from the water and try very hard to open my chest. Sparks as white as snow dart toward the heavens. The iceberg also emits purple smoke, with a deep rumble. [*zgxcxsx*, 369]

In this story, that world is composed of certain recurrent images: the ocean, ice, her body and chest. As we see in the other passage, the narrator is finally united with the friend in her imagination by sharing the imaginary experience of opening the chest. Here, again, sparks as white as snow dart from her open chest. In the end, "Mother's Shoe," a song which may be considered a strange theme song of their love, is also sung by the lovers in voices deep inside their chests. In other words, emotion, represented by sparks and song, can only be expressed through a fragmentation of the body, symbolizing sterility and death.

In that icy and sterile world, ice is shapeless, broken, and moving. In this sense, ice is similar not only to fire in its burning heat, but also to liquid in its fluidity. Can Xue's image of ice is itself a perfect oxymoron in its combination of heat and cold, as well as in that of solidity and fluidity. The water and ice of the ocean have become one single unity. In this boundless world even a faint line of demarcation tends to disappear. Liquid, fire, and solid bodies are transformable with one another. Thus, even the narrator's eyes are transformed into violets. To a large extent, this world of transformation is also a world of liquification in which everything turns into drops of water in the limitless and shapeless ocean. Female subjectivity, flexible and indeterminate as it is, emerges from this ocean.

In traditional China, since the time of *The Book of Changes*, one of the most ancient Chinese books, water has been considered a *yin* element, thus associated with femininity.[28] In addition, the colloquial expression "fluid nature" (*shuixin*) has been used for centuries to describe the changing nature of women. Interestingly, a modern French feminist, Luce Irigaray, also uses the expression "fluid" to describe femininity in contrast to the tendency of solidification in the world of male subjectivity:

And there almost nothing happens except the (re)production of the child. And the flow of some shameful liquid. Horrible to see: bloody. *Fluid* has to remain that secret *remainder*, of the one. Blood, but also milk, sperm, lymph, saliva, spit, tears, humors, gas, waves, airs, fire . . . light. All threaten to deform, propagate, evaporate, consume him, to flow out of him and into another who cannot be easily held on to. The "subject" identifies himself with/in an almost material consistency that finds everything flowing abhorrent. And even in the mother, it is the cohesion of a "body" (subject) that he seeks, solid ground, firm foundation. Not those things in the mother that recall the woman—the flowing things. He cathects these only in a desire to turn them in the self (as same). Every body of water becomes a mirror, every sea, ice.[29]

Love in Can Xue's story can occur only in a fluid world of female subjectivity. This specificity of love deliberately marks a refusal to provide the male subject with a firm ground for its solidification by means of sexuality. In her world of transformation, the father's logic is absent.[30] However, this absence of the name of the father[31] in Can Xue's fiction largely duplicates the situation in contemporary China. Since the patricide of the Confucian father by the socialist revolution in 1949, the communist father among Chinese people has also gradually become an agonizing figure, deadly wounded by the political struggles within the party, by the economic failures in the country, and by a resulting disillusionment with the current regime. Similar to other experimental works of the late 1980s, Can Xue's writings belong to post-Mao China where the name of the father has become increasingly absent.

Nevertheless, in the perverse, destructive, and subversive world of fiction created by most male experimental writers, one can always detect a vague sense of nostalgia for an origin. Generally speaking, most male writers, however timidly, still attempt to seek solid ground and a firm foundation implicity or explicitly based on a father's logic. Mo Yan's narrator, for example, attempts to reconstruct a precommunist past in which his grandfather's masculinity is kept intact in an idealized world.[32] Zhaxi Dawa's characters embark on numerous quests for something which may eventually combine an ancient Tibet and a modern West. Nevertheless, this combination has never truly been found.[33] Some of Su Tong's heroes desperately try to break away from the dead-end of sexual relations between men and women by taking recourse to male bonding. Unfortunately, male bonding has finally been proven to be another form of dead-end.[34] Yu Hua, however, tends to establish a rigorous new order of violence, which uncannily reminds us of the old order of communist domination.[35]

Contrary to all these male writers' search for a solidified firm ground, the liquification of all solid materials in the fatherless world of Can Xue's story is daringly celebrated as an exuberant renewal or even a rebirth. Can Xue's world does not offer any firm ground on which the subject, male or female, may search for an origin. The narrator's recognition of her fluid nature in a boundless world of ocean is the point of departure for a possible birth of her subjective world. This possible birth is based on a refusal to serve as a solid mirror for the male subject—a "pure and simple image fashioned by the father's spirit"[36] By means of its constant refusal and denial, the world of female subjectivity is identified with the boundless and shapeless ocean. Like the ocean, it can no longer be contained within the boundaries of any specific discourse.

At the same time, this world which denies the paternal authority also cuts itself off from any maternal ties, since the female narrator's refusal to solidify her body is expressed by a rejection of motherhood. In Can Xue's fatherless and motherless universe, deprived of any social, family, or personal ties, the lonely voice of the female subject cannot provoke any response other than its own echo. Since the woman's subjective voice is preserved at the price of absolute loneliness and sterility, Can Xue's reconstruction of female subjectivity can be accomplished only in an imaginary world as fiction within fiction.

In this sterile world of fiction, sensuality seems completely detached from its reproductive function, motherhood. In Can Xue's stories, the mother is very often described as an authoritarian, hostile, and repulsive figure. To mother a child—especially a male child—is very often part of a conspiracy to start a shameful and incurably doomed sexual liaison. Apparently, physical pleasure and motherhood in Can Xue's writings are mutually exclusive.

Can Xue's special resentment against motherhood may be perceived as a rebellion against the significant role of mother assigned to Chinese women by the traditional culture. In traditional China, since the only legitimate social function for a Chinese woman was to give birth to male descendants, motherhood was the only respectable identity for women. This identity, to a certain extent, could be considered a firm ground for a traditional Chinese woman in her otherwise liquid world of in(de)finity.[37] Furthermore, as carrier of the husband's son, she also performs the role of a mirror for the male ego.

In "A Mei's Melancholy Thoughts on a Sunny Day," the narrator gives birth to a son, but does not feel at all motherly. The role of mother is assumed by the narrator's own mother, who is particularly hostile to the narrator. Moreover, the grandmother uses her grandson to maintain a suspicious and hopeless liaison with her son-in-law. Similarly, in "What Happened to Me in That World—To a Friend," motherhood is as usual personified by an old woman. Identified with a tung-oil tree, the old woman also usurps the place of the narrator, who from time to time takes the form of a camphor tree. As soon as she takes the place of the camphor tree, the old woman is turned into cement. Thus, in Can Xue's story, the female body is solidified by two different processes: transformation into cement in this world, and into ice in that world. The former is irrevocable, whereas the latter is always subject to fluidification.

Transformation into cement can be perceived as an equivalent to motherhood. Woman, identified by her reproductive function, loses her fluidity—feminine identity—which is regarded as changeable, indefinable, and unreliable in a patriarchal society. Moreover, as the bearer of the male sign (the son), the mother's "cemented" body has also been transformed into the father's mirror. In contrast, the sterile process of glaciation in the narrator's imaginary world can be taken as an attempt to formulate a new kind of female subjectivity. Constantly changing, the narrator's imaginary world deconstructs the boundaries and definitions assigned to women by a patriarchal culture. The rejection of motherhood symbolizes a radical denial of woman's instrumental position in a patriarchal discourse. By means of this denial, female subjectivity emerges in its shapelessness and indeterminacy. The denial of motherhood largely cuts the traditional tie which binds a woman to a man as a sexual partner, or even more strikingly, the tie between women symbolized by the mother-daughter relationship. At the same time, a new tie either between the two sexes or between women has not yet been formed. As a result, Can Xue's world of female subjectivity can be said to exclude any man or woman, unless it is at a completely abstract level as in the case of this nameless and faceless friend. In other words, the male friend is transformed by female subjectivity into a formless liquid—a drop of water in the immense ocean.

In her "Power of Discourse," Luce Irigaray states:

> This "style," or "writing," of women tends to put the torch to fetish words, proper terms, well-constructed forms. This "style" does not privilege sight; instead, it takes each figure back to its source, which is among other things *tactile*. It comes back in touch with itself in that origin without ever constituting in it, constituting itself in it, as some sort of unity. *Simultaneity* as its "proper" aspect—a proper(ty) that is never fixed in the possible identity-to-self of some form or other. It is always *fluid*, without neglecting the characteristics of fluids that are difficult to idealize: those rubbings between two infinitely near neighbors that create a dynamics. Its "style" resists and explodes every firmly established form, figure, idea or concept.[38]

Like the ultimate signifier, the phallus in a Lacanian sense, which breaks into pieces at the end of Can Xue's "In the Wilderness," every firmly established form, figure, idea, or concept explodes in her writings. In accordance with a changing idiosyncratic map of identities, words are repeatedly broken and reconstituted so that every form—be it linguistic, stylistic, narrative, or metaphysical—is constantly subject to fragmentation. To use Irigaray's words, Can Xue's language "is never fixed in the possible identity-to-self of some form or other." This linguistic lack of identity-to-self is due to Can Xue's keen awareness of her identity as a woman, or more precisely to that of her lack of identity as a woman writer.

The lack of identity in a phallocentric discourse is precisely the "proper(ty)" of Can Xue's fiction. Can Xue's language of the body does not acknowledge any authority or order predicated on the ultimate signifier, the phallus. By privileging sensation and touching over rationality and vision, her language questions the traditional fetishist concept of women. In Chinese patriarchal society, women are frequently used either as visual and representational images or as reproductive instruments. In the first instance, women serve as visual or representational images in which the male subject invests his erotic desire or ideological belief. In the second instance, the female body is treated as a reproductive instrument by means of which the father's image can be multiplied in time and space. Thanks to the radical deconstruction of women's traditional position assigned by a patriarchal cultural and social discourse, Can Xue's language goes beyond any existing discursive boundaries. Therefore, it does not surprise us that her works are perceived as paranoid by a great number of Chinese avant-garde critics. To a large extent, the word "paranoid" may more properly be applied to those critics themselves, since their inappropriate use of this word reveals their own intense fear of a world created by a woman writer, which exceeds their expected discursive boundaries.

Moreover, most of these critics still believe that men actively shape language, whereas woman are passively shaped by language. Therefore, the experimental writings of a man reflect his consciousness or subjectivity, whereas those of a woman are the products of her unconscious and the symptoms of her mental illness. As a result, most male experimental writers, Such as Yu Hua and Ge Fei, have received enthusiastic praise from leading Chinese critics for their lucidity, discursive disruption, and courage to challenge the readers' expectations.[39] By contrast, Can Xue's daring experiments are interesting to the same critics mainly as symptoms of her paranoia.

The double standard generated by a gender bias not only discourages most women from participating in experimental fiction but also limits the subversive nature of this genre itself. Due to this pronounced gender bias, instead of transcending the cultural and ideological limitations of its objects of transgression, Confucian and communist patriarchies, Chinese experimental fiction of the late 1980s has unfortunately confined itself to a misogynistic discourse. At the level of literary criticism, this misogynistic tendency is expressed by an implicit attempt to use experimental fiction as an exclusively masculine property to reaffirm gender hierarchy. As a result, the subversion of communist ideology does not allow most experimental fiction writers or critics to break away from the structure of the patriarchal order implied in this ideology. Instead, this subversion only helps them establish a new order, largely modeled on the old patriarchal structure, which is defined by a master-slave logic.

As Frederick Engels points out:

The first class opposition that appears in history coincides with the development of the antagonism between man and woman in monogamous marriage and the first class oppression coincides with that of the female sex by the male.[40]

Class oppression does not simply coincide with gender hierarchy. To a large extent, gender hierarchy, perceived as biological and natural, can eventually be used to justify any discrimination of one group against the other in the name of differences in race, social position, or sexual orientation.[41] Those who want to be masters or slaves cannot avoid being subject to the same logic, which eventually leads to their own slavery. Following this logic, the use of women as subhumans in a large number of experimental fiction works leads to a certain worship of "the master" by these writers. Therefore, the male writers' misogynistic discourse largely limits the subversive potential of their works by reducing them to products of a newly established patriarchal clan. This clan can still present itself as dynamic and subversive mainly because it has not yet truly acquired political power.

In this context, Can Xue's marginalized position as a woman writer within this male order provides her with an edge to overcome the limits imposed on the writings of most of her male colleagues by a clan-oriented mentality. Her carefree attitude helped Can Xue break through the barriers which tended to exclude women from the world of experimental fiction. Since then, the lack of support from important literary critics who usually patronize certain male writers liberates Can Xue from the obligation to pay tribute to any master. Her success in experimental fiction mocks at the masters' efforts to monopolize this gender under the guardianship of certain new patriarchal figures. Moreover, this success also shows that the masculine monopolization of language is only another fiction by means of which these masters tend to justify their misogynistic discourse.

However, Can Xue's solitary voice, which demystifies the newly established phallological discursive order, does not consciously acquire any positive feminine identity. By choosing absolute solitude, this voice refuses to reverse the patriarchal order or to replace male bonding by female bonding as an easy and simple solution. But this choice also turns a majority of a potentially sympathetic audience interested in gender issues away from Can Xue's works. As a result, her subversive voice largely remains unheard among her potentially sympathetic listeners and has to a large extent been lost in a desert. The loss of this audience makes Can Xue's works more accessible to the newly established order of contemporary experimental fiction, which is indeed subversive but also not less patriarchal. Consequently, this order has reluctantly incorporated her fiction as a disturbed and disturbing element. Can

Xue's originality, deliberately misunderstood and misrepresented as the outcome of the author's madness by the defenders of this order, finally turns into a somewhat embarrassing but nevertheless harmless decoration of one of its targets of subversion—the myth of a masculine monopolization of language.[43]

NOTES

1. In Chinese, "name" (*ming*) also designates words. Confucian "rectification of names" means to readjust a linguistic sign with its original reference. The reference does not need to be objective, as long as the subject who decided on an original meaning of a word has been endowed with enough social authority, such as a prince, a king, or a sage. As Xunzi (approximately 313–238 B.C.), a Confucian philosopher, says: "Kings are the ones who define names. The names of criminal law were created in the Shang dynasty. The names of official titles have been formed since the Zhou dynasty. The names of ritual ceremonies originated from Zhou's *Book of Ritual.*" (Xun Kuang, *Xunzi jishi*, Li Di-sheng, ed. [Taipei: Taiwan xuesheng, 1979], 506).

2. In *The Great Leaning*, the rectification of names are explained in the following terms: "If names be not correct, language is not in accordance with the truth of things. If language be not in accordance with the truth of things, affairs cannot be carried on to success. If affairs be not carried on to success, proprieties and music cannot flourish. When proprieties and music do not flourish, punishments will not be properly awarded. When punishments are not properly awarded, the people do not know how to move hand or foot." (Confucius, *The Chinese Classic*, vol. 1, *Confucian Analects, The Great Learning, The Doctrine of the Mean*, trans. James Legge [Hong Kong: Hong Kong University Press, 1960], 263–64).

3. "Writing must carry the principle" (*Wen yi zaidao*), (*Tongshu*).

4. Li Tuo, an avant-garde critic, writes: "A Q (the protagonist of Lu Xun's 'The Official Story of A Q') and the discourse formulated on the basis of A Q's personality are now reshaping many Chinese people's mentalities. By the use of this discourse, they feel embarrassed by their Chineseness. Moreover, I believe that this ideological 'avalanche' has just begun. In the near future, A Q's discourse will more deeply influence the Chinese and thus, encourage radical changes in their concepts." (Li Tuo, "Where Did the Avalanche Start?", preface to Yu Hua's collection of short stories, *Shibasui chumen yuanxin* [To embark on a long journey at the age of eighteen] [Taipei: Yuanliu, 1990], 6).

5. During the 1980s, a number of important literary journals, such as *Beijing wenxue* (Beijing literature), *Shanghai wenxue* (Shanghai litera-

ture), *Zhongshan*, and *Shouhuo* (Harvest), at least for a period, were to a large extent controlled, if not monopolized, by this group of avant-garde literary critics.

6. Liu Suola may arguably be considered the only other woman writer who has gained a similar reputation, even though her works are much more traditional than Can Xue's.

7. Cheng Yongxin, "Editor's Note," *Zhongguo xinchao xiaoshuo xuan* (Selections of new-wave short stories in China) (Shanghai: Shanghai shehui kexueyuan chubanshe, 1989), 370. I shall indicate this book by *zgxcxsx* in the rest of the essay.

8. Cheng Depei, "The Dream Which Tortures Can Xue," *Shanghai wenxue*, 1987:6, 71.

9. Cheng Yongxin, *Zhongguo xinchao xiaoshuo*, 266.

10. See my introduction to this volume.

11. In most cases, Chinese literary critics still write comments on writers and their works mainly to praise them.

12. Yu Hua, for example, keeps referring to Li Tuo as his master in his collections and interviews. See his preface to *Shibasui chumen yuanxin* (To embark on a long journey at the age of eighteen) (Beijing: Zuojia chubanshe, 1989).

13. In her "Three Women's Texts and a Critique of Imperialism," for example, Gayatri Spivak shows us how the gender boundaries are deconstructed and reconstituted by the racial policy of Western imperialism. (Gayatri Chakravorty Spivak, "Three Women's Texts and a Critique of Imperialism," Catherine Belsey and Jane Moore, eds. *The Feminist Reader: Essays in Gender and the Politics of Literary Criticism* [New York: Basil Blackwell, 1989], 175–95).

14. Luce Irigaray, *Speculum of the Other Women*, trans. Gillian C. Gill (Ithaca: Cornell University Press, 1985), 237.

15. "A Mei's Melancholy Thoughts on a Sunny Day" (*A Mei zai yige taiyang tianli de chousi*), and Wu Liang et al., eds. *Huangdan pai xiaoshuo* (Absurd fiction) (Changchun: shidai chubanshe, 1988), 301–5. I shall indicate this book by *hdpxs* in the rest of the essay.

16. "In the Wilderness" (*Kuangye li*), ibid., 319–23.

17. "What Happened to Me in That World—To a Friend" (*Wo zai nage shijie de shiqing—gai youren*), Cheng Yongxin, ed. *Zhongguo xinchao xiaoshuo xuan*, 366–70.

18. Sima Xiangru (179–117 B.C.) writes: "One relies on the elegant lute to change the tone / Music of melancholy longing should not last long" (*Yuan yachin yi biandiao, zou chousi bu kechang*). (Sima Xiangru, "*Changmen fu*").

19. A socialist realist novel written by Hao Ran during the 1960s, for example, is entitled *Bright Sunny Day* (*Yanyang tian*).

20. "The red sun" (*hong taiyang*) appeared in a song entitled "The Red Light from the East" (*Dongfang hong*). During the Cultural Revolution, it was a daily ritual for Chinese people to sing this song in order to express their loyalty to their party leader, Chairman Mao.

21. "The reddest and reddest sun in our heart" (*women xinzhong zuihong zuihong de hong taiyang*) is an expression used by Lin Bao, the vice president of the Communist Party at the beginning of the Cultural Revolution, who excelled at flattering Mao Zedong. His expression, used in a speech delivered on Tian'anmen Gate in 1966, was repeated by several thousand millions of red guards and Chinese people during the Cultural Revolution. His art of flattery, however, did not spare him from the fate of a tragic ending. Politically dishonored, he died in a mysterious plane crash in Mongolia in 1969.

22. See my essay, " 'Red Sorghum:' Limits of Transgression," in Liu Kang and Tang Xiaobing, eds. *Politics, Ideology, and Literary Discourse in Modern China* (Durham: Duke University Press, forthcoming).

23. See Zhu Ling's essay "A Brave New World? On the Construction of 'Masculinity' and 'Femininity' in *The Red Sorghum Family*" in this collection.

24. See Su Tong's trilogy in Su Tong, *Qiqie chengqun* (Crowd of wives and concubines) (Taipei: Yuanliu, 1990).

25. See Yu Hua's collection of short stories: *Shibasui chumen yuanxing* (To embark on a long journey at the age of eighteen).

26. Paul Valéry, "La Jeune Parque."

27. The Chinese character *xiong* designates not only the chest but also the breast.

28. See *The I Ching or Book of Changes*, trans. Richard Wilhelm (Princeton: Princeton University Press, 1967).

29. Luce Irigaray, *Speculum of the Other Women*, 237–38.

30. Ibid., 238.

31. The name of the father, a Lacanian notion used by Luce Irigaray to refer to the law or central authority of a patriarchal order.

32. See Zhu Ling's essay "A Brave New World? On the Construction of 'Masculinity' and 'Femininity' in *The Red Sorghum Family*" in this collection.

33. For example, in one of Zhaxi Dawa's stories translated into English, "Souls Tied to the Knots of a Leather Rope," the protagonist, Taibei, embarks on a pilgrimage with his girl friend, Qiong. After his death, the narrator continues the quest, the aim of which remains unknown. Moreover, the narrator inherits Qiong as his girl friend from his dead character. (Zhaxi Dawa, "Souls Tied to the Knots of a Leather Rope," *Spring Bamboo*, ed. and trans. Jeanne Tai [New York: Random House, 1989], 135–69).

34. See Su Tong's trilogy in Su Tong, *Qiqie chengqun* (Crowd of wives and concubines).

35. See Yu Hua's collection of short stories: *Shibasui chumen yuanxing* (To embark on a long journey at the age of eighteen).

36. Luce Irigaray, *Speculum of the Other Woman*, 238.

37. Ibid., 237.

38. Luce Irigaray, *This Sex Which Is Not One*, trans. Catherine Porter (Ithaca: Cornell University Press, 1985), 79.

39. In his essay "Where Did the Avalanche Start?", Li Tuo chose Yu Hua as the best model for experimental fiction. At the end of the essay, he also mentions several other experimental writers, such as Ye Zhaoyan, Ge Fei, and Sun Ganlu—naturally all of them are men. This article serves as the preface to Yu Hua's collection of short stories: *Shibasui chumen yuanxing* (To embark on a long journey at the age of eighteen) published in Taiwan.

40. Frederick Engels, *The Origin of the Family, Private Property and the State*, trans. Alec West, rev. and ed. E. B. Leacock (New York: International Publishers, 1972), 129.

41. For a conceptualization of the relationship between gender hierarchy and other social inequalities, see Teresa de Lauretis's *The Technologies of Gender: Essays on Theory, Film, and Fiction* (Bloomington: Indiana University Press, 1987), 5.

42. In his "Exhausted Hearts" (*Pibei de xinling*), Wang Xiaoming uses Can Xue as an example of the limitations of women's works. In Wang's opinion, Can Xue cannot write true masterpieces because she is too radically individualistic. (Wang Xiaoming, "Exhausted Hearts" [*Pibei de xinling*], *Shanghai wenxue*, 88/5, 73). Taking into account individualism as a highly valued ideology among Chinese intellectuals of the post-Mao era, this criticism sounds surprisingly out-of-touch—especially com-

ing from an avant-garde critic. However, there is a certain truth in Wang's comment, since Can Xue's solipsism indeed imposes limitations upon her works—but not exactly in the sense of Wang's interpretation. Instead of writing as a man as this male critic has expected from a woman writer, Can Xue probably needs to acknowledge her specificity as a woman writer more publicly in order to overcome the limitations imposed by the solipsistic nature of her writings.

43. I would like to thank Yue Ming-bao for her suggestions for the revision of this chapter and Ruth Weil for her careful editing.